If The Brain Was An App, Would You Use It?

Perception, Programming, Consciousness and the Hidden Architecture of the Human Mind

James Miller

If The Brain Was An App, Would You Use It?

Disclaimer

This book is intended for **educational and informational purposes only**. It reflects the author's personal experiences, perspectives, and independent inquiry, and is not a substitute for professional medical, psychological, psychiatric, legal, or financial advice.

The concepts discussed, including nervous-system regulation, trauma-related patterns, communication dynamics, and the Mirror-Linguistic Hypothesis, are presented as a framework for reflection and exploration. They are not presented as clinical diagnoses, treatment protocols, or guarantees of outcome. Readers should not use this book to self-diagnose, to discontinue or modify prescribed treatment, or to delay seeking professional help.

If you are experiencing mental health distress, persistent anxiety or depression, intrusive thoughts, trauma symptoms, suicidal ideation, or any condition that affects your safety or daily functioning, please seek support from a qualified healthcare professional. If you believe you may be at immediate risk of harm to yourself or others, contact emergency services or your local crisis support provider right away.

Any references to research, theory, or physiology are included to support discussion and should be interpreted within the limits of this book's scope. The author is not providing medical or clinical services, and no professional relationship is created by reading this book.

To the fullest extent permitted by law, the author and publisher disclaim liability for any loss, injury, or damages arising from the use of, or reliance upon, the information in this book. You are solely responsible for how you interpret and apply the material.

Contents

Preface

This book did not emerge in isolation. It is part of a wider unfolding, a layered body of work shaped through years of observation, reflection, study, lived experience, and a persistent desire to understand what it means to be human in a world that so often fragments, conditions, and distorts that understanding. Each publication that came before this one moved me further towards the territory explored here, not only intellectually, but personally, emotionally, and spiritually. In many ways, this book feels like a point of convergence in that journey.

The Inversiverse: Waking Up In A World Built To Keep You Asleep opened the lens. It explored the structures of influence, perception, manipulation, and reality-framing that shape human experience, often without our full awareness. It asked difficult questions about the world, but also about the internal architecture through which the world is perceived. It was concerned not only with what surrounds us, but with the conditions under which we come to believe, comply, resist, fragment, or awaken.

My Inner Child Was Broken turned that lens inward.

Where earlier work often explored systems, symbols, perception, and power, this book moved more directly into the emotional terrain of the self. It examined childhood wounding, identity formation, inherited pain, emotional survival, and the long afterlife of early relational experiences. It was deeply personal, but also part of a wider psychological and philosophical inquiry into how a human being becomes who they become, and what remains possible when they begin to understand the roots of their own patterning.

The Resonance Matrix: The Anatomy of Influence & The Linguistic Somatic Decode took that inquiry further into the living field of language, tone, nervous-system response, and embodied communication. It marked an important stage in the development of my broader framework, including the Mirror-Linguistic Hypothesis, and explored how influence is not only ideological or conceptual, but physiological, relational, and somatic. It moved beyond the level of content alone and into the deeper question of how words, signals, states, timing, and implication participate in the shaping of human behaviour.

The Consciousness Code continued that trajectory by drawing together awareness, language, and the nervous system in a more integrated form. It explored how human beings are shaped not only by what they think, but by how awareness is structured, how attention is directed, how the body interprets experience, and how consciousness itself may be conditioned, narrowed, expanded, or reclaimed. That work helped clarify something essential for me: the human story cannot be understood through thought alone. It must be understood through the interwoven relationship between mind, body, memory, meaning, perception, regulation, and signal.

And so, this book emerged.

If the earlier works traced the social, emotional, linguistic, and conscious dimensions of being human, this one arrives at one of the most central questions beneath them all: what is the brain, really, and how does it participate in the making of human experience?

This is not simply a book about the brain as an organ in isolation. It is about the brain as interface, interpreter, filter, predictor, integrator, survival engine, storyteller, and adaptive bridge between body, self, world, and consciousness. It is about the architecture through which sensation becomes meaning, memory becomes identity, emotion becomes behaviour, and experience becomes reality. It is also about the brain as something far more dynamic than a machine: an evolving, embodied, responsive system shaped by biology, relationship, language, stress, curiosity, environment, and awareness.

In many respects, this publication reflects the continuing evolution of **This Place Called Earth.** What began as a platform for questioning the visible and invisible structures of life gradually became something more integrative. Over time, the work became less concerned with critique alone and more concerned with understanding the whole human being: perception, trauma, regulation, influence, consciousness, embodiment, ethics, adaptation, and the possibility of living with greater clarity, depth, and discernment.

This book stands as part of that maturation.

It brings together many of the recurring themes that have shaped my journey so far: the nature of reality, the body's role in meaning-making, the power of language, the shaping of perception, the tension between manipulation and awareness, the interdependence of emotion and intelligence, the mystery of consciousness, and the question of what it means to become more fully human in an age of increasing distraction, technological acceleration, and engineered capture of attention.

It also reflects something of my own path. The deeper I have explored these subjects, the more I have come to see that regulation, emotional balance, and intellectual clarity are not separate pursuits. As I learned to better stabilise my own inner world, I found I could retain more, observe more honestly, integrate more deeply, and desire learning not as escape, but as participation. This process has not only sharpened thought, but widened perception. It has changed how I read, how I listen, how I remember, how I speak, and how I relate to knowledge itself.

This book belongs to that phase of the journey.

It is not offered as a final word, nor as a closed system. Like all meaningful inquiry, it remains open. But it does mark an important threshold. It gathers together many of the threads running through the earlier books and reorients them around one of the most intimate and powerful structures we live through every day, yet rarely understand in full.

In that sense, it feels like one of the finishing touches in a much longer arc.

Beyond this work, one final publication remains to complete this particular phase of the wider journey: **Traversing the Darkness: A Spiritual Journey**. Where this book explores the brain, embodiment, consciousness, and the architecture of human experience through one lens, future work will bring the spiritual and existential dimensions into fuller view. Together, they represent not only books, but stages in an evolving map of inquiry.

For now, this is the next step.

A continuation.
A convergence.
And an invitation.

An invitation to look again at the system through which life is felt, filtered, interpreted, and lived.
An invitation to ask what the brain is doing, what it has learned, what it protects, what it distorts, and what it might yet become.
And perhaps above all, an invitation to become more conscious of the interface through which we meet the world.

Introduction - The Most Powerful Interface

Most people live through the brain every day without ever being taught what it is, how it works, how it adapts, how it distorts, or how profoundly it shapes the reality they experience.

We are taught fragments. We are told the brain controls the body. We are shown diagrams of hemispheres, neurons, chemicals, and regions with neat labels attached to them. We hear simplified ideas about memory, intelligence, emotion, logic, instinct, and behaviour. We are told that the brain stores information, processes the senses, and helps us survive. All of that is true in part. But none of it is enough.

What is often missing is the lived depth of the question.

What is the brain, really?

Is it simply an organ? A biological computer? A prediction engine? A control centre? A pattern-recognition system? A receiver? A filter? A storyteller? A translator between body and world? A survival mechanism dressed in memory and language? Or is it something stranger still, something we have not yet learned how to describe without reducing it too quickly to metaphor or mechanism?

This book begins from a simple but unsettling recognition: human beings use one of the most powerful, adaptive, and reality-shaping systems imaginable, yet most do so with only partial awareness of how it actually participates in their lives.

You do not merely have a brain.
You live through one.
You feel through one.
You remember through one.
You defend through one.
You interpret through one.
You become who you think you are through one.

And yet, for something so intimate, it often remains strangely invisible.

The brain rarely announces itself directly. It works through sensation, perception, memory, emotion, attention, anticipation, language, stress, desire, and pattern. It helps construct continuity where there is change, meaning where there is uncertainty, familiarity where there is repetition, and threat where there may only be ambiguity. It does not simply register reality like a camera. It interprets, predicts, edits, compresses, filters, and fills in.

In other words, the brain is not merely observing the world. It is participating in its construction.

That does not mean reality is imaginary, nor does it mean that nothing is true. It means that the human experience of reality is always mediated. We do not meet the world in a raw, untouched state. We meet it through biology, conditioning, memory, language, expectation, and embodied history. We meet it through a system shaped by evolution, vulnerability, adaptation, and relationship.

This is one of the central tensions running through the pages ahead.

The brain is both brilliant and limited.
It is plastic, yet patterned.
It is adaptive, yet often conservative.
It can learn, but it also protects what is familiar.
It can generate insight, but it can also trap us inside distortion.
It can widen perception, but it can just as easily narrow it under stress, fear, fatigue, trauma, ideology, or repetition.

For that reason, understanding the brain is not only a scientific project. It is also a human one.

To understand the brain is to ask how experience becomes meaning. How sensation becomes interpretation. How memory becomes identity. How emotion shapes thought. How language alters state. How relationships affect regulation. How the body influences the mind, people imagine to be separate from it. How behaviour is guided not only by belief, but by chemistry, physiology, attention, expectation, and subconscious patterning. And beyond all of this, how consciousness itself enters the picture.

These are not abstract questions. They are lived questions.

They shape how we remember childhood.
How we interpret conflict.
How we respond to danger.
How we fall into habits.
How do we become vulnerable to persuasion?

How we mistake familiarity for truth.

How we confuse intensity with meaning.

How do we inherit patterns we did not choose?

How we heal, learn, adapt, and sometimes awaken to the fact that much of what we took to be fixed was, in fact, conditioned.

This matters even more in the world we now inhabit.

We live in an age of unprecedented informational exposure, engineered distraction, algorithmic capture, chemical overstimulation, identity reinforcement, and persuasive design. Attention is harvested. Emotion is triggered. Belief is shaped through repetition, framing, social reward, outrage, and fear. The nervous system is pushed into cycles of activation and fatigue. Perception is increasingly mediated through screens, speed, and symbolic overload. Under such conditions, understanding the brain is not a luxury. It is becoming a form of literacy.

But this book is not written in the spirit of panic. Nor is it written to glorify the brain as some all-powerful master system that explains everything on its own.

It is written in the spirit of inquiry.

Its purpose is not merely to provide facts, though facts matter. Nor is it to reduce the human being to chemistry, circuitry, and tissue. Rather, it is to explore the brain as an embodied, adaptive, relational, and meaning-making interface through which life is interpreted and lived. It is to place the brain back into the wider context from which it is too often removed: the body, the senses, the nervous system, the immune system, development, language, relationship, environment, technology, culture, consciousness, and the long philosophical and spiritual struggle to understand what a human being actually is.

In that sense, this book moves across multiple layers.

It explores the biological brain: its architecture, signalling, chemistry, plasticity, memory systems, sensory integration, and predictive functions.

It explores the embodied brain: its relationship to the gut, the immune system, interoception, emotion, regulation, and the ongoing conversation between brain and body.

It explores the social brain: how attachment, language, co-regulation, cultural influence, identity, trauma, imitation, and belonging shape perception and behaviour.

It explores the programmable brain: how attention, repetition, fear, reward, media, ideology, and digital systems participate in the structuring of thought and feeling.

It explores the reflective and philosophical brain: the brain as it relates to the self, consciousness, ethics, free will, spirituality, artificial intelligence, genetics, and the possibility that our current models remain incomplete.

Running through all of this is an assumption that has become increasingly important in my own work: the human being cannot be properly understood by separating thought from feeling, brain from body, language from physiology, or intelligence from regulation.

Too often, we speak as though thought is clean and emotion is interference. As though rationality exists independently of the state. As though language is only symbolic rather than somatic. As though memory is a storage device rather than a reconstruction. As though behaviour is purely chosen rather than patterned through layers of development, adaptation, and neurobiological learning.

My own journey has taught me otherwise.

The more I have learned to regulate emotion, stabilise attention, and engage difficult material without becoming overwhelmed by it, the more I have found that memory improves, clarity deepens, discernment sharpens, and the desire to learn becomes more sustainable. Knowledge lands differently in a system that feels safer. Curiosity functions differently in a system that is not perpetually defending itself. Intelligence, in that sense, is not only a matter of information. It is also a matter of state.

That insight has fundamentally shaped this book.

It is one reason why the brain cannot be treated here as a detached object of cold inspection. It must be approached as part of lived experience, part of vulnerability, part of adaptation, part of the human search for orientation and coherence. It must also be approached ethically.

Because knowledge of the brain can be used in more than one way.

It can be used to heal, clarify, deepen, and reconnect.
But it can also be used to manipulate, engineer, persuade, fragment, and control.

The same understanding that helps a person regulate emotion can be used by another to exploit emotional triggers. The same knowledge that widens self-awareness can be repurposed into behavioural design, coercive messaging, addictive systems, and forms of influence that bypass genuine reflection. This is why any serious inquiry into the brain must also ask moral questions. Not only what the brain does, but what human beings do with the knowledge of how it works.

For that reason, this book is not only concerned with the mechanism. It is also concerned with responsibility.

It asks how we might understand the brain more deeply without reducing the person.
How we might honour science without collapsing into reductionism.
How we might remain open to philosophy and spirituality without abandoning rigour.
How might we explore new models without pretending certainty where none yet exists?

This matters especially as the comparison between the human brain and artificial systems becomes more common. We are increasingly surrounded by language that frames the brain as hardware, the mind as software, memory as storage, attention as bandwidth, and identity as information processing. These metaphors can be useful, but they can also quietly narrow our understanding. A human brain is not merely a computer made of tissue. It is a living organ embedded in a body, shaped by relationships, timing, metabolism, vulnerability, history, sensation, and meaning. It learns not only through data but through consequences, states, signals, emotions, and embodied life.

And yet, the comparison to AI and emerging technologies remains important. It forces us to ask where biological intelligence differs from synthetic systems, where the parallels are real, where they are overstated, and what the future may reveal about consciousness, learning, pattern recognition, and the architecture of cognition itself. These questions will appear later in this book, not as settled answers, but as part of a deeper inquiry into what makes human intelligence human.

There is also another thread running quietly beneath these pages: the possibility that our current models, however powerful, remain unfinished. Neuroscience has revealed extraordinary detail about structure, chemistry, networks, signalling, and function. But the full mystery of consciousness remains unresolved. So too do deeper questions of selfhood, free will, subjectivity, spiritual experience, and the possibility that human awareness exceeds the neat categories through which we currently attempt to define it.

That is not an excuse for vagueness. It is a reminder of humility.

The brain deserves precision.
But it also deserves wonder.

So this book is offered in both spirits: precision and wonder, grounding and openness, science and inquiry, embodiment and mystery.

If you are looking for a simple answer to what the brain is, this book will likely frustrate that hope. The deeper one looks, the more the brain appears not as a single thing, but as a layered and dynamic process: biological, electrical, chemical, relational, developmental, interpretive, and perhaps in some respects still beyond our current explanatory reach.

But that complexity is not a problem. It is part of the invitation.

To understand the brain even a little better is to understand something essential about perception, memory, suffering, behaviour, vulnerability, adaptation, and the strange beauty of being alive inside a system that is always doing more than we consciously notice.

That is where this inquiry begins.

Not with the claim that we have mastered the brain.
Not with the fantasy that we stand outside it.
But with the recognition that we are already living through its activity, whether we understand it or not.

And so we begin with the most powerful interface most
people have never truly learned to use

PART I - The Living Architecture

Before we can ask what the brain means, we must first ask what it is.

Not in the simplified language of diagrams, labels, and isolated functions alone, but in the fuller sense: as a living, adaptive, embodied system through which sensation, prediction, interpretation, and survival are organised. The brain is often spoken of as though it were a detached command centre, sealed away in the skull and issuing instructions to the rest of the body. But that picture is too small. The brain is not separate from the life it governs. It exists in constant conversation with the body, the senses, the environment, and the relational world in which human experience unfolds.

This first part lays the foundations for everything that follows. It explores the brain not merely as tissue, but as architecture: biological, electrical, chemical, perceptual, and embodied.

If later parts of this book examine memory, emotion, language, identity, influence, consciousness, ethics, and the future of human intelligence, then this opening section asks the more primary questions without which those later discussions lose their footing.

We begin in

Chapter 1, What Is the Brain, Really?

by establishing the basic orientation of the inquiry. What exactly is the brain, and what is it not? How does it differ from the mind, from consciousness, from the nervous system, and from the self we so often assume to be unified and obvious? Here, the brain is introduced not as a static object, but as an organ, network, signalling system, and adaptive model-builder through which experience is continuously shaped.

From there,

Chapter 2, The Brain and the Body Are Not Separate

widens the frame. Modern culture often treats the brain as though it sits above the body, governing it from a distance, but lived biology is far more integrated than that. This chapter explores the brain's dependence on bodily feedback, hormones, gut-brain communication, immune signalling, interoception, and the broader principle of embodied cognition. It asks the reader to reconsider the old division between "mental" and "physical," showing instead that the brain and body participate in one ongoing regulatory conversation.

In **Chapter 3, The Senses Do Not Show Reality, They Construct It**

The question becomes perceptual. What do the senses actually give us? Do they reveal the world as it is, or do they provide partial streams of information that the brain must organise into a usable model? This chapter explores vision, hearing, touch, taste, smell, proprioception, and interoception, while showing why perception is never a neutral recording of reality. Optical illusions, sensory distortions, and everyday examples help reveal how the brain actively constructs the world we take ourselves to be simply observing.

That naturally leads into

Chapter 4, The Brain as Prediction Engine

where perception is understood not as passive reception, but as active anticipation. The brain does not wait for reality to arrive fully formed. It predicts, fills in gaps, compares expectations with incoming data, and updates its model when necessary. This chapter explores predictive processing, pattern recognition, framing, priming, error correction, and bias, asking why human beings so often see what they expect to see and why interpretation can feel immediate, obvious, and unquestionable even when it is incomplete.

Chapter 5, Hemispheres, Networks, and the Myth of the "Logical vs Creative Brain"

Closes this opening part by challenging one of the most persistent simplifications in modern popular culture. The idea that one side of the brain is "logical" and the other "creative" has become widespread because it is tidy and easy to remember. But the truth is more complex, and therefore more interesting. This chapter explores hemispheric specialisation, distributed cognition, large-scale brain networks, and the integrated nature of human mental life. Rather than replacing one simplistic myth with another, it offers a more nuanced understanding of how multiple regions and systems cooperate to produce thought, feeling, perception, imagination, and action.

Taken together, these chapters form the ground beneath the entire book.

They show that the brain is not merely an object to be described, but a living interface through which the world is sensed, modelled, filtered, and made meaningful.

They also establish one of the central claims that will echo throughout everything that follows: the brain is not a detached machine observing reality from outside it. It is a participatory system, shaped by body, environment, prediction, relationship, and adaptation.

To begin with, here is to begin with foundations.

Not because foundations are simple, but because they are easy to overlook.

The better we understand the living architecture of the brain, the better we can understand memory, emotion, identity, language, conditioning, belief, consciousness, and the many ways human beings both inherit and construct the worlds they live within.

Chapter 1 - What Is the Brain?

The brain is one of the most familiar words in human language, and yet one of the least fully understood in human experience.

Most people know they have one. Most people know it matters. Most people know it is associated with thought, memory, intelligence, emotion, decision-making, perception, and survival.

But beyond that, the word "brain" often functions more as shorthand than understanding.

It is used to explain everything from behaviour to personality to genius to dysfunction, and yet the deeper question is rarely paused over with enough care:

What is the brain, really?

Is it simply an organ, a lump of biological tissue inside the skull?

Is it a command centre?

A processor?

A control system?

A prediction engine?

A storehouse of memory?

A survival machine?

A receiver?

A filter?

A model-builder?

A translator between body and world?

Or is it all of these at once, depending on the level from which we are looking?

The difficulty begins with the fact that the brain is not a single thing in the way language often suggests. It is not one function, one voice, or one cleanly bounded process.

It is a living organ, yes, but also a networked system. It is electrical and chemical. It is biological and adaptive. It is shaped by evolution, development, experience, relationships, and environment. It is both ancient and changing.

It contains specialised regions, but it does not behave like a collection of isolated boxes. It operates through interaction, timing, pattern, signalling, inhibition, reinforcement, and constant revision.

To say "the brain" as though that settles the matter is a little like saying "the weather" while ignoring the atmosphere, the ocean, pressure systems, temperature gradients, and the larger conditions that give rise to what is being observed. The word points us in the right direction, but it can also hide the complexity of what it names.

At its most basic level, the brain is a living organ composed of billions of nerve cells, support cells, vascular systems, chemical messengers, and dynamic circuits that coordinate sensation, movement, regulation, perception, learning, memory, emotion, and behaviour. But even this is only a partial beginning. Because the brain is not merely a device for doing tasks. It is part of the means through which we experience being alive.

The brain helps construct the continuity of your world. It helps turn sensation into meaningful perception. It helps decide what matters, what is ignored, what is remembered, what is feared, what is pursued, and what is treated as safe enough to approach.

It is not a neutral camera pointed at reality. It is an active participant in shaping what reality feels like, what it appears to contain, and how you are positioned within it.

This is where the brain becomes more than anatomy.

A diagram can show you the frontal lobe, the temporal lobe, the cerebellum, the brainstem, the limbic structures, the hemispheres, the folds and grooves, and the spinal continuation.

No diagram alone tells you what it is like to live through a system that is simultaneously sensing, predicting, evaluating, remembering, comparing, defending, and attempting to maintain enough coherence for the organism to function in a changing world.

The brain is not only a structure. It is a process.

It is not only material. It is an activity.

It is not only hardware. It is also timing, pattern, modulation, and adaptation.

Because of that, any serious attempt to understand the brain must resist the temptation to reduce it too quickly.

One of the most common ways the brain is oversimplified is by being treated as though it were equivalent to the mind. But the brain and the mind are not identical terms, even if they are deeply related.

The brain refers to the physical organ and its structures, signals, and processes.

The mind, by contrast, is often used to describe the more emergent realm of thought, feeling, imagination, memory, interpretation, intention, and awareness as they are lived and experienced.

The brain is embodied tissue and activity. The mind is the lived and felt dimension of cognition and subjectivity that seems to arise through, with, or alongside those processes.

Different philosophical traditions interpret this relationship differently. Some treat the mind as nothing more than brain activity described from the inside. Others regard the mind as a broader emergent phenomenon that cannot be fully reduced to neural mechanics.

Others still see consciousness itself as something not entirely explainable by the brain alone. This book does not need to settle that question immediately to proceed, but it does need to keep the distinction in view.

When we confuse the brain with the mind too casually, we risk flattening the richness of lived experience into mechanism, or else floating away from biology into abstraction. The task here is to hold both.

There is another distinction that matters just as much: the difference between the brain and the nervous system.

The brain is not the whole story. It is a central part of the nervous system, but not the entirety of it. The nervous system includes the spinal cord, peripheral nerves, autonomic regulation, sensory pathways, motor pathways, and the ongoing communication between the brain, body, organs, muscles, immune signals, internal states, and external demands.

In everyday life, people often speak as though the brain "controls" everything from above. But a better image is one of constant conversation.

The brain receives signals from the body, interprets them, predicts what they mean, and issues responses, while the body continuously feeds information back.

This is not a one-way command chain. It is an ongoing loop.

That matters because what people casually call "mental" life is often inseparable from bodily state. Fatigue changes thought. Fear changes perception. Inflammation changes mood. Breath alters regulation.

Hunger shifts patience. Hormones affect memory and motivation. Posture influences feeling. Safety widens attention.

Chronic stress narrows it. The brain cannot be understood properly if it is imagined in isolation from the living body that informs it moment by moment.

There is also the question of consciousness, which complicates matters further.

The brain clearly participates in conscious experience. Damage to it alters awareness, personality, language, perception, memory, and sense of self.

Sleep, drugs, injury, development, trauma, and disease all demonstrate that conscious life is intimately tied to neural processes.

Yet even with all this evidence, the precise relationship between brain activity and conscious experience remains unresolved.

How does electrical-chemical activity become the felt sense of pain, the visual of colour, memory, desire, grief, or selfhood?

How does matter generate subjectivity, if that is indeed what it does? These questions remain open.

So when we ask what the brain is, we are already standing at the edge of multiple layers at once:

a physical organ,

a signalling network,

a predictive system,
a regulatory interface,
a participant in conscious life,
and perhaps something still not fully captured by current frameworks.

Another confusion worth clearing early is the tendency to equate the brain with the self.

People often say things such as "my brain made me do it" or "my brain is wired this way", as though the brain were a separate entity inside the person.

At one level, this language can be useful. It helps point to patterns, predispositions, and automatic processes that do not feel consciously chosen.

But taken too far, it can subtly divide the person against themselves, as though the brain were a machine operating independently of the life it constitutes.

The truth is more paradoxical.

You are not reducible to your brain, but you are also not separate from it. The self you take yourself to be is shaped through neural development, memory, bodily feeling, relationships, language, and social experience.

Identity is not produced by the brain alone, but neither is it independent of it. What you call "me" emerges through layers of embodiment, pattern, narrative, and relational continuity that the brain helps sustain.

This means that the brain is neither the whole self nor irrelevant to it. It is one of the primary conditions through which selfhood becomes possible, stable, and revisable.

This is why the brain is perhaps best thought of not as a thing with one meaning, but as an interface made of many processes.

It is an interface between body and world.
Between sensation and interpretation.
Between memory and anticipation.
Between past learning and present response.
Between internal chemistry and external demand.
Between the organism and the reality it must navigate.

That interface is not passive. It does not merely record what is there. It selects, filters, predicts, edits, prioritises, amplifies, suppresses, and generates models that are useful enough for survival, social functioning, and behavioural continuity. In that sense, the brain is not designed to give human beings perfect truth.

It is designed, first and foremost, to help them remain viable organisms in changing environments.

This has enormous consequences.

It means that what feels obvious may be constructed.
What feels true may be familiar.
What feels threatening may be ambiguous.
What feels like direct perception may already be an interpretation.

What feels like a free decision may have been influenced by state, memory, and prediction before conscious awareness fully arrived.

This does not strip human life of meaning. It deepens the need for humility.

Because the more one studies the brain, the more one realises that certainty is often built on processes most people never notice. The brain gives the impression of seamlessness. It hides its own edits.

It presents its interpretations as immediate. It lets human beings feel that they are simply seeing, knowing, choosing, and remembering, when in fact layers of inference, filtering, and reconstruction are already at work beneath the surface.

None of this should make the brain seem cold or deceptive. On the contrary, it reveals how extraordinary it is.

The brain is not just managing threat. It is also managing the possibility.

It allows language, imagination, symbolism, humour, creativity, abstraction, empathy, rhythm, planning, reflection, and moral deliberation.

It enables us as beings not only to survive but to create worlds of meaning. Science, music, ritual, mathematics, storytelling, architecture, compassion, memory, grief, longing, philosophy, and prayer all emerge through a brain that is somehow both biological and open to dimensions of life that exceed simple description.

This is part of what makes the brain such a unique subject. It is at once mechanical and mysterious. Measurable and intimate. Material and meaning-bearing. It can be studied through scans, lesions, signals, neurotransmitters, and networks, but it also remains the medium through which the study itself is interpreted. The brain is both the object under investigation and part of the instrument doing the investigating.

That circularity matters.

It means that the brain is not like any other object of study. A rock does not study rocks.

A liver does not produce theories about the liver. But the brain becomes curious about itself.

It generates concepts about its own nature, then tests them, revises them, argues over them, and builds entire civilisations out of the interpretations it creates.

This reflexive dimension makes the brain not only a scientific subject but a philosophical one.

It is also increasingly a cultural and ethical one.

The more human beings understand about the brain, the more they gain power over perception, persuasion, learning, behaviour, memory, and emotional regulation. That knowledge can be used to heal trauma, improve education, deepen self-awareness, and create more humane systems.

But it can also be used to capture attention, engineer dependence, manipulate fear, shape identity, and design environments that exploit vulnerability.

Understanding what the brain is, therefore, carries consequences beyond academic curiosity. It changes how societies think about responsibility, intelligence, morality, health, freedom, and influence.

For that reason, the question "What is the brain?" cannot remain purely technical. It must also become existential.

What does it mean to live through a system that is adaptive but biased, brilliant but limited, embodied but often misunderstood, social but vulnerable to capture, predictive but prone to distortion?

What does it mean to become more aware of that system without reducing oneself to it?

These are the questions that begin here.

Not with a final definition, but with a reframing.

The brain is an organ, but not merely an organ.
It is a network, but not merely a network.
It is a processor, but not merely a processor.
It is a survival system, but not merely a defence mechanism.
It is a participant in consciousness, but not a settled explanation of consciousness.
It is part of the self, but not the totality of what a self is.

Most of all, the brain is a living, adaptive, embodied interface through which human beings encounter, interpret, and participate in reality. That is where this inquiry begins. Before we ask what the brain remembers, we must ask what it is.

Before we ask how it feels, we must ask how it organises experience.

Before we ask how it can be shaped, we must ask what kind of system is being shaped in the first place.

Once that foundation is clearer, we can move further.

Because the next truth follows naturally:
The brain does not stand apart from the body.

It lives in conversation with it.

Brain Observation

Notice how often you casually use the word *brain* in daily life.

Do you use it to mean thought, mood, memory, intelligence, instinct, self-control, or identity?

What assumptions are hidden in the way you speak about it?

Everyday Experiment

Write four short definitions in your own words:

- Brain
- Mind
- Nervous System

- Self

Then leave them for a day and return to them. Notice which definitions feel clear, which overlap, and which become vague the moment you try to separate them.

Create a simple four-column chart like this.

Create a simple four-column chart like this:

Brain	Mind	Nervous System	Self
• What is it? • Where does it operate? • Does it feel physical, experiential, or both?	• What is it? • Where does it operate? • Does it feel physical, experiential, or both?	• What is it? • Where does it operate? operaticinal • Does it feel physical, experiential, or both? One example from daily life	• What is it? • Where does it operate? • One example from daily life

Then draw lines between the columns where you notice overlap. The aim is not to get the "right" answer immediately, but to see how quickly these categories blur when examined closely.

Ethical Question

If greater knowledge of the brain gives human beings greater power to influence behaviour, who should be trusted to use that knowledge, and under what moral limits?

I think this is the right move. It makes the book more usable, more original, and more consistent with your style of inquiry.

Chapter 2 - The Brain and the Body Are Not Separate

One of the most persistent errors in modern thought is the habit of speaking about the brain as though it exists above the body, apart from it, governing it from a distance like a command centre sealed inside the skull.

This image is tidy, but it is misleading.

It encourages people to imagine that thought is somehow a clean mental process, while the body is merely physical. It reinforces the old split between mind and matter, reason and sensation, cognition and physiology.

It suggests that the brain is the real seat of personhood and the body is a kind of vehicle carrying it around. But lived biology tells a different story.

The brain does not stand apart from the body. It exists in continuous conversation with it. It depends on it. It is shaped by it. Much of what we casually call thought, mood, intuition, stress, instinct, clarity, fatigue, or emotional life is inseparable from this ongoing exchange.

To understand the brain properly, we must begin to abandon the fantasy that it is functioning alone.

The brain is an organ of the body, not an escape from it.

It is nourished by blood flow, oxygen, glucose regulation, immune signalling, hormonal fluctuation, sensory input, posture, movement, breath, sleep, gut activity, inflammation, and countless other processes taking place below the threshold of conscious attention.

At every moment, signals rise from the body to the brain, and responses travel from the brain back into the body. This is not a one-way chain of command. It is an ongoing loop of interpretation, regulation, adjustment, and meaning-making.

In that sense, the brain is not merely thinking about the body. It is thinking with the body, through the body, and often because of the body.

This becomes obvious in everyday life, the moment we pay attention.

A person who has not slept properly may become impatient, forgetful, emotionally reactive, or unable to concentrate.

A person whose blood sugar is unstable may suddenly feel anxious, weak, irritable, or mentally foggy.

A person under chronic stress may begin to perceive ordinary events as threatening, not because the world itself has changed, but because the body is already primed for danger.

A person who feels safe, fed, rested, and relationally supported may find that their thoughts are clearer, their attention wider, and their emotional responses less extreme.

These are not accidental side effects. They reveal something essential: cognition is state-dependent.

Thought is not floating above physiology. It is emerging through it.

This is one of the reasons the old separation between "mental health" and "physical health" is too crude to be fully accurate. Of course, the terms remain useful in practical settings, but in lived experience, the boundary is far less stable than language suggests.

The body influences mood, concentration, and memory.

The brain influences digestion, muscle tension, inflammation, hormonal response, and perception of pain. Emotions alter breathing, heart rate, posture, and immunity. Chronic physiological strain changes interpretation, motivation, and decision-making. The division is convenient, but the organism is integrated.

At the centre of this integration is a concept that has become increasingly important across neuroscience, psychology, and embodied approaches to cognition: interoception.

Interoception refers to the sensing of the body's internal condition. It includes signals related to heartbeat, breath, hunger, fullness, temperature, tension, discomfort, nausea, arousal, fatigue, and countless subtle shifts that tell the organism what is happening inside itself.

Much of this occurs automatically and never reaches conscious language. But even when we do not think about it directly, these signals still matter. They shape the background tone of experience. They influence mood, readiness, comfort, urgency, and the sense of being safe or under strain.

A person may say, "I have a bad feeling," or "Something feels off," without realising that the body has already detected a change in state before the conscious mind has organised it into an explanation.

That does not mean every bodily feeling is accurate about the outside world, but it does mean that the brain is constantly interpreting bodily signals as part of its model of reality.

This is crucial.

The brain does not merely perceive the external world. It also perceives the internal body.

And these two streams are not kept cleanly separate. They blend.

A racing heart may be interpreted as fear, excitement, anticipation, attraction, or danger, depending on context.

A tight chest may be read as anxiety, illness, grief, or simple tension.

A calm and regulated internal state may make the world appear manageable, while a dysregulated internal state may make the same world seem hostile or overwhelming.

In this sense, the body is not only something the brain monitors. It becomes part of the evidence from which reality is interpreted.

The philosopher and psychologist William James famously suggested that bodily changes are deeply intertwined with emotional experience.

Later research has developed this in many directions, but the broad insight remains important: emotion is not merely an idea in the head. It is lived through the body. Fear is not just a thought of danger. It is pulse, breath, readiness, contraction, and a narrowed focus.

Shame is not just a concept of social exposure. It is collapse, heat, aversion, and shrinking. Anger is not just mental disagreement. It is mobilisation, intensity, blood flow, and muscular preparation. Joy is not just an opinion that something is good. It is expansion, energy, movement, openness, coherence.

The brain does not generate these states in abstraction. It generates and interprets them through the body it inhabits.

This is one reason why regulation matters so much.

When the body is chronically dysregulated, cognition changes. Attention narrows. Memory retrieval becomes less reliable. Threat detection becomes hypersensitive. Ambiguity becomes harder to tolerate. Flexibility declines.

The person may become more reactive, more rigid, or more exhausted without fully understanding why. Conversely, when the body is more regulated, the brain often gains access to broader perception, greater patience, better memory integration, and more reflective decision-making.

This is not because regulation makes a person perfect. It is because a system not constantly defending itself has more capacity available for learning, nuance, and thought.

That insight has been central in my own work.

The more I have explored the relationship between emotion, regulation, and cognition, the more obvious it has become that intelligence is not only a matter of information or analytical ability.

It is also shaped by whether the organism can remain sufficiently stable to process complexity without becoming overwhelmed by it.

A dysregulated system may be highly intelligent in theory, but unable to access its own intelligence consistently in practice.

A more balanced system is often better able to retain information, engage with nuance, tolerate uncertainty, and stay curious without collapsing into defensiveness or overload.

In that sense, bodily regulation is not separate from intellectual life. It supports it.

The brain-body conversation also extends into the hormonal and chemical life of the organism.

Hormones such as cortisol, adrenaline, insulin, oestrogen, testosterone, thyroid hormones, and others affect energy, attention, mood, motivation, and perception. Neurotransmitters such as dopamine, serotonin, and GABA interact with wider bodily systems rather than operating in some sealed mental chamber.

Sleep rhythms alter hormonal cascades. Chronic inflammation can influence low mood and mental fatigue. Nutritional status shapes cognition.

Physical activity affects memory, mood regulation, and learning. Even the timing of meals and the quality of rest can subtly alter how the world is perceived.

This is one reason simplistic narratives about the brain so often fail. They isolate what in reality is distributed.

The brain is not a detached processor receiving clean data. It is embedded in a body that is alive with signals, each of which alters the conditions under which thought occurs.

A powerful example of this integration is the relationship between the brain and the gut.

The gut is sometimes casually referred to as a "second brain," a phrase that can be exaggerated if taken too literally, but points toward something real.

The digestive system contains extensive neural networks and communicates continuously with the brain through multiple pathways, including the vagus nerve, immune mediators, hormones, and microbial activity.

Gut health can affect mood, inflammation, energy, and even aspects of cognition. Stress can alter digestion.

Digestion can alter stress response. Appetite, satiety, nausea, comfort, and distress are not merely local bodily events. They enter the wider landscape of how the organism feels and functions.

This does not mean every emotional difficulty begins in the gut, nor that dietary reductionism can explain the complexity of human experience.

It does mean that the organism is more integrated than old mechanical models allowed.

The same can be said of the immune system.

Many people still think of immunity only in terms of infection and defence, but immune activity has consequences for mood, fatigue, clarity, and behaviour.

When the body is fighting illness or living with chronic inflammatory strain, the brain often shifts accordingly. Motivation may drop. Rest may become more necessary. Social appetite may shrink.

Thinking may feel slower or less precise. These are not simply failures of willpower. They are signs that the organism reallocates energy and changes priorities depending on internal conditions.

This matters because modern culture often moralises states that are actually physiological.

People are called lazy when they are depleted. Weak when they are dysregulated. Overly sensitive when their nervous system is overburdened.

Unmotivated when inflammation, sleep loss, hormonal disruption, or emotional overload have narrowed their capacity.

This does not mean people are without agency, but it does mean agency is embodied. The ability to act clearly depends on the condition of the system doing the acting.

To say this another way: the body is not an obstacle to cognition. It is one of its conditions.

The nervous system makes this even clearer.

While this chapter does not yet move into the full depth of autonomic regulation, it is important to note that the brain and body are connected through nervous system loops that continuously scan for safety, risk, novelty, relevance, and demand.

The organism does not wait for abstract reasoning before responding. Much of life is shaped by rapid assessments that occur beneath conscious awareness.

The body shifts first, then thought often follows with a story explaining the shift.

A person feels tension, then says, "I knew something was wrong."

A person feels relief, then concludes a situation is trustworthy.

A person feels heavy, then interprets the world as bleak.

The narrative may be sincere, but it often arrives after the body has already moved the system into a particular state.

This is why bodily awareness matters.

Not because every sensation should be obeyed blindly, but because a person who has no relationship with their internal state is more easily ruled by it without knowing.

The goal is not to become obsessed with bodily signals, but to become literate enough in them to notice when they are shaping interpretation.

A racing heart is real. The story attached to it may or may not be.

A tight stomach is real. The conclusion drawn from it may require further reflection.

A calm body is real. The sense of confidence that follows may be earned, or it may simply reflect temporary ease. In all cases, the body is participating.

Embodied cognition takes this even further by suggesting that thought itself is not only located in the brain as an isolated representation, but is shaped by movement, posture, spatial relation, gesture, sensory experience, and bodily engagement with the world.

We do not learn only by storing abstract information.

We learn through doing, repeating, orienting, acting, and situating knowledge in lived contexts.

Language itself is filled with bodily metaphors for this reason: we grasp ideas, carry burdens, feel weighed down, stand our ground, lose balance, warm to a person, recoil from disgust, or feel close to those we trust.

The body is not just decorating thought with imagery. It has helped structure thought from the beginning.

For this reason, a more accurate picture of the brain is not that of a solitary genius issuing commands, but of a participant in a living system.

The brain interprets the body.
The body informs the brain.
The nervous system mediates both.
The environment acts on them together.
And the person lives through the loop.

That loop is not only biological. It is existential.

Because once we understand that the brain and body are not separate, many assumptions begin to loosen. Emotional reactivity can no longer be dismissed as mere weakness of character.

Intellectual clarity can no longer be treated as something entirely independent of sleep, nutrition, safety, and regulation.

Healing can no longer be imagined as only changing thoughts while leaving physiology untouched. Influence can no longer be reduced to slogans or beliefs while ignoring tone, rhythm, stress, tension, and bodily state.

Even self-knowledge changes, because the self is no longer imagined as a detached thinker observing a bodily machine from above, but as an embodied being whose perception and identity are shaped through this continual interplay.

This has consequences for how we understand learning, therapy, trauma, behaviour, relationships, education, leadership, spirituality, and culture.

A frightened body does not learn the same way as a safe one. A depleted body does not reason the same way as a rested one. A shamed body does not interpret social signals the same way as a secure one. A rigid body does not experience possibility the same way as an open one.

And if all this is true, then the human story is even less separable than modern categories have allowed.

The brain is not trapped inside the skull, having thoughts about life at a distance.

It is part of a living, embodied field through which life is directly felt.

That is why any serious attempt to understand the brain must move beyond anatomy alone.

It must ask how sensation becomes meaning, how internal state alters perception, how physiology shapes thought, and how intelligence itself may depend not only on what a person knows, but on the condition of the organism through which that knowledge is being processed.

This is where the conversation deepens.

Because once we see that the brain and body are not separate, another question follows naturally:

If the brain does not simply receive the world, but constructs it through sensation and prediction, then what exactly are the senses giving us?

That is where we go next.

Brain Observation

Notice how your thinking changes when your body changes. Pay attention over the course of a day to moments of hunger, tiredness, stress, relief, tension, movement, stillness, or calm. How often does your interpretation of reality shift with your bodily state?

Everyday Experiment

Choose one short task that requires concentration, such as reading a dense paragraph, recalling a list of ten words, or solving a simple reasoning puzzle.

Do it once when you feel physically settled and once when you are hungry, tense, rushed, or mildly fatigued. Compare your clarity, patience, memory, and emotional response.

The aim is not to cause distress, only to observe how cognition changes with bodily conditions.

Visual Aid

Create a simple two-column page titled:

Body State | Mental Effect

Over the next three days, make short notes such as:

- poor sleep | slower recall
- calm walk | clearer thinking
- hunger | irritability
- deep conversation | mental sharpness
- shallow breathing | anxious interpretation
- physical tension | narrow focus

At the end, review the page and circle any repeated links.

This gives you a simple black-and-white printable self-map of how physiology and thought interact in daily life.

Body State	Mental Effect
• poor sleep	slower recall
• calm walk	clearer thinking
• hunger	irritability
• deep conversation	mental sharpness
• shallow breathing	anxious interpretation
• physical tension	narrow focus
•	
•	
•	
•	

Ethical Question

If human thought and behaviour are deeply shaped by bodily state, where should we draw the line between personal responsibility and physiological limitation?

Chapter 3 - The Senses Do Not Show Reality, They Construct It

We often speak as though perception is simple.

We look, and we see.
We listen, and we hear.
We touch, and we know.
We smell, taste, orient, and move through the world as though the senses are transparent windows opening onto reality exactly as it is.

But they are not.

The senses do not present the world in its raw, complete form. They provide streams of partial information which the brain must select, organise, compare, interpret, and shape into a usable model.

What we call perception is not a direct copy of reality. It is a construction built from signals, filtered through biological limits, prior experience, expectation, context, bodily state, and the brain's ongoing attempt to make the world coherent enough to navigate.

This is not a flaw in the system. It is one of its defining features.

The world contains more information than the human organism could ever consciously process in full. Light arrives across a vast spectrum, but human vision detects only a narrow band. Sound waves extend far beyond what the ear can hear. Countless chemical signals pass unnoticed by the nose and tongue. Internal bodily shifts occur continuously beneath conscious awareness.

Even within the information that does reach us, far too much is happening at once for the brain to treat everything as equally important.

So perception is selective from the beginning.

The brain must decide what matters, what belongs together, what should remain in the background, and what should be brought to the front.

It must detect pattern amidst noise, stability amidst change, threat amidst ambiguity, and relevance amidst excess. It must do this quickly enough to support survival and social life, yet flexibly enough to update when conditions shift.

That means what we experience is never the whole world. It is the world as rendered through the capacities and priorities of a particular organism.

This is why two people can encounter the same situation and not fully perceive the same thing.

One notices facial tension. Another notices tone of voice. One sees opportunity.

Another sees risk. One hears humour. Another hears an insult. One focuses on the central object. Another absorbs the atmosphere around it.

These differences are not always matters of opinion after perception has taken place. There are often differences in perception itself, shaped by attention, training, memory, fear, expectation, and the internal state of the body at that moment.

To say that perception is constructed is not to say it is invented from nothing. The world is not being hallucinated at random.

The external environment places real constraints on what can be perceived. But the route from signal to experience is not passive. The senses provide data. The brain provides organisation. Meaning emerges through the interaction.

Vision offers one of the clearest examples.

People often trust sight more than any other sense. Seeing feels immediate and persuasive. If something appears obvious to the eye, it often feels beyond dispute. Yet vision is full of hidden construction.

The eye does not send a complete photograph to the brain. It detects contrasts, edges, motion, light intensity, colour wavelengths within a narrow range, and spatial relations. From there, the brain assembles continuity, depth, shape, object boundaries, and significance.

What seems like effortless seeing is the result of extraordinary interpretive labour.

The brain fills in blind spots. It stabilises a moving world despite constant eye movements. It groups separate elements into coherent forms. It infers depth from cues rather than receiving depth directly. It uses context to decide what object is likely present, what background can be ignored, and what anomaly demands attention.

This becomes visible in optical illusions.

An illusion does not merely trick the eye. It reveals the rules by which perception is normally built. Lines of equal length appear unequal because the surrounding context alters judgement. Still images appear to move because contrast and pattern trigger motion-processing tendencies.

One image flips between two interpretations because the brain cannot hold both constructions equally at once. A shape appears brighter, darker, larger, smaller, nearer, or farther depending on what surrounds it.

The illusion is not an error added to perception from outside. It is a window into the constructive process itself.

The same principle extends beyond vision. Hearing also depends on interpretation.

We do not neutrally hear raw sound. We hear organised significance.

A sound may register as speech, threat, rhythm, atmosphere, interruption, comfort, machinery, or music, depending on context and expectation. In a noisy room, the brain can suddenly foreground one voice and let the rest fall back.

A creak in the house at midday is ignored; the same creak at night may feel ominous. A phrase spoken in one tone sounds affectionate; in another, contemptuous. The acoustic signal matters, but meaning emerges through the brain's interpretation of timing, emphasis, prior knowledge, and situational framing.

This is one reason language cannot be reduced to words alone. The sensory system is already shaping what the words feel like before conscious analysis catches up.

Touch is equally interpretive. Temperature, pressure, texture, pain, and bodily location are not simply delivered as finished truths.

They are mapped and evaluated. The same contact can feel soothing, invasive, neutral, or painful depending on state, trust, expectation, and context.

A hand on the shoulder may calm one person and alarm another. Bodily sensation is real, but sensation does not arrive free of interpretation.

Smell and taste, though often given less cultural attention, reveal another dimension of construction.

They are deeply tied to memory, emotion, and association.

A scent can trigger comfort, disgust, grief, or nostalgia almost instantly.

A flavour can feel familiar, medicinal, luxurious, dangerous, or repellent according to experience and cultural conditioning.

What is delicious in one context may be intolerable in another. Perception is not just sensory input. It is sensory input meeting biography.

There are also many senses that many people pay less conscious attention to, though they shape daily life profoundly.

Proprioception helps us know where the body is in space. It allows us to move without constantly staring at our limbs. It gives a sense of position, reach, balance, and coordination.

Interoception, discussed in the previous chapter, gives a sense of internal bodily condition: tension, heartbeat, hunger, breath, nausea, arousal, comfort, depletion.

Together, these make clear that perception is not only outward-facing. We do not merely perceive a world "out there." We also perceive a body "in here," and the two continuously influence one another.

This matters because perception is never only about information. It is about relevance.

The brain is constantly asking, often outside awareness: What is this? Does it matter? Is it safe? Is it familiar? What should I do with it?

This is why context changes everything.

A raised voice in a theatre rehearsal is different from a raised voice in a family argument. A rapid heartbeat after exercise is interpreted differently from the same heartbeat in a silent room while awaiting bad news. A stranger approaching quickly in daylight may seem ordinary; at night, in a tense state, threatening. The sensory data may overlap, but context reorganises meaning.

Perception, then, is not merely sensation. It is sensation plus interpretation, structured by history and current conditions.

Expectation plays a major role in this.

If the brain expects one thing, it often prepares perception in advance. This can be helpful. It speeds recognition and allows efficient interaction with a familiar world. But it can also narrow awareness.

People often see what they are prepared to see, hear what fits their model, and miss what does not fit cleanly enough. This is not because they are foolish. It is because perception is economical. The brain uses prior patterns to reduce uncertainty.

Without this, life would be overwhelming. With it, life becomes navigable but vulnerable to distortion.

This is one reason first impressions feel so powerful. Once an interpretation begins to settle, incoming information may be pulled into its orbit.

A person seen as trustworthy may have ambiguous behaviour overlooked.

A person framed as suspicious may have the same behaviour treated as evidence. A news story introduced with emotional language will be read differently from one framed neutrally. An image presented alongside certain words will appear to mean more than the image alone contains.

Perception is always in dialogue with framing.

This has enormous implications for influence.

If perception were merely a passive recording, manipulation would be much harder. But because we construct what they perceive through context, repetition, emotional priming, and expectation, perception can be shaped.

Attention can be guided. Salience can be engineered. Certain cues can be amplified while others are suppressed.

A person can be led not only towards certain conclusions, but towards certain experiences of what feels obvious, threatening, urgent, or true.

This is one reason modern environments are so powerful. Screens, headlines, edits, sound design, repetition, symbols, slogans, colour, pacing, and social cues all participate in the shaping of perceptual reality.

The brain is not simply decoding neutral information. It is moving through designed stimuli built to attract, intensify, and organise attention.

That is why literacy of perception matters.

To understand that the senses construct rather than merely reveal is not to become paralysed by doubt.

It is to become more discerning. It is to realise that what feels immediate may still require reflection. It is to notice that perception is strongest where it feels most self-evident. It is to develop humility in the face of how easily context can reshape what appears clear.

This does not mean trusting nothing. It means learning how trust should be earned.

It also changes how we think about disagreement. Some conflicts are not simply disputes over interpretation after the fact.

They begin with different perceptual worlds. People are not always arguing over the same thing, seen differently at the level of opinion.

Sometimes they have genuinely attended to different cues, organised them differently, and lived through different bodily and emotional states while doing so.

Understanding this does not solve every conflict, but it softens simplistic assumptions about why others perceive as they do.

There is another important implication.

If perception is constructed, then the self that moves through the world is partly shaped by those constructions.

The world you inhabit is not only external geography. It is also a perceptual organisation.

What stands out to you, what recedes, what alarms you, what comforts you, what you fail to notice, what you repeatedly anticipate, all of this contributes to the reality you live within.

This is why learning to observe perception is itself transformative.

To notice that context alters sight is to weaken naïve certainty.
To notice that tone alters meaning is to deepen relational awareness.
To notice that bodily state alters interpretation is to become less ruled by immediate impressions.
To notice that attention can be guided is to reclaim some freedom from automatic capture.

The senses are extraordinary. They do not imprison us in illusion. They make human life possible. But they do not hand us reality in finished form. They offer partial contact with a world too vast to absorb directly, and the brain builds from there.

That construction is shaped by biology.
It is shaped by experience.
It is shaped by memory.
It is shaped by the state.
It is shaped by expectation.
And it is shaped by the environments in which perception is being trained.

This is not bad news. It is an invitation to maturity.

Because once we understand that the senses construct the world we experience, another question emerges naturally:

If perception is built through interpretation, then how much of that interpretation is happening before conscious awareness even catches up?

That takes us to the predictive brain.

Brain Observation

Notice one ordinary situation today in which context changes what you perceive. It might be a message read in one tone and then another, a facial expression that feels different depending on your mood, or a sound that seems harmless in daylight and unsettling at night.

Everyday Experiment

Look at one ambiguous image or optical illusion and stay with it for at least thirty seconds. Notice whether your perception changes. Then place it beside a caption or interpretation suggested by someone else and look again. Ask yourself: did the image change, or did my interpretation change?

Visual Aid

Create a simple black-and-white page titled: **Signal | Context | What I Perceived.** Use three columns and fill in a few short examples, such as:

- raised voice | busy café | enthusiasm
- raised voice | family argument | threat
- silence | peaceful walk | calm
- silence | after conflict | rejection
- fast heartbeat | exercise | energy
- fast heartbeat | uncertainty | anxiety

Leave extra blank lines underneath for your own examples. At the end of the page, underline any entries where the same signal produced a different perception because the context changed.

Signal | Context | What I Perceived

Signal	Context	What I Perceived
raised voice	busy café	enthusiasm
raised voice	family argument	threat
silence	peaceful walk	calm
silence	after conflict	rejection
fast heartbeat	exercise	energy
fast heartbeat	uncertainty	anxiety
.		
.		
.		
.		

Ethical Question

If perception can be shaped by context, framing, and expectation before conscious reflection begins, what responsibilities do media, institutions, teachers, designers, and leaders have when presenting information to others?

Chapter 4 - The Brain as Prediction Engine

It is tempting to imagine perception as something that happens in a simple sequence.

First, the world presents itself.
Then the senses receive it.
Then the brain processes what has arrived.
Then consciousness notices the result.

This picture feels intuitive, but it is incomplete.

The brain does not merely wait for reality to arrive and then react to it. It anticipates. It projects. It generates expectations about what is likely to happen, what signals are likely to appear, what they are likely to mean, and how the organism should prepare. In that sense, the brain is not only a receiver of information. It is a prediction engine.

This may be one of the most important things to understand about human cognition.

Much of what feels like immediate perception is already shaped by what the brain expected to find. Much of what feels like certainty is supported by prior patterning.

Much of what feels like a direct reading of reality is actually a comparison between incoming signals and an internal model built from memory, learning, repetition, context, and survival relevance.

The brain is not asking only, *What is here?*
It is also asking, *What is most likely here?*
What usually happens next?
What should I prepare for?
What fits what I already know?

This predictive function is not a strange extra feature. It is one of the reasons the brain can operate with such speed.

If the brain had to build every perception from nothing, moment by moment, human life would be far too slow and cognitively expensive to sustain. Prediction reduces uncertainty. It allows the organism to move through a changing world without re-learning the meaning of every sound, face, object, tone, or environment from scratch. The brain uses prior knowledge to guide present interpretation. It fills in likely patterns before all the evidence has arrived.

This is efficient.
It is adaptive.
And it is also the source of many distortions.

The predictive brain works, in simple terms, through an ongoing process of modelling and correction.

It builds expectations based on experience. Incoming sensory information is then compared with those expectations. When the incoming signal matches the model closely enough, perception feels smooth and immediate. When the signal does not fit, a mismatch appears. The brain must then decide whether the signal is noise to be ignored, an anomaly to be noted, or evidence that the model itself needs updating.

This mismatch is often described as a **prediction error**.

Prediction error is not a mistake in the moral sense. It is the gap between what the brain expected and what actually arrived. In many cases, this gap is how learning happens. The brain predicts, reality differs, and the model is revised. But not all prediction errors are treated equally. Some are dismissed. Some are minimised. Some are absorbed into the old model. Some force a more substantial update. Which response occurs depends on attention, emotional salience, bodily state, prior belief, and perceived stakes.

This helps explain why people often fail to revise their views even when faced with new information.

The issue is not always simple stubbornness. Sometimes the brain is treating the new signal as less important than the stability of the existing model. The familiar interpretation may feel safer, more coherent, or less costly than the uncertainty required to update it. Under stress, this tendency often becomes stronger. When the organism feels threatened, efficiency and certainty are prioritised over openness and nuance.

That is why prediction is not merely cognitive. It is embodied and emotional.

A person who has learned, through repeated experience, that raised voices signal danger may react before conscious reasoning begins. A person who has learned that silence predicts rejection may interpret distance quickly and painfully. A person living under chronic tension may predict threat where ambiguity exists. Another person, raised in more stable conditions, may predict manageability and remain open longer. The signal may be the same. The model beneath it is not.

Prediction is therefore not only about objects and events. It is also about relationships, safety, identity, belonging, and meaning.

This begins early.

The developing brain not only learns facts. It learns regularities. It learns which facial expressions tend to precede comfort or criticism. It learns whether emotional expression is met with support, dismissal, intrusion, or punishment. It learns whether the world tends to feel chaotic or coherent, whether closeness feels nourishing or risky, and whether attention brings safety or exposure. These patterns become predictive templates. Later in life, they shape how quickly a person trusts, defends, withdraws, over-explains, anticipates loss, or braces for conflict.

Many adult reactions are not merely responses to the present moment. They are predictions carried forward from past environments.

This helps explain why some experiences feel so immediate and disproportionate. The system is not only reacting to what is there. It is reacting to what the brain predicts, which means, based on previous patterning.

The predictive nature of the brain also shapes attention.

Attention is not just a spotlight we direct consciously. It is deeply guided by what the brain expects to matter. If a person is worried about a threat, attention becomes biased towards cues of danger. If a person is searching for approval, attention may become tuned to signs of acceptance or rejection. If someone is repeatedly immersed in outrage-driven media, attention may become sensitised to provocation and conflict. What stands out in the environment is influenced not only by what is objectively present, but by what the predictive system is already primed to detect.

This is why expectation can alter perception before deliberate thought begins.

When people say, "I had a feeling something was off," sometimes that feeling reflects real pattern detection below the level of language. At other times, it reflects a prediction template that has become too ready to impose itself. Distinguishing the two is part of the work of discernment.

The brain predicts not only the outside world but also the body.

It anticipates the likely meaning of internal signals. A quickened heart might be interpreted as exertion, fear, anticipation, attraction, or panic, depending on context and prior modelling. A dip in energy might be read as rest needed, personal failure, illness, sadness, or boredom, depending on what the system expects such a shift to mean. Prediction shapes interoception just as it shapes perception of the external world.

This matters because bodily states can become self-reinforcing through prediction.

If a person notices a bodily shift and predicts danger, the body may intensify. The intensified body then appears to confirm the prediction. The person says, "I knew something was wrong," while the loop has partly been driven by interpretation itself. This does not mean the distress is imaginary. It means the brain-body system is participatory. Expectation can amplify experience.

In calmer forms, the same dynamic appears in everyday life. A person who expects a conversation to go badly may enter a tense, guarded, and narrow in attention. That state alters tone, posture, and interpretation, making misunderstanding more likely. Another person who expects openness may hear more generously, respond with less defensiveness, and help create a better outcome. The future is not fully determined by expectation, but expectation shapes the conditions under which the future is met.

Prediction, then, is closely tied to **framing**.

A frame is not merely an opinion. It is a structure of expectation. It tells the brain what kind of thing this is likely to be. Once the frame is in place, interpretation begins to organise around it.

Call a policy a protection, and it is perceived differently than if it is called a restriction.

Call a person intense, and their behaviour is read differently than if they are called committed.

Introduce an event as inspiring, suspicious, dangerous, sacred, trivial, or historic, and the perceptual field changes before the details are even examined.

Frames matter because they pre-load meaning.

This is why headlines, introductions, labels, authority cues, and emotional tone are so powerful. They do not only communicate information. They prepare a prediction. They condition what the brain is likely to notice, foreground, dismiss, or infer. By the time a person thinks they are assessing the facts neutrally, the interpretive field may already be structured.

Closely related to framing is **priming**.

Priming refers to the way prior exposure to certain cues can influence subsequent interpretation, behaviour, or response without requiring explicit awareness. A word, image, tone, emotional atmosphere, or repeated association can subtly shape what comes next. Prime someone with fear, and ambiguous information is more likely to be perceived as threatening. Prime someone with scarcity, and decisions may become narrower. Prime someone with belonging, and their openness may change. These influences are not always dramatic, but they are real enough to reveal how porous conscious interpretation can be.

The predictive brain also explains why habits feel natural once established.

Repeated experiences become compressed into expectations. The brain learns that certain routines, reactions, and thoughts are likely. The more often a pattern is repeated, the less effort is needed to produce it. This is useful when the pattern is healthy, skilled, or stabilising. It becomes limiting when the pattern is rigid, defensive, or self-defeating. In both cases, prediction reduces effort by leaning on prior learning.

That is why change can feel uncomfortable even when it is beneficial.

A new way of thinking, regulating, or responding may be better in principle, but the brain has not yet learned it as the most reliable prediction. The unfamiliar can initially feel wrong simply because it is unfamiliar. This is especially important in healing and development. People sometimes assume that what feels natural must be what is true for them. Often, what feels natural is simply what has been predicted for the longest.

The predictive brain is not only vulnerable to error. It is also the basis of skill.

A musician predicts timing, rhythm, and sequence.
A driver predicts movement and flow.
A speaker predicts audience response and adjusts in real time.

A reader predicts the likely end of a sentence.
A close friend predicts mood shifts before they are named.

Much of competence is prediction refined through experience. The more skilful the system becomes, the less obvious its predictive work appears. Expertise often feels intuitive because the brain has built highly tuned models.

But expertise has limits, too. It can harden into an assumption. A person can become so confident in their model that they stop noticing disconfirming evidence. The same brain that learns beautifully can become over-committed to its own predictions. This is why humility remains essential even in mastery.

Prediction also helps explain social and political perception.

People do not enter information environments empty. They arrive with narrative models already in place: about institutions, identity, morality, danger, truth, competence, and betrayal. New events are filtered through these models. Often, opposing groups are not just disagreeing over data. They are predicting different realities from the same signals. One sees defence, another sees aggression. One sees censorship, another sees protection. One sees liberation, another sees chaos. Once prediction templates become socially reinforced, they can become very difficult to revise.

This is one of the reasons repetition is so effective in shaping belief.

Repetition not only makes an idea familiar. It makes it easier for the brain to predict and, therefore, easier to experience as coherent, plausible, and available. Familiarity can begin to feel like truth, not because truth has been established, but because the predictive burden is lower. The repeated narrative becomes the expected narrative. The expected narrative becomes the smoother one to inhabit.

This should not make us cynical. It should make us more aware.

To understand the brain as a prediction engine is to recognise that certainty is often supported by expectation beneath awareness. It is to realise that perception and interpretation are not only about what is present, but also about what the system is already preparing for. It is to see that learning requires not only new information, but sometimes enough safety and attention for prediction itself to be revised.

This brings us to an important point: the brain is not trying to be philosophically objective. It is trying to keep the organism functioning.

If an existing model works well enough for navigation, the brain often prefers it over costly revision. That is adaptive. But it also means human beings must sometimes do something effortful and unnatural: pause, reflect, and ask whether what feels obvious is actually accurate, or simply predicted.

This is one of the foundations of critical thinking.

Critical thinking is not only about logic applied to facts. It is also about noticing the predictions that arrive before the logic does. It is about seeing the frame beneath the conclusion, the emotional tone beneath the certainty, the expectation beneath the perception. It is about widening the gap between immediate interpretation and deeper evaluation.

That widening can feel uncomfortable. But it is one of the ways awareness matures.

Once we understand this, many familiar experiences begin to look different.

Why do first impressions stick?
Why do misunderstandings escalate so quickly?
Why does anxiety distort ambiguous cues?
Why do people remain attached to narratives despite contradictions?
Why does repeated media exposure shape what feels obvious?
Why does calm improve discernment?

In each case, the predictive brain is involved.

It is constantly modelling.
Constantly anticipating.
Constantly comparing.
Constantly deciding whether to hold, ignore, or revise.

The brain does not merely receive the world. It attempts to stay one step ahead of it.

That is not a defect. It is part of how life remains possible. But it means that reality, as we experience it, is always partly shaped by what the brain thought was likely before the moment fully arrived.

And once that becomes clear, another question emerges:

If prediction shapes perception so profoundly, then what happens when those predictions are repeatedly shaped by culture, media, trauma, language, and social reinforcement?

That takes us further into the architecture of influence still to come.

Brain Observation

Notice one moment today when you reacted to something quickly and later realised you had filled in part of the meaning before all the information was available.

What did you predict, and what made that prediction feel so immediate?

Everyday Experiment

Ask someone to send you a short, ambiguous text message such as "We need to talk later" or "Interesting." Read it once when you feel calm and once when you feel tired, stressed, or uncertain.

Notice how the predicted meaning shifts with your internal state, even though the words remain the same.

Visual Aid

Create a simple black-and-white page titled:

What Happened | What I Predicted | What Actually Happened

Fill in a few examples over several days, such as:

- delayed reply | they are annoyed with me | they were busy

- tight chest | something is wrong | I was over-caffeinated

- silence in meeting | they disliked the idea | people were thinking

- unexpected call | bad news | routine check-in

Leave extra lines underneath for your own examples. At the end of the page, mark any repeated patterns where your first prediction leaned consistently towards threat, rejection, certainty, or reassurance.

What Happened	What I Predicted	What Actually Happened
delayed reply	they are annoyed with me	they were busy
tight chest	something is wrong	I was over-caffeinated
silence in meeting	they disliked the idea	people were thinking
unexpected call	bad news	routine check-in

Ethical Question

If we as beings are constantly predicting before we consciously reflect, how easily can those predictions be shaped by people or systems that understand how expectation works?

Chapter 5 - Hemispheres, Networks, and the Myth of the "Logical vs Creative Brain"

Few ideas about the brain have travelled further in popular culture than the claim that one side is "logical" and the other is "creative".

It is repeated in classrooms, personality quizzes, business workshops, self-help language, casual conversation, and social media shorthand. People describe themselves as "left-brained" if they are analytical, orderly, mathematical, or verbally structured.

They describe themselves as "right-brained" if they are artistic, intuitive, emotional, imaginative, or visually expressive. The distinction is appealing because it is simple. It gives people an easy way to classify themselves and others. It turns the complexity of cognition into a neat story.

The trouble is that the story is too neat.

Like many enduring myths, it contains a fragment of truth wrapped in a great deal of oversimplification. The brain does have hemispheres.

Those hemispheres do show certain patterns of specialisation. Some functions are more strongly associated with one side than the other. But the popular idea that people are essentially ruled by one hemisphere, as though half the brain dominates personality and ability, is not an accurate reflection of how human cognition works.

The deeper truth is more interesting.

The brain is lateralised in some respects, integrated in many others, and profoundly networked overall. Thought, feeling, language, imagination, planning, movement, memory, attention, and perception emerge through cooperation across regions and systems, not through a simple battle between two different personalities living on either side of the skull.

To understand why this matters, we need to begin with the hemispheres themselves.

The human brain is divided into left and right hemispheres, connected by a thick bundle of fibres called the **corpus callosum**, which allows rapid communication between them. This division is not decorative. It reflects real developmental and functional organisation. The hemispheres are not identical mirror copies performing all tasks in the same way. Research over decades has shown that some functions tend to be more dominant in one hemisphere than the other.

For example, in most right-handed individuals, and in many left-handed individuals as well, aspects of language production and grammatical sequencing are more strongly associated with the left hemisphere. Certain forms of spatial processing, facial recognition, broad attentional awareness, and aspects of prosody or emotional tone have often been more associated with the right. This is real lateralisation.

But lateralisation is not the same as isolation.

Language is not "only left-brained". Creativity is not "only right-brained". Emotion does not belong neatly to one side, nor logic to the other. Even highly lateralised functions rely on broader cooperation. To speak meaningfully involves not just grammar and word retrieval, but tone, memory, timing, social interpretation, motor control, emotional context, and self-monitoring.

Creating art involves not just imagination, but planning, sequencing, attention, motor coordination, memory, symbolic association, and decision-making. In real life, cognitive acts are composite.

The myth survives because the brain is easier to talk about when reduced to binaries.

Human beings like clear oppositions:
logic versus feeling,
order versus spontaneity,
structure versus freedom,
analysis versus intuition.

These oppositions are culturally powerful because they map onto personality stereotypes, educational habits, gender narratives, and modern identity language. But the brain does not organise itself around these social simplifications. It operates through layered coordination.

A person solving an equation may use imagination.
A poet may rely on structure.
A musician may depend on counting and timing.

A scientist may need intuition to ask the right question.
An artist may be highly methodical.
A strategist may rely deeply on embodied feeling.

The false split between "logical" and "creative" minds often hides how intertwined these capacities really are.

It can also become limiting.

When people are told they are "not creative," they may stop exploring forms of thought that were never absent, only underused or undertrained. When people are told they are "not analytical," they may confuse lack of confidence or practice with fixed cognitive architecture. The myth encourages identity foreclosure. It invites people to live inside simplified labels rather than dynamic possibilities.

This matters because the brain is plastic. Networks strengthen with use. Skills deepen with training. Modes of thinking interact. A person may have predispositions, but predisposition is not destiny. The more rigidly someone identifies with one side of a simplified binary, the less likely they are to develop across the full range of their capacities.

So if the brain is not usefully understood as "left versus right," how should it be understood?

A better model is one of **distributed networks**.

The brain contains regions with different tendencies and roles, but complex cognition emerges through communication among them. Perception, attention, memory, emotion, planning, language, self-monitoring, and imagination are all supported by overlapping systems. These systems form dynamic networks that shift depending on task, state, context, and learned habits.

In recent decades, neuroscience has increasingly moved towards network-based thinking for precisely this reason. Rather than asking only which single region "does" a function, researchers increasingly examine how sets of regions cooperate. This does not make anatomy irrelevant. It makes anatomy more relational.

Take attention as an example.

Attention is not one thing. It involves orienting, sustaining focus, filtering distraction, shifting between stimuli, and balancing narrow concentration with broad situational awareness. Different brain regions participate in these processes, but they do so as networks rather than isolated modules. Likewise, memory involves encoding, consolidation, retrieval, emotional weighting, contextual placement, and bodily state. It is not housed in one neat location. It is coordinated across systems.

The same is true for selfhood.

The experience of "being me" involves interoception, autobiographical memory, social reflection, internal narrative, emotional tone, and moment-to-moment sensory integration. No single brain region contains the self in finished form. What feels like a unified identity arises through ongoing coordination.

This network view also helps correct another misleading assumption: that specialised regions imply rigid compartments.

It is useful to know that some areas are particularly important for speech production, visual processing, motor control, emotional salience, or memory consolidation. But these are not tiny isolated offices doing one job forever in total independence. Their function depends on input, output, context, and communication with other areas. Damage to one part of the network may have cascading effects. Compensation may emerge elsewhere. The system is not infinitely flexible, but it is more dynamic than static maps imply.

This is why people can recover functions after injury in ways that would seem impossible under a strictly compartmental model. Not because the brain is magical, but because it is adaptive and networked.

The idea of the "logical brain" versus the "creative brain" also becomes less persuasive when we look at how real-world problem-solving works.

A person trying to navigate a difficult conversation must read tone, infer meaning, regulate emotion, remember context, choose words, predict consequences, and adapt in real time. Is that logic? Creativity? Emotion? Intuition? It is all of these interacting.

A person writing a chapter, composing music, designing a system, raising a child, teaching a class, or building a business is drawing on multiple forms of cognition at once. Human intelligence is rarely pure in the categories culture gives it.

There is also a deeper point here.

The binary myth often mirrors the broader habit of splitting cognition from feeling. One hemisphere becomes associated with rationality, the other with emotion or intuition, as though integrated human life were somehow less valuable than tidy separation. But some of the most important capacities in mature cognition come from integration, not division. Insight often depends on emotional sensitivity plus conceptual clarity. Good judgement often requires both analysis and felt sense. Discernment frequently emerges when pattern recognition, memory, bodily regulation, and reflective reasoning are all available together.

The healthiest question is not, *Which side am I?*
It is. *How integrated is my system?*

This brings us naturally to large-scale networks that have become increasingly influential in understanding the brain.

Without turning this chapter into a technical catalogue, it is useful to note that researchers have identified recurring patterns of activity across distributed systems. Different networks are involved in focused task engagement, salience detection, internal reflection, bodily awareness, executive control, and broad attentional orientation. These networks are not little personalities, but functional groupings that help explain why the brain can shift between different modes of operation.

For example, there are systems associated with:

- focused attention and deliberate task execution

- noticing what is important or emotionally salient

- internal reflection, autobiographical thought, and mind-wandering

- sensory and bodily integration

- motor coordination and timing

What matters for this book is not memorising the names of every network, but understanding the principle: the brain works through coordinated patterns, not simplistic dualisms.

This also helps explain why we can feel fragmented.

When attention is hijacked, emotion is dysregulated, bodily awareness is muted, and internal narrative becomes repetitive or defensive, the system may lose integration. A person may feel split between what they know and what they feel, between what they want and what they do, between their values and their reactions. This does not necessarily mean their "right brain" is fighting their "left brain". More often, it means multiple systems are struggling to coordinate under strain.

Likewise, states of coherence may feel like clarity, flow, alignment, or groundedness because more of the system is working together.

This is one reason oversimplified brain myths can be subtly damaging. They do not merely misinform. They can distract people from the deeper issue, which is not hemispheric identity but systemic integration.

There is also a cultural allure to brain myths because they explain without responsibility.

A person can say, "I'm more right-brained," to avoid building structure. Another can say, "I'm more left-brained," to avoid risk, ambiguity, or emotional literacy. The label becomes a story that freezes development. But the brain is not asking to be reduced in this way. It is asking to be understood as dynamic, trainable, relational, and context-sensitive.

This does not mean there are no meaningful differences between people. Of course there are. Temperament varies. Training varies. developmental history varies. Strengths vary. Interests vary. Some people more readily lean into abstraction. Others into pattern, image, sound, or relational nuance. Some people naturally prefer sequence and structure. Others thrive in exploration and synthesis.

These differences matter. But they do not justify the crude fiction that one half of the brain is the "real" source of who someone is.

A more mature understanding allows both variation and complexity.

You may be drawn towards certain styles of thought.
You may have stronger habits in one direction than another.
You may have been reinforced, educated, praised, or shamed

into particular modes.

But you are not best understood as a hostage of one hemisphere.

You are better understood as a person whose cognitive life emerges through multiple interacting systems shaped by biology, experience, culture, and use.

This chapter closes Part I for a reason.

The first part of this book has established that the brain is not merely an organ to be named, but a living architecture: embodied, perceptual, predictive, and networked. We began by asking what the brain is, then moved into its ongoing conversation with the body, its constructive role in perception, and its predictive relationship to the world. Now, by stepping beyond one of the most familiar simplifications in popular neuroscience, we arrive at a more grounded image of cognition itself.

The brain is not a tidy machine of isolated compartments.
It is a coordinated system.
Not a set of simplistic binaries, but an adaptive whole.
Not merely left or right, logical or creative, but distributed, dynamic, and integrative.

This matters because the next stage of the inquiry moves deeper into function.

Once we understand that the brain is an embodied and networked architecture, the next question becomes: how does it operate through signalling, chemistry, timing, and adaptation? How do electrical impulses, neurotransmitters, memory processes, and emotional states shape the lived reality of thought and behaviour?

That is where Part II begins. If Part I has given us the structure, Part II turns to process. We move from architecture to activity.

From form to function. From the living brain as a system to the living brain as a signal. Once the chemistry and electricity of that signal come into view, the human story becomes deeper still.

Brain Observation

Notice when you casually describe yourself or others using narrow cognitive labels such as "logical," "creative," "left-brained," "right-brained," "book smart," or "not wired for that." What do those labels simplify, and what do they hide?

Everyday Experiment

Choose one small task you usually associate with a particular kind of mind. If you see yourself as analytical, do something expressive: sketch, improvise, free-write, or rearrange a room aesthetically. If you see yourself as creative, do something structured: organise a page of notes, solve a logic puzzle, map a sequence, or break a process into steps. Notice what feels difficult, what feels possible, and whether the old label is describing a limit or merely a habit.

Visual Aid

Create a simple black-and-white page titled:

Task | Which Abilities It Actually Uses

Fill in examples such as:

- writing a poem | memory, rhythm, language, emotion, structure
- solving a problem | logic, imagination, pattern recognition, patience
- having a difficult conversation | empathy, self-control, language, timing, prediction
- learning music | repetition, listening, movement, sequencing, feeling
- teaching an idea | comprehension, communication, creativity, organisation

Leave extra blank lines for your own entries.

At the end, underline any task where you initially assumed only one ability was involved but later noticed several working together.

Task	Which Abilities It Actually Uses
writing a poem	memory, rhythm, language, emotion, structure
solving a problem	logic, imagination, pattern recognition, patience
having a difficult conversation	empathy, self-control, language, timing, prediction
learning music	repetition, listening, movement, sequencing, feeling
teaching an idea	comprehension, communication, creativity,
•	
•	
•	
•	
•	

Ethical Question

When simplified brain myths are repeated in schools, workplaces, therapy language, and media, do they merely make science easier to talk about, or can they quietly shape people into narrower versions of themselves?

PART II - Chemistry, Electricity, And Adaption

If Part I established the living architecture of the brain, Part II turns to its movement, signalling, and change.

The brain is not only a structure. It is an activity. It is not simply made of regions and networks that can be named on a diagram. It is alive with transmission, modulation, timing, reinforcement, inhibition, adaptation, and revision.

Electrical impulses travel across cells. Chemical messengers alter readiness, mood, motivation, attention, and learning. Memories are formed, reshaped, and sometimes distorted. Emotional states influence cognition.

Repetition strengthens patterns. Novelty interrupts them. Through all of this, the brain remains neither rigid nor infinitely fluid, but paradoxically both stable enough to preserve continuity and plastic enough to change.

This second part explores that dynamic life directly. If the first part asked what the brain is, this part asks how it functions as a living signalling system. How does electricity become communication?

How do neurotransmitters and hormones participate in shaping behaviour and experience? How does memory work if it is not simple storage? Why do emotion and logic depend so heavily on one another? And how does the brain remain adaptable without becoming chaotic?

We begin in **Chapter 6, Electricity, Neurochemistry, and the Language of Signalling**, where the brain is approached as an electrical-chemical system rather than a static object. This chapter introduces neurons, glial cells, synapses, action potentials, neurotransmitters, and the wider principles of signalling through which the brain coordinates communication.

It also begins to show that information in the brain is not only about content, but about timing, rhythm, intensity, and relation.

The brain does not merely contain signals. It lives by them.

From there, **Chapter 7, Dopamine, Serotonin, Cortisol, Oxytocin, and the Myth of Simple Mood Chemicals**, widens the chemical picture while resisting pop-science simplifications.

Modern culture often treats these substances as though each were responsible for one tidy emotional function: dopamine for pleasure, serotonin for happiness, cortisol for stress, oxytocin for love. But the truth is far more layered.

This chapter explores how these chemicals participate in motivation, attachment, anticipation, novelty, vigilance, reward, bonding, regulation, and adaptation, while challenging the reductionist myths that so often flatten them into slogans.

In **Chapter 8, Memory Is Not Storage, It Is Reconstruction**, the inquiry turns to one of the most intimate and misunderstood functions of the brain. Memory does not simply archive reality like a hard drive. It selects, edits, compresses, links, and rebuilds experience through changing contexts. This chapter examines working memory, short-term and long-term memory, emotional memory, procedural memory, and the reasons recall is often unstable, selective, and vulnerable to distortion. It also opens the deeper question of how memory becomes narrative, and how narrative becomes identity.

That naturally leads into **Chapter 9, Emotion, Logic, and Why the Best Thinking Is Not Emotionless**, where one of the most persistent modern misconceptions is challenged directly. Emotion is often framed as the enemy of reason, something primitive that interferes with clarity.

Yet lived experience and research both show that emotion is not separate from thinking, but central to it.

This chapter explores emotion as a signal, the narrowing effects of dysregulation, and the degree to which memory, judgement, discernment, and learning depend on the stability of the system as a whole.

It also returns to a recurring theme of this book: that regulation, emotional balance, and intellectual clarity are deeply intertwined.

Finally, **Chapter 10, Plasticity, Adaptation, and the Paradoxical Brain**, closes this part by bringing the previous themes together into the broader question of change. The brain can learn, reorganise, and adapt, but not without limit.

It is shaped by repetition, attention, habit, recovery, stress, environment, and use.

This chapter examines neuroplasticity without romanticising it, showing both the possibility of transformation and the constraints that give continuity to identity and functioning.

The paradox at the heart of the chapter is the paradox at the heart of the brain itself: it must remain stable enough to preserve a world, yet flexible enough to survive one.

Taken together, these chapters move the inquiry from architecture into process.

They reveal that the brain is not just a thing one has, but a living system of activity through which mood, meaning, memory, habit, motivation, and adaptation emerge.

They also deepen one of the central themes that has been building since the beginning of the book: thought is never separate from the state.

The quality of perception, memory, learning, and judgement depends profoundly on the signalling conditions through which the system is operating.

If Part I gave us the scaffolding, Part II gives us the current moving through it.

Here, the brain begins to appear less like a fixed object and more like an ongoing event: electrical, chemical, emotional, rhythmic, adaptive, and in constant negotiation with both body and world.

Once that becomes clear, the next stage of the inquiry begins to sharpen.

Because if the brain is shaped so profoundly by its signals, states, and repetitions, then the question is no longer only how it works. It becomes what it is shaped by relationship, culture, language, conditioning, attention, and social life itself.

That is where Part II will take us.

Chapter 6 - Electricity, Neurochemistry, & Language of Signalling

If the brain is to be understood as a living system rather than a biological mass of cells, then sooner or later we must turn towards its signals.

The brain does not merely contain thoughts, memories, or emotions in some silent, finished form. It lives through activity. It functions through communication.

It depends on cells that signal, support, regulate, amplify, inhibit, connect, and adapt. Beneath every perception, movement, memory, anticipation, impulse, and mood is an extraordinary interplay of electrical and chemical events unfolding across time.

This does not make our experiences less meaningful. It reveals one of the ways meaning becomes possible.

A thought is not only an idea.

It is also a pattern of activity.
A feeling is not only subjective.

It is also embodied signalling.
A memory is not only narrative. It is also reactivated circuitry.
An urge is not only psychological. It is also chemical readiness and neural preparation.

To understand the brain as a signal is not to reduce our experiences to being mechanical. It is to recognise that the machinery is alive, adaptive, and relationally organised in ways far more subtle than older mechanical metaphors ever captured.

At the centre of this signalling world is the neuron.

Neurons are often introduced as the primary signalling cells of the nervous system, and that description is broadly correct. They are specialised cells able to receive, process, and transmit information through electrochemical means.

But even here, the simplified textbook image can mislead if it becomes too static. A neuron is not merely a little wire. It is a living cell with structure, metabolism, thresholds, timing properties, and the ability to alter its connectivity over time.

In simple terms, a neuron typically receives inputs through branching structures called dendrites, integrates that information in the cell body, and, if enough activation is reached, sends a signal down a long projection called the axon. That signal can then influence other neurons, muscles, or glands. The basic principle sounds simple. The reality is astonishingly complex.

The brain contains billions of neurons, each connected to many others in dynamic patterns.

What matters is not only whether a neuron fires, but when it fires, how often, in relation to what other cells, under what chemical conditions, and within which larger network.

The brain is not merely a collection of switches turning on and off. It is a coordinated field of timing and relation.

The electrical side of this process begins with differences in charge across the neuron's membrane.

Neurons maintain a kind of resting electrical potential through the distribution of ions such as sodium, potassium, chloride, and calcium.

This potential is not static in the sense of being inactive. It is a readiness state, a condition of possibility. When inputs arrive, they alter that electrical balance. Some inputs make the neuron more likely to fire. Others make it less likely. The neuron integrates these influences, and if the threshold is crossed, an action potential occurs.

The action potential is often described as an electrical impulse. That description is useful, but again, it should not be imagined too crudely. It is a rapid, self-propagating change in membrane voltage travelling down the axon. This allows the signal to move with speed and reliability across distance. Once it reaches the axon terminal, the electrical event triggers a chemical.

And here the story becomes even more interesting.

Most neurons do not physically touch the next cell directly. Between them is a tiny gap known as the synapse. At this junction, the arriving electrical signal causes the release of chemical messengers called neurotransmitters.

These molecules cross the synaptic gap and bind to receptors on the next cell, influencing whether that cell becomes more or less likely to fire.

So the brain is not purely electrical and not purely chemical. It is an electrical-chemical system. Electrical events trigger chemical release. Chemical signals alter electrical readiness. The two are inseparable.

This is one reason simplistic metaphors often fail. The brain is not like a battery alone. It is not like a plumbing system alone. It is not like a computer circuit alone. It shares something with all of these metaphors and also exceeds them. Its signals are living, context-sensitive, state-dependent, and deeply shaped by relationships across scales.

Not all synaptic effects are the same.

Some neurotransmitters are generally excitatory, meaning they increase the likelihood that the next neuron will fire. Others are generally inhibitory, decreasing that likelihood. This balance between excitation and inhibition is fundamental.

Too much excitation without enough inhibition can produce instability, overload, or seizure-like dynamics. Too much inhibition can suppress responsiveness and flexibility. Healthy brain function depends on patterned balances rather than raw intensity alone.

This matters philosophically as well as biologically.

Many people imagine intelligence as more activation, more stimulation, more firing, more input. But the brain depends just as much on what it suppresses as on what it amplifies. Focus is not only about what becomes active. It is about what is inhibited. Clarity often depends on selective exclusion. Coherence depends on patterned restraint as much as expression.

The synapse, then, is not a trivial detail. It is one of the primary sites where learning, adaptation, and regulation become possible. Synapses strengthen, weaken, sensitise, habituate, and reorganise over time. They are part of how repetition becomes habit, how new learning becomes stabilised, and how old pathways can become more or less dominant.

For many years, neurons received most of the cultural attention, as though they alone were the stars of the nervous system. But that picture has changed. We now know that support cells, especially glial cells, are far more significant than older accounts allowed.

Glia were once treated almost as passive scaffolding, a kind of neural glue keeping things in place. The name itself reflects that history. But glial cells do much more than support structure. Different types of glia help regulate the chemical environment, clear waste, influence inflammation, assist in the insulation of axons through myelin, contribute to repair processes, and participate in signalling conditions that affect how neurons function.

In other words, the brain's intelligence does not emerge from neurons alone.

This is important because it reminds us that living systems are rarely driven by one glamorous component. Support, maintenance, modulation, and context matter as much as primary transmission. There is a lesson here beyond neuroscience. What appears central often depends on what culture learns to overlook.

Myelin offers a useful example.

Many axons are wrapped in myelin, a fatty insulating layer that helps electrical signals travel more efficiently. This insulation is essential for speed and coordination. Without it, signalling becomes slower or disrupted. Diseases that affect myelin demonstrate how fundamental this support structure is. Again, the brain is not merely about firing. It is about the conditions that allow signalling to remain coherent.

This takes us into an important idea: signalling is never only about content. It is also about timing.

The same signal arriving at a different moment can produce a different effect. Synchronisation matters. Rhythm matters. Temporal coordination matters.

The brain functions across multiple timescales, from rapid sensory discrimination to slower mood regulation to even longer cycles shaped by sleep, hormonal rhythms, and learning history. It is not enough to say that the brain "communicates". One must ask how signals are timed, grouped, repeated, inhibited, and woven into larger patterns.

This is where the language of brain rhythms or neural oscillations becomes relevant.

Different large-scale patterns of rhythmic activity have been associated with different states of wakefulness, attention, sleep, memory processing, and integration. It would be too simple to assign fixed meanings to each rhythm in a rigid one-to-one way, but the broader point remains: the brain is not only active, but it is patterned. Its activity has a cadence. States of consciousness are not merely different amounts of activity, but different organisations of activity.

A calm, attentive mind is not just "less stimulated" than a distressed one. It is differently organised. A sleeping brain is not inactive. It is active in another mode. Memory consolidation, emotional processing, and bodily restoration all depend on these changing patterns of coordination.

This brings us closer to the lived dimension of signalling.

When people think of brain chemistry, they often imagine single molecules responsible for single emotions. But before we get to specific neurotransmitters in the next chapter, it is important to understand that signalling never happens in a vacuum.

A neurotransmitter does not "mean" one thing in all places and times. Its effect depends on receptor type, network context, current state, developmental history, bodily conditions, and interaction with many other processes.

The same broad principle applies to electrical activity. A firing neuron is not meaningful in isolation. Meaning emerges in relation: which cells are involved, how patterns repeat, how the body is functioning, what the organism has learned, and what environment is currently being navigated.

This should already begin to reshape how we think about mood, thought, and behaviour.

A mental state is not just "in your head" as a vague phrase. It is part of a signalling condition. Anxiety, for example, is not only a fearful idea. It is a configuration involving attention, bodily arousal, prediction, chemical readiness, muscular tension, and often learned expectation. Likewise, calm is not only the absence of bad thoughts. It is an integrated signalling state in which the organism has sufficient regulation to widen perception and reduce defensive urgency.

The same can be said of motivation.

Motivation is not merely a moral property, as though some people possess it and others do not. It depends on energy availability, anticipated reward, salience, emotional tone, bodily state, habit, and neurochemical readiness.

This does not remove responsibility, but it does deepen our understanding of what responsibility is working through.

It also helps explain why some experiences change us so powerfully.

A repeated pattern of signalling can become familiar. Familiar patterns become easier to reactivate. Pathways strengthen. Responses become more efficient.

This is useful when the pattern reflects learning, skill, or healthy regulation. It is limiting when the pattern reflects chronic stress, defensive loops, compulsive checking, attentional hijack, or repeated emotional narrowing. The brain learns through signalling histories.

This is why repetition matters so much in education, healing, addiction, ritual, and manipulation alike.

Each repeated experience is not just an event. It is also a training signal.

Say a child repeatedly receives criticism in moments of vulnerability. The words matter, but so do the tone, the timing, the bodily state, and the repeated anticipation.

Over time, the system learns a signalling expectation: openness predicts pain. Likewise, if a person repeatedly enters calm, structured, encouraging environments while learning, the system may begin to associate difficulty with growth rather than humiliation.

These are not merely psychological beliefs floating above the body. They become patterns in the signalling life of the organism.

Seen this way, the brain is less like a storage vault and more like a dynamic regulatory conversation.

Signals arrive.
Thresholds are crossed.
Chemicals are released.

Patterns repeat.

Some pathways strengthen.

Others weaken.

Meaning becomes embodied.

This is one reason the phrase "the language of signalling" is so useful.

The brain does not speak in sentences, but it does communicate through differences, intensities, repetitions, absences, timings, and relations. It uses gradients and thresholds.

It marks salience. It amplifies some pathways and quiets others. Over time, the organism learns this language not consciously at first, but bodily. It learns what tends to happen next. It learns what states are familiar. It learns what kinds of signals mean urgency, safety, opportunity, loss, novelty, or depletion.

And because this signalling language is so fundamental, it shapes not only behaviour but interpretation.

A person living in chronic hyperarousal does not merely have a "stress problem". They are living in a signalling environment where vigilance becomes normal.

A person in prolonged under-activation may not simply lack will. They may be inhabiting a low-energy signalling condition in which mobilisation feels expensive. A person in a more regulated state may be able to think, remember, plan, and relate more effectively, not because they are morally superior, but because the underlying conditions of signalling are different.

Again, this does not erase agency. It refines what agency must work through.

It also reveals why reductionism is so inadequate. To say "it's just chemistry" misses the point entirely. Chemistry here is not trivial. It is one of the forms through which life is organised. The electrical and chemical language of the brain is not beneath meaning. It is one of the ways meaning becomes embodied, and behaviour becomes possible.

There is a further lesson here for how we think about influence.

If we are shaped by signalling environments, then tone, repetition, rhythm, stress, sensory load, and relational timing matter deeply. Influence is not only about explicit persuasion. It is also about what kinds of signalling conditions are being created. A fast, fragmented, alarm-laden environment trains one kind of brain state.

A calm, coherent, relationally safe environment supports another. The brain is always learning from the conditions in which it repeatedly operates.

This is one of the bridges between neuroscience and the wider concerns of this book.

If The Brain Was An App, Would You Use It?

Language matters, yes.
Belief matters, yes.
But beneath both are signalling conditions.

How fast something is said.
How often is it repeated?
What emotional tone surrounds it?
Whether the body is calm or braced while receiving it.
Whether the environment is coherent or fragmented.
Whether the signal is associated with safety, pressure, reward, threat, approval, or exclusion.

All of this shapes what lands and what stays.

So, before we move into specific neurotransmitters and their wider cultural mythology, this chapter asks us to hold one foundational image clearly:

The brain is alive with signals. It is electrical and chemical.
Its cells do not merely exist; they communicate.
Its networks do not merely sit there; they coordinate.
Its patterns do not merely describe experience; they help generate it.

Once that becomes clear, the next question naturally deepens:

If the brain lives through signalling, what kinds of chemicals shape motivation, mood, stress, bonding, novelty, vigilance, and reward, and why have these substances been so badly simplified in public understanding?

That is where we go next.

Brain Observation

Notice how often you describe your inner state with all-or-nothing language such as "switched on", "drained", "foggy", "wired", "flat", or "overloaded".

These phrases are often everyday descriptions of signalling conditions.

What do they reveal about how your system is functioning?

Everyday Experiment

At three points in a single day, pause for one minute and briefly note your current state using simple words: alert, tired, calm, tense, scattered, focused, heavy, energised, restless, clear. Then ask:

What might be contributing to this state right now: sleep, food, conversation, stress, movement, environment, anticipation, noise, or quiet?

The goal is not to diagnose, only to begin noticing that cognition is always arriving through conditions.

Visual Aid

Create a simple black-and-white page titled:

Time of Day | My State | Possible Contributors

Fill in a few example rows, such as:

- morning | clear but tense | poor sleep, strong coffee
- midday | scattered | noise, interruptions, hunger
- afternoon | focused | quiet room, steady pace
- evening | flat | mental fatigue, screen overload

Leave extra lines for your own entries over several days. At the end, circle any repeated contributors that seem to influence your clarity, tension, energy, or focus.

Time of Day	My State	Possible Contributors
morning	clear but tense	(poor sleep, strong coffee)
midday	scattered	noise, interruptions, hunger
afternoon	focused	(quiet room, steady pace)
evening	flat	mental fatigue, screen overload
•		
•		
•		
•		
•		
•		

Ethical Question

If environments can shape human signalling states before conscious reflection begins, how much responsibility do institutions, workplaces, schools, media systems, and digital platforms have for the kinds of states they repeatedly induce?

Chapter 7 - Dopamine, Serotonin, Cortisol, Oxytocin, and the Myth of Simple Mood Chemicals

Modern culture loves quick explanations.

Dopamine becomes the pleasure chemical.
Serotonin becomes the happiness chemical.
Cortisol becomes the stress chemical.
Oxytocin becomes the love chemical.

These labels are memorable, and that is precisely why they spread. They offer the comfort of simplicity. They make the inner life appear easier to explain than it really is. But they also mislead. The brain does not run on neat one-word chemicals with single emotional jobs.

Neurochemistry is relational, contextual, and dynamic. These substances do matter profoundly, but they do not mean only one thing, nor do they act in isolation from the wider system.

This chapter, then, is not about dismissing these chemicals. It is about rescuing them from oversimplification.

To understand brain chemistry properly, we must begin with a principle already established in the previous chapter: signalling in the brain is never only about one molecule.

It is about patterns, receptor activity, timing, location, bodily state, previous learning, and interaction with other systems. The same chemical can contribute to different experiences depending on what else is happening in the organism. Its effects may vary across different brain regions, different developmental stages, different thresholds of activation, and different social or physiological environments.

This is why chemical shorthand can be so misleading. It takes a living system and turns it into a slogan.

Consider **dopamine**.

Dopamine is often described as the pleasure chemical, but that is too narrow. Dopamine is deeply involved in motivation, salience, anticipation, reinforcement, and learning. It is not simply what makes life feel good. It is part of what makes things feel worth moving towards. It helps mark what matters, what is novel, what may lead to reward, and what should be remembered as significant.

This means dopamine is not only about enjoyment after the fact. Often, it is more active in wanting, seeking, anticipating, and orienting than in satisfaction itself.

It helps energise the approach. It is part of why novelty can feel compelling, why uncertainty can become addictive, why scrolling can continue long after real pleasure has faded, and why habits of pursuit can take on a life of their own.

This matters because human beings often confuse stimulation with fulfilment.

A person may feel highly driven by dopamine-mediated seeking and mistakes that drive for genuine satisfaction. But wanting and liking are not identical. The brain can become caught in pursuit loops that intensify action without deepening contentment.

That is one reason modern digital systems are so effective. They are often structured around intermittent reward, novelty, anticipation, and unresolved completion, conditions under which dopamine-linked motivation can remain engaged without genuine satisfaction ever fully arriving.

Dopamine also plays a role in learning. When outcomes differ from expectations, especially in reward-related ways, the system updates. This ties dopamine not only to pleasure, but to the prediction and reinforcement processes discussed in the previous chapter. It helps the organism learn what to repeat, what to pursue, and what to treat as salient. So while dopamine can contribute to enjoyment, it is better understood as part of a broader system of motivation, salience, and adaptive learning.

Now consider **serotonin.**

Serotonin is often treated as the happiness molecule, yet this, too, is misleading. Serotonin is implicated in mood regulation, but also in appetite, sleep, impulse control, sensory processing, social status dynamics, and broader forms of behavioural regulation. It is not a bottled version of happiness circulating through the skull. Rather, it is part of the wider regulation of stability, flexibility, and internal balance.

This is one reason simplistic public narratives about serotonin have become increasingly unsatisfying. Mood cannot be reduced to one neurotransmitter deficit straightforwardly, and depression is not a single chemical event. Human emotional life emerges through neurochemistry, yes, but also through meaning, stress, trauma, sleep, inflammation, hormones, environment, relationships, and history. Serotonin matters, but it does not explain the whole landscape by itself.

Still, serotonin remains important because it points towards regulation rather than mere excitement. Where dopamine is often associated with pursuit and salience, serotonin is more often discussed in relation to balance, modulation, and the governance of impulse and mood over time. These are not opposites, but different dimensions of the chemical life of the system.

Then there is **cortisol**.

Cortisol is commonly called the stress hormone, and this label is not entirely wrong, but it is too negative and too simple if left there. Cortisol is part of the body's response to challenge, energy demand, and adaptation. It helps mobilise resources. It is involved in circadian rhythms, alertness, glucose regulation, and the organism's response to perceived threat or pressure.

In acute circumstances, cortisol is not the enemy. It is part of what allows the body to meet demand. The problem arises when stress becomes chronic, unresolved, or repeatedly activated without sufficient recovery.

In such cases, the very systems designed to help adaptation can begin to wear the organism down. Attention narrows. Sleep may suffer. Mood may become brittle. Memory and learning can be affected. The body may begin to live in a state of anticipatory strain.

This is one reason so much modern discourse around stress feels incomplete. It is not merely that people "have cortisol". They live in environments that repeatedly induce the conditions under which stress signalling is normalised: uncertainty, overload, emotional capture, speed, performance pressure, fractured attention, social comparison, lack of rest, lack of safety, lack of coherent recovery.

The chemical is real, but it is always part of a wider ecology.

Next, consider **oxytocin**.

Oxytocin is often called the love hormone or bonding chemical. Again, there is truth here, but not enough. Oxytocin is involved in social bonding, trust, affiliation, attachment, and aspects of caregiving. It participates in intimate and relational life. But to call it simply the love chemical risks sentimentalising what is actually more complicated.

Oxytocin does not make every social interaction warm and universally open. Its effects are shaped by context, familiarity, prior learning, perceived safety, and in-group versus out-group dynamics. Under some conditions, it may support closeness and trust. Under others, it may intensify bonding with the familiar while heightening suspicion of what feels outside the circle. Human social chemistry is not morally pure. It is adaptive, relational, and shaped by evolutionary pressures as well as lived experience.

This should caution us against chemical romanticism. There is no single molecule of love, no single molecule of happiness, no single molecule of stress in the way popular discourse often implies.

What there are, instead, are signalling systems participating in complex emotional and behavioural lives.

We could widen the picture further.

GABA is a major inhibitory neurotransmitter involved in calming neural activity and supporting regulation.
Glutamate is one of the major excitatory neurotransmitters involved in learning, plasticity, and activation.
Noradrenaline contributes to alertness, vigilance, orientation, and mobilisation.
Endorphins are associated with pain modulation and relief.
Acetylcholine contributes to attention, learning, and memory.

But even here, the same rule applies: each matters, none acts alone, and none can be understood properly outside context.

This has direct implications for how we think about mood and behaviour.

When someone says, "I just need a high," or "I'm feeling low," they may be pointing vaguely towards real phenomena, but the language is often a cultural shortcut rather than an accurate account.

A person's motivational collapse, anxiety, compulsive seeking, emotional flatness, or social withdrawal may involve neurochemistry, but also sleep deprivation, chronic stress, nutritional issues, trauma history, overstimulation, lack of movement, inflammatory burden, hormonal changes, social isolation, or repeated cognitive-emotional patterns.

To say this clearly: chemistry matters, but chemistry is never merely chemistry in the abstract. It is lived chemistry.

This also helps us avoid one of the most common mistakes in contemporary self-understanding: moralising chemical states. People are often judged for being "lazy", "unmotivated", "too emotional", "addicted to stimulation", or "unable to focus" without enough attention paid to the signalling conditions under which those states emerge.

Again, this does not remove responsibility. But it changes the question from blame alone to inquiry.

What conditions is this system living in?
What is being repeatedly reinforced?
What is being depleted?
What is being anticipated?
What is being numbed, sought, avoided, or chemically compensated for?

These are better questions than simply assigning virtue or failure.

There is also a philosophical caution here.

The more brain chemistry enters public discussion, the easier it becomes to imagine that we are as beings nothing more than chemical weather.

But that is not the argument of this book. Chemistry is part of the story, not the whole story. A person is not reducible to neurotransmitter levels.

Human life includes meaning, interpretation, biography, symbol, relationship, culture, morality, and consciousness. At the same time, none of those dimensions is free-floating.

They are lived through embodied chemistry.

So the challenge is to avoid both extremes:
neither reductionism nor vagueness,
neither "it is just chemicals" nor "chemistry does not matter".

The truth lies in integration.

Chemistry affects attention.
Attention affects interpretation.
Interpretation affects the state.
State affects behaviour.
Behaviour affects future learning.
Future learning reshapes chemistry.

This loop is why repeated experience matters so much. The brain and body are always being trained through what is rehearsed, anticipated, rewarded, feared, or endured. Neurochemistry does not sit outside life commenting on it. It participates in the making of life as it is felt.

This is especially relevant for addiction, compulsion, attachment, and mood regulation.

Human beings often become trapped not by one bad choice but by repeated loops in which anticipation, reward, relief, habit, and chemistry reinforce one another. Likewise, healing rarely happens through insight alone. The system often needs new repeated conditions: safety, sleep, stable rhythm, supportive relationships, movement, attention retraining, emotional processing, and environments that stop rewarding fragmentation. This is one reason deeper change can take time. It is not only the mind changing its opinion. It is the signalling life of the system learning a new pattern.

In that sense, the myth of simple mood chemicals is not just scientifically inaccurate. It can be spiritually and psychologically flattening.

It can encourage people to misunderstand themselves as broken dispensers of the wrong molecules rather than as living systems shaped by biology, experience, environment, and meaning. The chemistry is real, but so is the life in which the chemistry is embedded.

To understand dopamine, serotonin, cortisol, oxytocin, and related signalling substances properly is not to memorise one-word labels. It is to see how motivation, regulation, vigilance, bonding, and adaptation arise through dynamic systems rather than isolated causes.

And once that is clearer, another important question emerges.

If the brain's chemistry shapes what gets repeated, noticed, and reinforced, then how does the brain actually remember? How are experiences retained, rebuilt, altered, and carried forward?

That takes us next into memory.

Brain Observation

Notice when you casually use chemical shorthand to explain a state, "I need a high", "I'm stressed", "I'm burnt out", "I'm low", "I'm overstimulated".

What does that phrase point to in lived experience: reward-seeking, fatigue, vigilance, flatness, isolation, overload, anticipation, or something else?

Everyday Experiment

Over one day, notice one moment of wanting and one moment of satisfaction.

They do not have to be dramatic. It could be checking your phone, reaching for coffee, wanting a reply, looking for praise, finishing a task, or hearing good news.

Ask yourself: was the strongest feeling in the seeking, or in the receiving? This helps distinguish anticipation from fulfilment.

Visual Aid

Create a simple black-and-white page titled:

State or Urge | What It Felt Like | What May Have Been Driving It

Fill in a few example rows, such as:

- checking phone again | restless anticipation | novelty, uncertainty, wanting update
- craving sugar | low energy and irritability | fatigue, hunger, reward-seeking
- feeling flat after overload | numb, unfocused | mental fatigue, overstimulation
- strong need for reassurance | tension, urgency | uncertainty, attachment, stress

Leave extra lines for your own entries. At the end, underline any repeated drivers such as novelty, exhaustion, social tension, boredom, stress, or reward-seeking.

State or Urge	What It Felt Like	What May Have Been Driving It
checking phone again	restless anticipation	novelty, uncertainty, wanting update
craving sugar	low energy and irritability	fatigue, hunger, reward-seeking
feeling flat after overload	numb, unfocused	mental fatigue, overstimulation
strong need for reassurance	tension, urgency	uncertainty, attachment, stress
•		
•		
•		
•		
•		

Ethical Question

If human behaviour can be shaped by systems that repeatedly trigger anticipation, reward, stress, bonding, and reassurance, when does influence become exploitation?

Chapter 8 - Memory Is Not Storage, It Is Reconstruction

Memory is often imagined in technological terms.

People speak of storing information, retrieving facts, filing away events, losing data, or keeping things in reserve, as though the brain were a biological hard drive and experience were simply deposited into it.

These metaphors are understandable. They are convenient and sometimes useful in limited ways. But they are also misleading. Memory is not a passive archive. It is not a sealed vault of unchanged recordings waiting to be replayed on demand.

Memory is active.
Selective.
Context-bound.
Emotionally shaped.
And, most importantly, reconstructive.

This means that when we remember, we are not simply opening a drawer and pulling out a perfect copy of the past. We are rebuilding the past from traces, patterns, associations, emotional tone, bodily state, narrative framing, and current conditions.

Some parts are vivid. Some are missing. Some are inferred. Some are altered by repetition itself. Some memories become stronger through rehearsal. Others weaken, blur, or merge with later interpretation. What feels like recall is often an act of reconstruction.

This is not a flaw in our memories. It is part of how it works.

The brain is not designed to preserve every detail of lived experience with equal fidelity. That would be inefficient and, in many cases, overwhelming. Instead, memory helps the organism retain what is useful enough for navigation, survival, identity, learning, and relationships. It compresses. It links. It prioritises. It tags emotionally significant events. It stores procedures differently from facts, and feelings differently from timelines. It is less like a camera roll and more like a layered and evolving map.

To understand memory properly, it helps to distinguish between some of its forms.

Working memory refers to the temporary holding and manipulation of information in the present moment. It is what allows a person to remember a sentence long enough to interpret it, hold a number in mind briefly, follow multi-step instructions, or compare two ideas while thinking. Working memory is not designed for long-term preservation. It is more like the mental workspace of the present.

Short-term memory overlaps with this immediate holding function, though the boundaries between working memory and short-term memory are often discussed differently across contexts. What matters here is that not all remembered information is remembered for long. Much of what enters awareness passes quickly unless it is reinforced, rehearsed, emotionally marked, or integrated more deeply.

Long-term memory refers to more enduring retention. But even here, long-term memory is not one single thing.

There is episodic memory, the memory of events and experiences situated in time and place. This includes remembering a conversation, a birthday, an argument, a journey, a room, or a feeling attached to a specific occasion.

There is semantic memory, which involves general knowledge, concepts, meanings, and facts less tied to a particular moment. Knowing what a tree is, what a word means, or what year an event occurred belongs more to this domain.

There is procedural memory, which involves skills and habits: riding a bicycle, typing, tying shoelaces, playing an instrument, and driving a familiar route. These kinds of memory can remain even when explicit recall is imperfect.

There is also emotional memory, which is not always neatly verbal or narrative. A person may not consciously remember every detail of an event, yet their body, mood, or relational reaction carries the imprint of what has been learned. A smell may produce unease.

A tone may trigger contraction. A place may feel wrong before the mind can explain why. Memory does not only live in what can be narrated fluently.

This is where the idea of reconstruction becomes especially important.

When people think of remembering, they often imagine a straightforward return to the past. But in practice, memory is shaped by the present. What you remember today is influenced by your current emotional state, your current interpretation of your life, what has happened since, what parts of the event have been repeated in conversation, and what the memory now means to you.

This means memory is never only about what happened. It is also about how what happened has been integrated.

For example, two people can experience the same event and later remember it quite differently. This is not always because one is lying. It may be because they attended to different features, encoded different elements, felt different emotions, and later reconstructed the event through different identities and meanings. Even within the same person, a memory can change its emotional tone over time. What once felt humiliating may later be understood as formative. What once seemed trivial may later appear significant. Memory is not stable because the person remembering is not stable.

Each new act of remembering can become an act of editing.

This has been shown repeatedly in psychological research. When a memory is reactivated, it becomes, in a sense, temporarily open again. New context, new emotional tone, new framing, and new information can subtly alter how it is stored going forward. Memory can be strengthened by repetition, yes, but repetition does not guarantee accuracy. It may instead strengthen the current version of the memory, whether or not that version is fully faithful to the original event.

This is one reason confident memory is not always reliable memory.

Certainty can feel persuasive because the mind experiences coherence as truth. But the vividness of a memory is not identical to its accuracy. A person may remember something with great force and still be mistaken about details, sequence, motive, or wording.

Memory often prioritises meaning over perfect fidelity. It preserves the shape of significance more readily than the precision of fact.

This is not only a legal or scientific issue. It is a human one.

Many people live inside stories built from memory. They remember who cared, who abandoned, what they were taught about themselves, what was possible, what was dangerous, what kind of person they became in response to experience. These stories matter deeply.

They shape identity, expectation, attachment, and behaviour. But the stories are not always simple mirrors of the past. They are often reconstructions formed from repeated acts of remembering under emotional and relational conditions.

This means identity itself is partly mnemonic.

Who you believe yourself to be depends, in part, on what you remember and how you remember it. If memory becomes organised around failure, betrayal, shame, rejection, or helplessness, identity may contract accordingly. If memory becomes integrated through greater nuance, context, compassion, or truthfulness, identity may widen. This does not mean inventing a prettier past. It means recognising that the relationship between memory and self is dynamic, not fixed.

It also means that memory is highly sensitive to emotion.

Emotion does not merely accompany memory. It helps shape what is encoded, what is retrieved, and what is repeated. Events that carry a strong emotional charge are often remembered more powerfully, but that power does not guarantee precision. A frightening event may be remembered with intense bodily vividness while its timeline remains confused. A painful conversation may leave a strong emotional residue, while exact wording becomes uncertain. Under threat, the brain may prioritise salience over sequence, survival relevance over narrative completeness.

This helps explain why trauma memory can feel different from ordinary memory.

Traumatic experiences are often not stored as calm, coherent stories from beginning to end. They may remain fragmented, sensory, bodily, emotionally intense, or difficult to place in linear time. A person may remember flashes, sensations, sounds, bodily states, or emotional floods more readily than an ordered narrative. This does not make the experience unreal. It reflects the conditions under which the system encoded it.

When the organism is overwhelmed, memory may be shaped more by survival processing than by reflective integration.

That is why healing traumatic memory is not always about "remembering more" in a simplistic sense. Often, it is about creating enough safety and integration for the memory to be held differently, linked into context, and no longer relived as though it were fully present.

At the other end of the spectrum, routine and repeated actions can become deeply remembered without much conscious effort.

This is the domain of habit and procedure. A person may not remember learning to tie their shoelaces, yet they can do it.

A musician may not consciously narrate each finger movement.

A driver may reach a destination while barely remembering the individual turns.

This kind of memory is not absent. It is embodied through repetition. The brain has learned a pattern so thoroughly that it can be enacted with minimal conscious load.

This reveals something important: memory is not one thing because learning is not one thing.

Some memories support a conscious narrative.

Some support skilled action.

Some support emotional anticipation.

Some support identity.

Some support rapid prediction without explicit recall.

In all of these cases, the brain is preserving not the entire past, but enough of it to shape the future.

This is one reason memory and prediction are so closely related.

The brain remembers to anticipate. Experience becomes a guide to future expectation. If someone has repeatedly learned that silence means rejection, their memory does not sit quietly as history.

It becomes a prediction in the present. If someone has learned that effort leads to growth, that too becomes an expectation. Memory is not only backwards-looking. It is a major part of how the future is pre-loaded.

This also explains why repeated narratives can become so powerful.

Each time a person tells a story about themselves, others, or the world, they are not merely reporting memory. They may be reinforcing a version of it.

The more often a certain interpretation is repeated, the more available it becomes. Over time, that narrative can begin to feel inevitable, even if other dimensions of the memory were once available too.

This is why reflection matters.
Not because memory can be made perfect, but because it can become more conscious.

A person can begin to ask:
What do I remember most easily?
What do I leave out?
What emotional tone dominates the memory?
What story have I attached to it?
What has repetition strengthened?
What has been forgotten because it did not fit?

These are not trivial questions. They are part of self-understanding.

The reconstructive nature of memory also has consequences for social life.

People argue about "what really happened" not only because they disagree, but because they may have encoded and reconstructed events differently from the beginning. In conflict, people rarely remember a conversation as though they were impartial recording devices.

They remember through self-protection, emotion, expectation, and significance. This does not mean truth is impossible. It means truth often requires more humility than memory alone naturally provides.

It is also why witness memory can be less reliable than popular culture assumes.

We as beings do not store experience in perfect narrative sequence waiting to be replayed in court, conversation, or self-explanation.

They rebuild. They infer. They compress. They remember what mattered most to them, and even that may shift.

If this sounds unsettling, it need not be.

Reconstructive memory is one of the reasons human life can remain adaptive.

The past is not locked away as dead data. It is carried forward as a living meaning. That allows learning, flexibility, reinterpretation, and integration. It allows painful experiences to be revisited differently.

It allows identity to change. It allows memory to become wiser without pretending the past never happened.

But this adaptability comes with vulnerability. Memory can be shaped by suggestion, authority, repetition, emotional state, and social reinforcement.

It can be narrowed by stress and widened by safety.

It can become rigid through rumination or softened through reflection. Like much else in the brain, it is both powerful and fallible.

To understand memory, then, is to abandon the fantasy of internal recording technology and accept something richer and more human.

Memory is a living reconstruction.
It is built from traces, not replicas.
It serves a meaning, not perfect storage.
It shapes identity, but does not imprison it.
It carries history forward, but always through the present.

And once that becomes clear, another question begins to press forward.

If memory is shaped so powerfully by emotion, state, and significance, then how separate can logic really be from feeling? Can the best thinking ever be emotionless, or does clarity depend on a more integrated relationship between reason and emotional life?

That is where we go next.

Brain Observation

Notice one memory that returns to you often. Ask yourself not only what happened, but what emotional tone now comes with the memory, what meaning you have attached to it, and whether that meaning has changed over time.

Everyday Experiment

Write down a short memory from childhood or early adulthood in five or six lines. Leave it for a day. Then return and rewrite it without looking at the first version. Compare the two. Notice what stayed the same, what shifted, what details were added or omitted, and what emotional tone became stronger or softer.

Visual Aid

Create a simple black-and-white page titled:

Memory | What I Recall Clearly | What Feels Uncertain | What Meaning I Attached

Fill in a few example rows, such as:

- school presentation | feeling exposed, room layout | exact words spoken | "I am bad under pressure"

- difficult argument | tone of voice, tension | sequence of events | "conflict leads to disconnection"

- family holiday | warmth, sunlight, laughter | what year it was | "that was a safe time"

Memory
What I Recall Clearly
What Feels Uncertain |What Meaning

Memory	What I Recall Clearly	What Feels Uncertain	What Meaning I Attached
school presentation	feeling exposed, room layout	exact words spoken	"I am bad under pressure"
difficult argument	tone of voice, tension	sequence of events	"conflict leads to disconnection"
family holiday	warmth, sunlight, laughter	what year it was	"that was a safe time"
•			
•			
•			
•			
•			
•			

Ethical Question

If memory is reconstructive rather than perfectly archival, how careful should we be when using remembered pain, certainty, or narrative as the basis for judging ourselves or others?

Chapter 9 - Emotion, Logic, and Why the Best Thinking Is Not Emotionless

One of the most persistent myths in modern culture is the idea that the clearest thinking is emotionless thinking.

Reason is imagined as clean, detached, and objective. Emotion is imagined as messy, unreliable, disruptive, or primitive. To be rational, people are told, is to remain unaffected. To think well is to rise above feeling. To be intelligent is to keep emotion at a distance, as though the best version of the mind were one that could somehow operate outside the body that gives rise to it.

This picture is appealing because it flatters control.

It suggests that thinking becomes better the more it resembles machinery. It offers a fantasy of pure cognition untouched by vulnerability, attachment, desire, fear, shame, grief, longing, love, fatigue, and bodily state. But the fantasy is false. We as Beings do not think from nowhere. We think from somewhere. We think through a nervous system, a body, a history, a chemistry, a memory structure, and a current state of regulation.

Emotion is not the enemy of thought.
Emotion is part of the conditions under which thought occurs.

This does not mean every feeling is wise. It does not mean emotion should rule judgement unchecked. It means that good thinking depends on a better relationship with emotion, not on the fantasy of escaping it.

If The Brain Was An App, Would You Use It?

By the time we reach this chapter, the foundations for that claim are already in place.

We have seen that the brain is not separate from the body, that perception is constructed rather than passively received, that prediction shapes interpretation before conscious awareness fully catches up, that signalling and neurochemistry alter the conditions under which cognition unfolds, and that memory is reconstructive rather than archival. All of these points towards a deeper conclusion: what a person thinks cannot be separated cleanly from how a person feels, and how a person feels cannot be separated cleanly from the state of the system through which thinking is happening.

Emotion, then, is not just a colouring added to thought after the fact. It helps shape salience, priority, interpretation, motivation, memory, and readiness. It tells the organism what matters. It narrows or widens attention. It biases prediction. It influences whether uncertainty feels tolerable or threatening, whether another person appears safe or suspect, whether a memory remains accessible or collapses under pressure, and whether an idea feels exciting or exhausting.

This is why emotion is better understood as a signal

Fear signals possible danger.
Shame signals social exposure or a threat to belonging.
Anger signals violation, frustration, or blocked movement.
Sadness signals loss, unmet need, or contraction.
Joy signals expansion, coherence, or reward.

Anxiety often signals uncertainty combined with heightened anticipatory vigilance.

Relief signals a reduction in perceived threat or burden.

These signals are not always accurate in their conclusions, but they are real in their presence. Emotion tells the organism something about its current relation to the world, even if that relation still requires reflection and interpretation.

The problem is not that emotion exists. The problem is that emotion can become dysregulated, overwhelming, misread, suppressed, or fused so completely with thought that the person no longer notices how strongly their interpretation has been shaped by the state.

When that happens, thinking changes.

A dysregulated person rarely thinks in the same way as a regulated one. Under threat, ambiguity becomes harder to tolerate. Nuance often collapses. Certainty rises. Attention narrows. Memory retrieval shifts. Defensive narratives become more persuasive. Contradictory information becomes harder to integrate. The system begins to privilege speed, simplicity, and self-protection over complexity, openness, or patient reflection.

This is not a character flaw. It is a biological and cognitive consequence of the state.

A person in fear may confuse urgency with truth.

A person in shame may interpret neutral reactions as condemnation.

A person in anger may become highly certain while losing subtlety.

A person in despair may mistake temporary collapse for permanent reality.

A person in chronic stress may come to treat vigilance as wisdom.

Again, this does not mean emotion is useless. It means state matters.

It also means that what many people call "logic" is often far less detached than it appears. Human reasoning frequently serves emotional coherence as much as factual precision. People do not only think to discover. They also think to protect identity, reduce uncertainty, justify reaction, preserve belonging, and stabilise self-image. Logic can be used beautifully in the service of clarity, but it can also be recruited into the defence of a state the person has not yet recognised.

This is why highly intelligent people are not immune to distortion.

A person may reason brilliantly and remain captive to emotional blind spots they do not observe. They may build elegant arguments around conclusions their nervous system has already reached for defensive reasons. They may confuse their capacity to explain with their capacity to see clearly. In that sense, intelligence without self-awareness can become highly sophisticated self-protection.

This is where the chapter deepens.

If the best thinking is not emotionless thinking, then what kind of thinking is it?

It is thinking that can feel without being wholly ruled by feeling.

Thinking that can register emotion as data without collapsing into it.

Thinking that can recognise the state while still examining the interpretation.

Thinking that can remain in contact with the body without surrendering discernment.

Thinking can slow down enough for awareness to notice what the system is doing.

This is where metacognition enters the picture.

Metacognition is often defined as thinking about thinking. That is correct, but incomplete. In lived experience, metacognition is the capacity to become aware of the mind in motion.

It is the ability to notice thought while thought is happening, to recognise that one is interpreting, predicting, reacting, remembering, assuming, or defending in real time rather than mistaking those processes for transparent reality.

At a deeper level, metacognition is not only about thought. It includes noticing how feeling is shaping thought, how bodily state is altering certainty, how memory is influencing interpretation, how prediction is organising expectation, and how language inside the mind is reinforcing or softening the emotional field.

It is, in short, the mind's capacity to observe its own activity.

This capacity is one of the most important forms of human freedom.

Without metacognition, a person is largely embedded in their reactions as they happen. They do not merely feel angry; they become the anger and its narrative. They do not merely notice shame; they become the shame and its certainty.

They do not merely have a thought; they inhabit it as though it were reality itself. The stimulus comes, the state shifts, the interpretation forms, and the person is carried along inside the sequence.

With metacognition, a space begins to appear.

Not a cold distance, but a reflective gap.

In that gap, the person may begin to notice:
I am tense.
I am rushing to a conclusion.
I am filling in meaning.
My body feels unsafe.
I want certainty more than accuracy right now.
I am reacting from memory, not only from the present.
This thought may reflect my state as much as the situation itself.

That noticing does not instantly solve everything. But it changes the structure of the moment.

It turns pure reaction into possible reflection.
It weakens fusion.
It creates room for discernment.
It allows a person to think with more honesty because they are no longer wholly inside the first layer of thought.

This is one reason metacognition belongs so naturally in this chapter. It is not an abstract academic add-on. It is one of the main capacities that allows emotion and logic to be integrated rather than split.

A person who notices their own emotional state can think differently from a person who is unknowingly ruled by it. A person who can recognise the onset of shame, urgency, defensiveness, or collapse has a greater chance of staying with complexity. They may still feel deeply. They may still struggle. But they are less likely to confuse the first feeling with the final truth.

This has profound implications for learning.

A dysregulated student may not only know less. They may be less able to access what they know. A person in shame may perform below their real capacity. A person in fear may misread information as a threat. A person whose system feels safe enough may retain more, connect more, tolerate challenge better, and remain curious for longer. In that sense, cognition is not just about content entering the mind. It is about whether the system can stay open enough to receive, organise, and work with what is arriving.

This helps explain something I have become increasingly conscious of in my own life.

The more I have learned to notice my own internal states rather than being unconsciously driven by them, the more my thinking has changed. As regulation increased, memory improved. As emotional charge became easier to observe without immediate fusion, clarity widened. As I became more aware of how the state was shaping interpretation, I found I could remain with difficult material for longer without collapsing into urgency, defensiveness, or overload. The desire to learn became less frantic and more grounded. Knowledge no longer felt like something to chase compulsively or force through tension. It began to feel more like participation.

That shift mattered.

It changed how I read.
How I listen.
How I speak.
How I remember.
How I tolerate not knowing.
I notice when a thought is being pushed by fear, intensity, or the need for control.

I do not say this as a claim of mastery. I say this because it illustrates the larger argument of this chapter: the best thinking is not achieved by suppressing emotion but by becoming more conscious of the relationship among emotion, state, and interpretation.

Metacognition is part of that consciousness.

It is the difference between:
"I am right."
and
"I notice I feel very certain right now."

It is the difference between:
"This person is dangerous."
and
"I notice my body has gone into alarm, and I need to examine what is actually present."

It is the difference between:
"I cannot handle this."
and
"I notice my system is overwhelmed, and my thinking is narrowing."

These distinctions matter because they protect humility without collapsing agency. They allow a person to honour emotion without handing it total authority.

They also improve relationships.

Many relational breakdowns are not simply failures of communication after the fact. They are failures of awareness in the moment. One person becomes defensive without realising it. Another becomes flooded and starts interpreting everything through abandonment or criticism.

The mind then recruits logic to justify a state already in motion. By the time words are exchanged, both people may feel certain they are only responding to the other, while in reality, both are also reacting to their own signalling histories.

Metacognition does not eliminate this, but it can soften it.

It allows a person to pause and ask:
What am I bringing into this moment?
What is my body doing right now?
Am I hearing what was said, or what I expected to hear?
Am I defending against the present, or against a remembered past?

This is one of the reasons reflective awareness is central to discernment.

Discernment is not merely choosing between good and bad arguments.

It is also noticing the conditions under which judgement is being formed. It asks whether the system is clear enough, regulated enough, spacious enough, and honest enough to evaluate well.

It asks whether a person's certainty is coming from truth or from urgency. Whether their conclusion arises from integrated reflection or from the emotional need to resolve tension quickly.

This does not mean endless self-doubt. Metacognition is not the destruction of trust in one's own mind. It is the refinement of trust. It allows trust to become more earned, because it is no longer built only on immediacy.

There is another important point here.

Emotion is not simply something metacognition watches from afar. Often, emotion is what first reveals where metacognition is needed. A sudden rush of shame, anger, or anxiety can become a doorway into self-observation if the person has enough capacity to pause. The question is not, "How do I stop feeling this?" but "What is this state doing to my perception, my memory, my certainty, my story?" That is a different orientation altogether.

It turns emotion into information rather than dictatorship.

This also means that the ideal of "emotionless logic" is not only unrealistic. It can be dangerous. People who believe they are acting from pure reason are often the least aware of the emotional and identity forces shaping their conclusions.

The person who says, "I am just being objective," may in fact be deeply organised by fear, contempt, shame, pride, or the need for control without recognising it.

Unexamined emotion often hides most effectively beneath the language of detached logic.

The alternative is not emotional chaos. It is integrated cognition.

Integrated cognition means:

emotion is felt,

state is noticed,

thought is examined,

Memory is questioned,

prediction is recognised,

and interpretation is held with enough humility to be revised.

This is what mature thinking begins to look like.

Not the absence of feeling, but a deeper capacity to remain with feeling without surrendering discernment.

This is also where emotional regulation becomes inseparable from intellectual life. A regulated system is not simply more comfortable. It is often more cognitively available. It can hold ambiguity longer. It can be revised more honestly. It can tolerate complexity without needing premature closure. It can remember better, listen better, and reason with greater depth.

That does not mean calm is always correct. It means chronic dysregulation often comes with predictable cognitive costs.

These costs include:

- narrowed focus

- defensive reasoning

- Reduced working memory

- Higher threat bias

- greater reliance on familiar narratives

- quicker certainty

- poorer tolerance for contradiction

Seen this way, emotional regulation is not merely therapeutic. It is epistemic. It affects how a person knows, what they can take in, and what kinds of truth they can stay with.

This is one reason Chapter 9 sits at the heart of Part II.

If Chapter 6 showed that the brain lives through signalling, Chapter 7 challenged simple chemical myths, and Chapter 8 revealed memory as reconstruction, then this chapter makes one of the book's deeper implications explicit: thought cannot be fully understood apart from feeling, and clear thinking depends not on the eradication of emotion, but on a more conscious relationship with it.

That relationship is made possible, in part, through metacognition.

The more aware a person becomes of their own inner processes, the less they are wholly driven by them. The more they can observe thought and feeling as processes rather than absolute reality, the more room opens for wisdom, honesty, and self-correction. And the more the system is regulated, the more likely that room is to remain available under pressure.

This does not create perfection. It creates possibility.

A possibility to think more clearly without pretending to be disembodied.

A possibility to feel deeply without becoming wholly fused

with feeling. A possibility to remain human and still become more discerning. Once that becomes clear, the next question naturally follows.

If emotion, cognition, and metacognition all depend on a brain capable of adaptation, then how does that adaptive capacity actually work? How can the system change, learn, stabilise, reorganise, and yet remain recognisably itself?

That takes us into plasticity.

Brain Observation

Notice one moment today when you felt emotionally certain about something.

Ask yourself: was I only feeling the emotion, or was I also able to notice how that emotion was shaping my thinking?

Everyday Experiment

The next time you feel rushed, irritated, ashamed, defensive, or intensely certain, pause and write two short sentences:

1. What I am thinking right now

2. What I am feeling right now

Then add a third:

3. How this feeling may be shaping my thoughts

This is a simple metacognitive practice. The aim is not to stop the emotion, but to observe the relationship between state and interpretation.

Visual Aid

Create a simple black-and-white page titled:

Situation | What I Thought | What I Felt | What I Noticed About My Thinking

Fill in a few example rows, such as:

- delayed reply | they are ignoring me | anxious, tense | I moved quickly towards rejection

- criticism at work | I have failed | shame, contraction | I treated feedback as identity

- argument with partner | they do not understand me | anger, urgency | I wanted to win before I understood

- difficult task | I cannot do this | frustration, heaviness | my thinking narrowed under pressure

Leave extra lines for your own entries. At the end, underline any repeated patterns in how emotion shapes certainty, self-judgement, defensiveness, urgency, or collapse.

Situation
What I Thought
What I Felt | What I Noticed About My
Thinking

Situation	What I Thought	What I Felt	What I Noticed About My Thinking
delayed reply	they are ignoring me	anxious, tense	I moved quickly towards rejection
criticism at work	I have failed	shame, contraction	I treated feedback as identity
argument with partner	they do not understand me	anger, urgency	I wanted to win before I understood
difficult task	I cannot do this	frustration, heaviness	my thinking narrowed under pressure
•			
•			
•			
•			
•			

Ethical Question

If many people are unaware of how strongly emotion shapes their thinking in real time, what ethical responsibility do communicators, institutions, media systems, and leaders carry when they knowingly trigger emotional states to steer interpretation?

Chapter 10 - Plasticity, Adaptation, and the Paradoxical Brain

Few ideas about the brain have captured the modern imagination more than the idea of plasticity.

People hear that the brain is plastic and conclude that it can become almost anything.

They hear that neural pathways can change and assume the human being is endlessly rewritable.

They hear that habits can be replaced, memories reshaped, new skills learned, old wounds softened, and entire ways of living transformed. At one level, this enthusiasm makes sense.

Plasticity is one of the most hopeful discoveries in brain science because it reveals that the brain is not fixed in the way older models once implied.

But like many hopeful ideas, it can become distorted when oversimplified.

The brain is plastic, yes.
But it is not infinitely plastic.
It can adapt, but it cannot become anything whatsoever.
It can change, but not without cost, repetition, time, condition, and constraint.
It can preserve continuity while reorganising function, but the very continuity it preserves also places limits on how change occurs.

This is the paradox at the heart of the brain.

It must remain stable enough to hold a world together, yet flexible enough to survive that world as it changes.

Without stability, there would be no continuity of self, skill, memory, language, or orientation. Every experience would fall apart before it could become meaningful. Without plasticity, there would be no learning, no recovery, no refinement, no adaptation to new demands, and no transformation through lived experience.

The brain's extraordinary achievement is that it does both at once. It holds, and it changes. It conserves, and it updates.

Plasticity, then, should not be understood as limitless freedom. It should be understood as adaptive responsiveness within living constraints.

At the biological level, plasticity refers to the brain's capacity to alter its structure, connectivity, efficiency, and patterns of activation in response to experience, repetition, injury, development, and use.

Neural pathways strengthen when repeatedly engaged. Some weaken when neglected. Synapses can become more or less efficient.

Networks can reorganise. In certain contexts, regions may partially compensate for loss elsewhere. Habits of perception, attention, movement, and response become more established through rehearsal. New learning can literally alter the functional shape of the system.

This is not a metaphor. It is one of the central realities of brain function.

Every repeated act is, in some sense, a vote for a pathway.

Each time a person practises a skill, revisits a thought pattern, rehearses an emotional response, scrolls for stimulation, regulates through breath, enters panic, returns to a memory, or pauses in reflective awareness, something is being reinforced or weakened. The brain learns not only from what is taught formally, but from what is lived repeatedly.

That is why adaptation is so powerful and so morally significant.

The brain adapts to music, language, reading, movement, safety, relationships, and challenge. It also adapts to stress, fragmentation, overstimulation, chaos, humiliation, and reward loops.

Plasticity does not distinguish automatically between what is good for the organism in the long term and what is merely repeated often enough to become familiar.

This is why the modern world can shape people so deeply. Repetition trains. Pace trains. Stress trains. Social media trains. Silence trains. Attention trains. Family atmosphere trains.

The workplace trains. Schooling trains. Trauma trains. Ritual trains. Relationship trains. Whether those trainings widen a person or narrow them depends on the conditions under which adaptation is occurring.

Plasticity, in that sense, is neither inherently liberating nor inherently dangerous. It is a capacity. What matters is what it is being asked to adapt to.

This is one reason habit becomes so central to brain life.

A habit is not merely a repeated action. It is a repeated reduction of effort. The more often a pattern is used, the easier it becomes for the brain to anticipate, initiate, and stabilise it. This is efficient. It allows the organism to conserve energy and move through familiar routines without re-deciding everything from scratch.

That efficiency can be beneficial. A person who practises music, writes daily, exercises regularly, reads deeply, or learns to regulate under stress is not only choosing those things anew each time. The brain is gradually making those pathways more available. Over time, what once required effort can become more natural.

But the same is true of less helpful patterns.

Compulsive checking becomes easier with repetition. Defensive interpretation becomes easier. Catastrophising becomes easier. Withdrawal becomes easier. Numbing becomes easier.

The person may later say, "This is just how I am," when in fact what feels like identity may be a deeply rehearsed adaptation.

Plasticity can make temporary states look permanent simply because they have been repeated long enough.

This matters especially in the context of stress and survival.

When the organism lives for long periods under pressure, the brain may adapt in ways that are useful in the short term but costly in the long term. Hypervigilance may become normal. Rest may feel unsafe. Ambiguity may be read as a threat. Narrow focus may replace spacious attention.

Quick defensive reaction may become more accessible than reflective thought. None of these adaptations is irrational in its original context. They may have been necessary. The problem arises when a brain trained in one environment continues to operate by the same rules long after the environment has changed.

This is the deeper tragedy and brilliance of adaptation.

The brain learns faithfully.
But it does not always know when the lesson has outlived its usefulness.

That is why healing is rarely as simple as insight.

A person may understand intellectually that they are no longer in danger, yet their system still predicts danger because prediction itself has been trained through repetition.

A person may know they want change, yet their brain still returns to the familiar path because the familiar path is easier to activate. This is not hypocrisy. It is plasticity plus history.

Change, therefore, requires more than intention. It usually requires repeated new conditions.

New conditions of safety.
New conditions of pacing.
New conditions of practice.
New conditions of interpretation.
New conditions of embodied experience.
New conditions in which the brain learns, not abstractly, but through repeated contact, that another way of being is possible and can be stabilised.

This is why neuroplasticity should never be used as a motivational slogan detached from reality. Telling people "your brain can change" may be true, but it is not enough. The real questions are harder.

Under what conditions can it change?
How long will the change take?
What is being reinforced daily without notice?
What old pattern is still being rewarded by familiarity?
What new pattern is being asked to stabilise without enough repetition, support, or safety?

These are more honest questions.

Plasticity also includes pruning.

Not all change is additive. The brain not only builds more connections. It also trims, simplifies, and removes pathways that are less used or less efficient. This is particularly evident in development, where the early brain forms an abundance of possibilities and later sculpts itself through experience. In this sense, growth is not merely accumulation. It is a selection.

This too has philosophical implications.

To become is also to lose.
To specialise is also to exclude.
To stabilise one pattern is often to weaken another.
Every repeated life narrows and deepens in certain directions.

The developing brain illustrates this vividly. Children are born into extraordinary plastic possibilities, but development is not about keeping every possibility equally open forever. It is about patterned shaping.

Language exposure tunes sound discrimination. Culture shapes attention and meaning. Relationship shapes regulation. Education shapes cognitive habits.

What becomes easy is not only a reflection of innate potential, but of repeated engagement.

Adult brains remain plastic, but differently so.

The myth that "children learn faster" is partly true in some domains, but it should not obscure the adult capacity for meaningful change.

Adults can still learn languages, alter habits, build skills, regulate more effectively, and reorganise aspects of their lives.

Adult change often requires more deliberate repetition, more conscious effort, and more work against the sediment of established patterns. The older brain is not frozen. It is layered.

This brings us to an important insight: plasticity is shaped by attention.

What is attended to repeatedly becomes more likely to be strengthened. This is one reason attention is so precious. It is not merely a spotlight for the present. It is a sculpting force for the future. To attend again and again to resentment, threat, shame, novelty, comparison, or outrage is to give those pathways rehearsal. To attend repeatedly to reflection, bodily awareness, skill-building, calm, or meaningful challenge is also to rehearse a future brain.

This does not mean people can simply "think positive" and rewire themselves instantly. That would be another misuse of plasticity language. But it does mean attention is not trivial. Where attention goes repeatedly, adaptation follows.

Sleep also plays a profound role here.

Plasticity does not occur only during deliberate effort. Consolidation depends heavily on rest. Learning stabilises through sleep. Memory is reorganised. Emotional experience is processed differently. The exhausted brain can still repeat patterns, but often with less nuance, less flexibility, and poorer integration. This is one reason chronic sleep loss is so corrosive. It does not merely make a person tired. It undermines the conditions under which healthy adaptation can occur.

The same is true of recovery more generally.

The brain does not change best under relentless pressure. It often requires oscillation: challenge and rest, effort and integration, activation and settling. A system that is never allowed to recover may still adapt, but often around survival rather than around flourishing. This matters because many modern environments push people into constant stimulation while denying the slower rhythms through which meaningful change becomes embodied.

There is also a social dimension to plasticity.

Brains do not adapt only in private. They adapt in a relationship. The tone of a household, the consistency of a caregiver, the rhythm of conversation, the emotional climate of a workplace, the rewards of a peer group, the moral atmosphere of a culture — all of these become part of the training field. People often imagine personal change as an individual project of will. But the brain is deeply social, and what it rehearses is often cued relationally.

A person trying to become calmer in an environment that continually rewards reactivity faces a different task from someone doing the same work in conditions of support and coherence.

A person trying to widen their thinking in a culture of speed, certainty, and outrage is working against more than private habit. They are working against distributed reinforcement.

This is why the environment matters so much.

Plasticity also helps explain why people can be transformed by meaningful practices.

Meditation, deep study, music, therapy, training, contemplative ritual, disciplined craft, physical skill, reflective writing, and relational repair all matter not only because of what they symbolise, but because of what they repeatedly ask the brain to do. They train attention. They alter pacing. They cultivate inhibition or openness. They stabilise new interpretations. They strengthen capacities that may once have been fragile.

The same is true, in darker form, of repeated manipulation.

Propaganda works partly because repetition trains. Addictive systems work partly because repetition trains. Coercive environments work partly because repetition trains. The plastic brain can be educated or captured, widened or narrowed, humanised or instrumentalised, depending on what kinds of conditions are repeatedly installed.

This is why plasticity belongs not only to science but to ethics.

Knowledge that the brain adapts can be used to support healing, development, literacy, and humane education. But it can also be used to design compulsive systems, engineer dependence, and shape populations through repeated emotional capture. The capacity for change is not automatically liberating.

It becomes liberating only when it is held within an ethical vision of what human beings are for.

There is another reason this chapter closes Part II.

The previous chapters have shown the brain as a signalling and adaptive system. Electricity, chemistry, memory, emotion, and metacognition all reveal a brain in motion rather than a brain as object. Plasticity now brings these themes together by showing how repeated signalling becomes structure, how repeated experience becomes pattern, and how pattern becomes the living architecture of a person's ongoing responses.

This is the paradoxical brain:
stable enough to remain itself,
plastic enough to become more than it has been.

Neither infinitely free nor mechanically fixed.
Neither trapped in the past nor untouched by it.
A living system capable of learning, but also of being trained without consent.
Capable of healing, but also of being shaped by harmful repetition.
Capable of growth, but only through conditions that allow growth to stabilise.

This is what Part II has been moving towards all along.

If Part I gave us the architecture of the brain, Part II has shown us the brain as an active process: signalling, chemical, reconstructive, emotional, metacognitive, and adaptive. It has been shown that the human mind is not born each day anew, but shaped by repeated electrical, chemical, emotional, and behavioural histories.

It has been shown that state and pattern are inseparable. And it has shown that the very capacity which makes transformation possible also makes conditioning powerful.

That brings us naturally into the next part of the book.

Because once we understand that the brain is shaped by repetition, relationship, reward, stress, and environment, the next question becomes impossible to avoid:

Who and what is doing the shaping?

How does the brain form itself in the presence of other people?
How do language, attachment, culture, schooling, media, ideology, and digital systems participate in that process?

How much of what feels personal is, in fact, social training carried into the nervous system?

This is where we move next.

Part III, The Social & Programmable Brain, begins with a truth that has been present from the start but now comes fully into view: the brain is not only biological.

It is relational. It is influenceable. It is trainable through the worlds it inhabits.

If Part II explored how the system functions, Part III explores how that system is shaped.

And once the brain is understood as social and programmable, the moral and cultural stakes of everything we have covered so far become sharper still.

Brain Observation

Notice one repeated pattern in your daily life that feels automatic.

Ask yourself: does this feel "natural" because it is deeply true to me, or because it has been rehearsed often enough to become easy?

Everyday Experiment

Choose one small pattern you would like to alter for three days only.

It could be pausing before checking your phone, taking one slow breath before replying, reading for ten minutes before opening social media, or walking briefly after work instead of sitting immediately.

Do not aim for transformation. Aim only to observe how quickly the old pathway tries to reassert itself and what conditions help the new one feel more possible.

Visual Aid

Create a simple black-and-white page titled: Repeated Pattern | What Reinforces It | What Might Weaken or Replace It

Fill in a few example rows, such as:

- checking phone constantly | boredom, uncertainty, habit loop | delayed check-in, walking, focused task

- harsh self-talk | shame, old memory, perfectionism | pause, evidence check, kinder reframe

- late-night scrolling | overstimulation, avoidance, fatigue | set cutoff, dim lights, different wind-down

- shallow breathing under stress | urgency, body tension, anticipation | longer exhale, posture shift, pause before action

Leave extra lines for your own entries. At the end, circle any patterns where repetition seems stronger than conscious intention.

Repeated Pattern
What Reinforces It
What Might Weaken or Replace It

Repeated Pattern	What Reinforces It	What Might Weaken or Replace It
checking phone constantly	boredom, uncertainty, habit loop	delayed check-in, walking, focused task
harsh self-talk	shame, old memory, perfectionism	pause, evidence check, kinder reframe
late-night scrolling	overstimulation, avoidance, fatigue	set cutoff, dim lights, different wind-down
shallow breathing under stress	urgency, body tension, anticipation	longer exhale, posture shift, pause before action

Ethical Question

If the human brain is plastic enough to be shaped by repeated environments, habits, signals, and social pressures, what obligations do families, schools, workplaces, media systems, and technologies have in relation to the kinds of brains they are helping to build?

PART III - The Social & Programmable Brain

By this point in the book, the brain should no longer appear as a detached organ sealed away from life.

We have seen it as living architecture. We have seen it in conversation with the body, constructing perception, anticipating reality, signalling through electricity and chemistry, rebuilding memory, integrating emotion with thought, and adapting through repetition. But if the previous parts have clarified how the brain functions, the next question becomes sharper and more unsettling:

What is shaping that function over time?

Because no brain develops in isolation. No nervous system learns alone. No mind arrives fully formed and untouched by relationship, language, culture, timing, reward, fear, or the wider social worlds in which it is embedded. Human beings are not only biological. They are relational. They are influenceable. They are trainable. And the same plasticity that makes learning and healing possible also makes conditioning, persuasion, and capture possible.

This is where the inquiry now turns.

Part III explores the brain not simply as a living system, but as a **social and programmable** one. That does not mean human beings are machines waiting to be coded. It means that repeated environments, emotional climates, linguistic patterns, relational dynamics, technologies, institutions, rituals, ideologies, and attention systems all participate in shaping what the brain comes to expect, defend, desire, fear, and normalise. The person who says, "This is just how I think," may in fact be speaking from a system that has been trained for years by forces far wider than private choice alone.

We begin in **Chapter 11, The Brain in Relationship**, because relationship is one of the earliest and most powerful contexts in which the brain is shaped. This chapter explores attachment, co-regulation, social pain, emotional contagion, mimicry, and the ways human beings borrow states from one another. It asks how a nervous system learns safety, threat, closeness, anticipation, and defence in the presence of others — and how many adult patterns are best understood not as isolated traits, but as relational adaptations carried forward.

From there, **Chapter 12, Language, the Brain, and the Mirror-Linguistic Hypothesis**, moves directly into one of the central frameworks of this wider body of work. Here, language is not treated as a neutral symbolic tool alone, but as embodied signalling: a force shaped by tone, pacing, implication, timing, and emotional atmosphere. This chapter explores how words do not merely describe reality but participate in regulating the state, framing perception, and shaping meaning in real time. It brings the Mirror-Linguistic Hypothesis into fuller view, showing how language interacts with physiology, attention, and relationship rather than floating above them.

In **Chapter 13, The Programmed Brain**, the frame widens further. This chapter turns to repetition, conditioning, propaganda, ideology, digital reinforcement, ritual, schooling, trauma loops, and social reward systems. It asks how brains are shaped "matrix style" in everyday life — not through fantasy, but through repeated exposure, emotional priming, social pressures, institutional language, and designed environments that install expectation and narrow possibility. The chapter explores how what feels personal can often be patterned through the repeated structure of the world itself.

That naturally leads into **Chapter 14, Attention Hijack and the Economy of Capture**, where the modern environment becomes central. This chapter examines how social media, outrage cycles, novelty-seeking, algorithmic design, fragmented focus, and constant stimulation reshape the brain's attentional landscape. The issue here is not only distraction, but capture: the way systems compete to hold salience, trigger emotional response, and condition what feels urgent, meaningful, or impossible to ignore. It asks what happens to a human mind repeatedly trained by environments designed less for wisdom than for engagement.

Finally, **Chapter 15, Belief, Identity, and the Need to Be Right**, closes this part by moving from attention to identification. This chapter explores why brains defend identity structures so fiercely, why cognitive dissonance can feel threatening at the level of self, and why belonging, tribe, meaning, and narrative often matter more to people than detached factual accuracy. It examines group loyalty, protective reasoning, certainty, and the emotional weight carried by the worldview itself. In doing so, it shows that the social brain is not merely trained in what to notice, but also in what must be defended.

Taken together, these chapters reveal that the brain is not simply a private organ generating private thought. It is shaped in the presence of others. It is shaped by language. It is shaped by emotional climates, by relational feedback, by repeated narratives, by reward structures, by media systems, by institutions, and by the invisible atmospheres of social life. What feels natural may be conditioned. What feels like instinct may be repetition carried into identity. What feels like certainty may be belonging in disguise.

This is why Part III matters so much.

It takes everything from the earlier parts and places it into the living field, where human beings actually become who they are. A brain that predicts is shaped by what it has repeatedly encountered. A brain that remembers is shaped by what relationships are made memorable. A brain that adapts is shaped by what environments reward. A brain that signals is shaped by what emotional climates it has learned to survive.

In that sense, Part III marks a shift in the book.

Until now, we have focused largely on the internal architecture and adaptive life of the system. From here, we move more directly into the shaping power of relationship, language, social structure, and cultural reinforcement. The question is no longer only how the brain works, but how the world works upon it.

And once that becomes clear, the deeper moral stakes of the book begin to sharpen.

Because if the brain is social and programmable, then the question of influence can never be treated lightly. It becomes a question not only of psychology, but of ethics, culture, education, technology, and power.

That is where we now begin.

Chapter 11 - The Brain in Relationship

No brain develops alone.

It may sit within an individual skull, but from the beginning, it is shaped in the presence of other nervous systems. It learns through faces, tone, rhythm, touch, absence, attention, unpredictability, closeness, rupture, repair, and repeated emotional climate. The brain is not only a biological organ responding to the physical world. It is also a relational organ responding to other people.

This is one of the deepest truths of human development.

A child does not first become a fully formed self and then enter a relationship. The self begins in a relationship. Regulation begins there. Expectation begins there. Trust begins there. Fear begins there. The meaning of closeness, attention, distance, conflict, safety, approval, criticism, repair, and abandonment begins there. Before a person has language for any of it, the brain is already learning what kind of world other people make.

This is why the social brain cannot be treated as a secondary topic. Relationship is not an optional layer added onto an already finished system. It is part of how the system is built.

From the earliest stages of life, the developing brain depends on interaction. Eye contact, tone of voice, pacing, touch, and responsiveness do more than comfort a child emotionally. They help organise the nervous system. They shape expectation.

They contribute to the regulation of arousal, attention, and stress. They help teach the organism what can be anticipated from human contact.

When care is consistent enough, the brain begins to predict that need may be met, distress may be soothed, and proximity may be survivable. When care is chaotic, intrusive, rejecting, or absent, different lessons begin to form. The brain may learn that closeness is unreliable, that vulnerability is risky, that emotion must be hidden, that attention is inconsistent, or that self-protection must come early.

These are not abstract beliefs at first. They are relational patterns becoming biological expectations.

This is why attachment matters.

Attachment is often reduced to a psychological label or parenting concept, but at a deeper level, it concerns the brain's learned expectations about safety, connection, and regulation in the presence of others.

It asks: what happens to the organism when it reaches outward?

What is learned about co-regulation, repair, and responsiveness? Does closeness settle the system, confuse it, overstimulate it, or threaten it? Is help associated with relief, intrusion, disappointment, or inconsistency?

The answers to these questions are rarely held only as ideas. They become patterned into anticipation, emotional response, and relational behaviour.

A person who learned that care was relatively available may still struggle in life, but they may find it easier to return to baseline after conflict, to trust repair, to tolerate uncertainty in a relationship, and to believe that misunderstanding is not the end of connection.

A person who learned that care was inconsistent or unsafe may experience relationships differently. Delay may quickly become an alarm. Silence may feel like rejection. Closeness may trigger both longing and defence. A small shift in tone may seem larger than it appears to someone whose system is less sensitised. Again, this is not because the person is irrational. It is because the brain learned relational prediction early, and that prediction became part of how later experience is organised.

This helps explain why adult relationship patterns often feel so immediate.

A person does not merely "choose" every relational response from a neutral place. Much of what unfolds between people is shaped by learned expectation, bodily state, prediction, memory, and the need for safety. One person pursues closeness quickly because distance feels intolerable. Another withdraws because proximity feels exposing. One over-explains to prevent rupture. Another shuts down to avoid conflict. One becomes hyper-attuned to tone. Another struggles to read, feeling at all, because they learned long ago that inward withdrawal was safer than contact.

The adult brain carries forward many relational lessons it did not consciously design.

This is one reason the concept of co-regulation is so important.

Human beings are not self-regulating in isolation from the beginning. Regulation is first learned in the presence of others. A calm, responsive caregiver can help settle a distressed infant before the infant has any independent means of doing so. Over time, repeated experiences of being soothed, mirrored, and responded to help the child internalise patterns of regulation. They do not become calm from nowhere.

They become calmer by living through calm enough contact often enough for the system to learn it.

Co-regulation does not disappear in adulthood.

Adults continue to affect one another's states constantly. Tone calms or escalates. Presence settles or pressures.

A certain person may make the body soften; another may make it brace.

One conversation may widen thought; another may collapse it. One room may feel emotionally breathable; another may feel like a field of surveillance. Human beings borrow states from one another all the time, often without fully noticing.

This is not a weakness. It is part of social neurobiology.

The nervous system is highly responsive to relational atmosphere. A regulated person can make reflection more available to another. A dysregulated person can spread urgency, panic, agitation, or defensiveness rapidly. Groups intensify this even further. The emotional tone of a classroom, family, team, or audience can alter individual cognition dramatically. In such settings, people may feel more capable, more threatened, more open, more performative, or more inhibited depending not only on their own internal state, but on the relational field surrounding them.

This is one reason emotional contagion is real.

Emotional states can spread. Not magically, but through tone, facial expression, gesture, pacing, language, mirrored activation, and shared attention. A tense room can make tension feel obvious. A laughing group can make relief spread. Panic can escalate through a crowd not only because each individual has independently concluded danger is present, but because the relational field itself is amplifying alarm.

At the level of the brain, this makes sense. Human survival has long depended on social attunement. If one member of a group notices something threatening, rapid sensitivity to others' signals can be adaptive. If others are calm and coordinated, that calm may help regulate the group.

The social brain is therefore tuned not only to isolated stimuli, but to what others appear to feel, intend, avoid, and prioritise.

This sensitivity is closely related to mimicry and mirroring.

People subtly mirror one another all the time. Posture shifts. Speech rhythms align. Facial expressions echo. Emotional tone is reflected and absorbed. Some of this is conscious, much is not. This does not mean that every form of mirroring is healthy or that every person mirrors equally. But it does mean that the brain is built for relational resonance. It notices other humans deeply. It tracks them. It calibrates around them. It uses them as part of its own orientation system.

That is one reason loneliness can be so psychologically and physiologically significant.

Human beings often speak of loneliness as though it were merely the absence of company. But at a deeper level, loneliness can be understood as the absence of meaningful co-regulation, recognition, and relational anchoring.

A person can be surrounded by others and still feel profoundly alone if their system does not experience attunement, safety, or genuine contact. Conversely, a single stable relationship can sometimes offer more nervous-system nourishment than many superficial interactions.

The brain does not only need stimulation. It often needs attuned presence.

This also helps explain social pain.

Rejection, exclusion, humiliation, ridicule, dismissal, abandonment, and relational uncertainty can affect the brain with striking intensity. Social pain is not simply a metaphorical wound. For human beings, belonging has long been tied to survival.

To be cast out, ignored, or devalued is not processed as trivial by the organism. It can alter mood, attention, bodily state, memory, and self-perception.

A criticism may linger for hours.

A cold silence may echo long after the event. A repeated feeling of exclusion may become part of identity itself.

This is not because people are overly sensitive by nature. It is because the social brain treats relationships as consequential.

This can be seen in everyday life.

A person receives a warm message, and their whole day changes.
Another receives no reply and begins scanning for what went wrong.
A look of approval widens confidence.
A mocking tone can collapse it.
A safe conversation sharpens thought.
A hostile one narrows it.

The brain is always asking relational questions:
Am I safe here?
Am I seen?
Am I welcome?
Am I too much?

Am I not enough?
Can I relax?
Do I need to defend?
Will this connection hold?

These questions are not always conscious, but they shape behaviour all the same.

This is why many adult difficulties are relational not only in content, but in structure.

A person may think they have a problem with anger, but the deeper issue may be relational unsafety. Another may think they have a problem with overthinking, when in fact their brain is attempting to manage anticipated relational rupture. Someone else may struggle with self-expression, not because they lack ideas, but because the nervous system associates being seen with exposure, criticism, or rejection. The behaviour is real, but the brain in relationship often explains it better than isolated character judgement does.

This also has consequences for learning and performance.

A person can know something privately and lose access to it in a relational field that feels evaluative, shaming, or threatening. Another can become more articulate, thoughtful, and creative in the presence of someone calm, interested, and non-defensive. Intelligence is not always evenly available across contexts because the brain is not functioning in a vacuum.

Relationships can shut cognition down or help it come online.

That is why the relational field matters in therapy, education, leadership, friendship, partnership, and parenting alike.

What kind of brain does a person become in your presence?
More defended?
More collapsed?
More performative?
More scattered?
Or more coherent, spacious, and able to think?

This is one of the central ethical questions of the social brain.

Because once we understand that brains regulate in relationships, influence must be understood differently. Influence is not only persuasion through explicit ideas. It is also the shaping of the state through presence, tone, timing, approval, pressure, and repeated atmosphere. A person can guide another without ever "arguing" with them at the level of content. They can reward one state, punish another, normalise one emotional climate, destabilise another, and, over time, help train what the other person comes to expect.

This is one reason manipulative relationships are so powerful.

They not only provide bad information. They alter the relational conditions under which information is interpreted. They confuse safety cues. They distort repair. They create unpredictability. They reward compliance and punish independent reality-testing. They train the brain not only in what to believe, but in how to feel in the presence of certain beliefs, doubts, or disclosures.

At the other end of the spectrum, healing relationships can do something equally powerful in another direction. They can create repeated experiences of being met without intrusion, challenged without humiliation, seen without being consumed, corrected without being shattered, and close without being trapped. Over time, such conditions can help the brain revise what it once predicted from a relationship.

This is part of why repair matters more than perfection.

No relationship remains ideally attuned at all times. Misunderstanding happens. Friction happens. Timing breaks. But the possibility of repair teaches something crucial: disconnection does not always equal abandonment. Conflict does not always equal destruction. Rupture can be survived and reworked. This is one of the most stabilising lessons a social brain can learn.

Without repair, many people come to equate any relational disturbance with final collapse. With repair, the system gains a wider tolerance for reality.

This also brings us close to the role of language, which will deepen in the next chapter.

Because in a relationship, words are never just words. They arrive through tone, pacing, implication, hierarchy, history, and nervous-system state. The same sentence can regulate or destabilise, depending on how it lands in the field between people. A phrase such as "We need to talk" may signal openness in one relationship and threat in another. "I'm fine" may calm or intensify depending on tone. Silence may communicate respect, fear, punishment, or thoughtfulness depending on the relational pattern surrounding it.

In this sense, the brain in relationship is always interpreting more than content. It is interpreting the atmosphere.

That is why relationships often feel complicated even when the words themselves seem simple. The brain is not only listening to statements. It is listening for position, status, danger, softness, exclusion, uncertainty, invitation, contradiction, and hidden consequence. It is listening with memory.

This chapter matters because it makes something explicit that has been building quietly throughout the book: the human brain is not just embodied. It is social to its core.

It is shaped by attachment.
It is regulated through presence. It borrows states. It learns expectation through repeated interaction. It is wounded relationally and often healed relationally. It becomes itself in the company of others. That does not mean individuality is unreal.

It means individuality is never formed in isolation from the relational field.

And this leads us directly into the next chapter. If the brain is deeply shaped in a relationship, then one of the most powerful forces within a relationship is language itself. Not just what is said, but how it is said, how it is timed, what it implies, what state it induces, and how it becomes part of the signalling environment through which meaning is made.

That is where we go next.

Brain Observation

Notice one person in your life whose presence tends to change your state quickly.

Do you become calmer, sharper, more guarded, more scattered, more self-conscious, or more open around them? What does your brain seem to expect in their presence?

Everyday Experiment

Over the next two days, pay attention to one interaction in which you feel more settled and one in which you feel more tense.

After each, write a few words about:

- your body state

- your thoughts

- the other person's tone, pace, and emotional atmosphere

Do not analyse the entire relationship. Just observe how differently your system functions in different relational fields.

Visual Aid

Create a simple black-and-white page titled:

Relationship / Interaction | How My System Felt | What I Seemed to Expect

Fill in a few example rows, such as:

- close friend after honest conversation | settled, clearer, more open | that I could be myself

- delayed reply from partner | tight, watchful, anxious | possible rejection

- meeting with a critical manager | tense, self-monitoring, narrow | that I might be judged

- time with calm relative | slower breathing, grounded | that nothing urgent was required

Leave extra lines for your own entries. At the end, underline any repeated expectations such as rejection, safety, performance pressure, emotional labour, or permission to relax.

Relationship / Interaction

*How My System Felt | What I Seemed
to Expect*

Relationship / Interaction	How My System Felt	What I Seemed to Expect
close friend after honest conversation	settled, clearer, more open	that I could be myself
delayed reply from partner	tight, watchful, anxious	possible rejection
meeting with critical manager	tense, self-monitoring, narrow	that I might be judged
time with calm relative	slower breathing, grounded	that nothing urgent was required
•		
•		
•		
•		
•		

Ethical Question

If human beings regulate each other so powerfully, what responsibility do we carry for the kinds of nervous-system states we repeatedly evoke in those close to us?

Chapter 12 - Language, the Brain, and the MLH

If the previous chapter made clear that the brain is shaped in relationship, then this chapter turns towards one of the most powerful forces operating within the relationship itself:

language.

Not language merely as vocabulary, definition, grammar, or symbolic exchange, but language as a living signal. Language as timing, tone, implication, rhythm, pressure, invitation, threat, orientation, and nervous-system consequence. Language is not only something we use to describe reality, but also something that helps shape the reality we can perceive, endure, and inhabit.

This is where the inquiry begins to converge more explicitly with one of the central frameworks of my wider work: the Mirror-Linguistic Hypothesis, MLH.

The basic intuition behind this hypothesis is simple, though its implications are wide-reaching: language is not merely representational. It is also regulatory, relational, and somatic. Words do not land in a vacuum. They land in bodies. They arrive within nervous systems already carrying histories, expectations, stress loads, attachment patterns, and emotional states. The same sentence can soothe one person, activate another, shame a third, and go almost unnoticed by a fourth, not because the words changed, but because the state into which they landed was different, and because the language itself carried different signalling properties than its literal meaning alone would suggest.

This is why language cannot be understood fully at the level of content alone.

A sentence is never only what it says.
It is also how it arrives.
How fast.
How sharply.
With what tone?
With what implication?
Inside what relationship?
Against what history?
In what state?
Towards what anticipated consequence?

Most modern discussions of language still treat it primarily as symbolic transmission. Words are taken to refer to things, ideas, categories, facts, and feelings. At one level, this is obviously true. Language does represent. It describes, labels, explains, requests, argues, narrates, and records.

If we stop there, we miss something crucial. Language also modulates attention, affects physiological arousal, shapes anticipation, and participates in the regulation or dysregulation of the person receiving it.

This is not mystical. It is observable.

A softly timed sentence can slow the body.

A clipped phrase can tighten it.

A repeated accusation can reorganise self-perception.

A steady voice can widen tolerance.

An ambiguous message can trigger spirals of prediction.

A skilfully framed narrative can make one interpretation feel inevitable before evidence has even been examined.

Language moves through the social brain as a signal.

This is where the Mirror-Linguistic Hypothesis becomes useful. It proposes, in essence, that speech functions not only as content but as embodied signalling that can modulate nervous-system state in real time. The mirror element of the hypothesis points towards the interpersonal field: how people reflect, shape, cue, and condition one another through the manner and pattern of speech.

Human beings do not only exchange information. They entrain, mirror, pace, pressure, regulate, confuse, invite, signal safety, signal urgency, signal hierarchy, signal approval, and signal threat.

The linguistic element points towards the structure of language itself: wording, syntax, emphasis, metaphor, implication, framing, and repetition.

Together, these suggest that language is not merely a vehicle for thought. It is part of the live shaping of thought, feeling, and behaviour within a relationship.

This is why the same phrase can mean radically different things depending on tone and timing.

Take a simple phrase such as:

"We need to talk."

At the literal level, this is minimal content. It states that a conversation is needed. But almost no one receives it as neutral. The body reacts. Why? Because the brain is not only processing semantics. It is a processing pattern, memory, relationship, and anticipatory consequence. In one relationship, the phrase may signal healthy honesty.

In another, it signals rupture.

In one tone, it invites clarity. In another, it threatens exposure. The body often responds before the mind has formed a full explanation.

This happens constantly.

"I'm fine" can mean regulation, withdrawal, irritation, protection, dismissal, exhaustion, or concealed injury, depending on how it is spoken.
"Interesting" can communicate curiosity or contempt.
"Calm down." can settle or inflame.
"I'm here." can reassure or crowd.
Silence can regulate or destabilise.

The literal content matters, but it is not enough.

Tone carries relational instruction.
Pacing carries urgency or spaciousness.
Emphasis marks salience.
Volume marks force.
Timing alters interpretation.
Repetition conditions expectation.
Implication often lands more powerfully than explicit wording.

This is why language is so central to the nervous system.

A person does not only hear what was said. They hear what it appears to mean for their safety, belonging, dignity, agency, and place in the relational field. That appraisal may be conscious or not. Either way, the body participates.

This is also why some forms of speech remain in the body long after their literal content has faded.

A person may not remember every sentence used to shame them as a child, yet they may still carry the echo of its signal: *Do not take up space. Do not make mistakes. Do not need too much. Do not be visible unless you are useful.* These may later become self-talk, not because the person consciously chose them, but because repeated linguistic environments helped train expectation and identity.

The same is true in more positive directions. Repeated language of attunement, steadiness, and accurate naming can help widen internal space. A child repeatedly told, with genuine presence, *"You're overwhelmed right now, but you're safe, and we can slow down"*, is not just receiving information.

They are receiving a regulatory pattern that may later become internally available. Language here becomes part of how the nervous system learns to organise.

This is one reason naming matters.

To name an experience clearly and accurately can change the person's relationship to it. A state that felt global and consuming may become more workable once named. *This is anxiety.*

This is a shame. This is overstimulation. This is grief. This is not the whole of me; it is the state I am in. Such language does not magically fix the experience, but it can reduce fusion. It can create metacognitive distance.

It can bring implicit distress closer to reflection.

This is not only psychological. It is physiological in consequence.

A better name can produce more space.
A more distorted name can intensify the state.

Call a state panic, and the system may escalate.
Call it activation, and curiosity may remain possible.
Call a person too sensitive, and shame may rise.
Call them overloaded, and the frame shifts towards care and regulation.
Call a difference non-compliance, and one field emerges.
Call it distress, and another field emerges.

Frames are linguistic, but they are not merely semantic. They reorganise what becomes emotionally and morally available.

This is why institutions wield so much power through language.

Schools, governments, workplaces, therapy cultures, media systems, and ideological movements all use language to organise perception and state. A population can be softened, frightened, polarised, soothed, normalised, divided, or activated through repeated linguistic framing. Again, this does not happen only because of the explicit content of a message.

It happens because of the total signalling package: repetition, emotional tone, authority positioning, symbolic load, speed, rhythm, and consequence.

Words can become environments.

A slogan repeated often enough can begin to feel like reality. A phrase used repeatedly within a family can define the emotional possibilities available there. A diagnostic label can offer relief to one person and confinement to another.

A spiritual phrase can become a resource or a bypass. A political phrase can become tribal shorthand that pre-loads certainty before thought even begins.

This is where the Mirror-Linguistic Hypothesis becomes especially helpful, because it keeps us from collapsing language into either pure abstraction or crude manipulation. It invites a more layered view.

Language is:

- representational

- relational

- regulatory

- performative

- anticipatory

- embodied

It not only tells us what something is. It tells the system how to position itself in relation to what is being named.

This is why self-talk matters too.

The brain, in relationship, internalises linguistic patterns and begins to reproduce them inwardly. Over time, external voices can become internal ones. The way a person speaks to themselves often mirrors past relational fields: critical, rushed, dismissive, demanding, panicked, soothing, clear, fragmented, or patient. This is not just a metaphor. Internal language can alter bodily state, attention, and perceived possibility much like external language can.

A sentence such as *"I always mess this up"* does more than describe. It narrows.

A sentence such as *"This is difficult, but I can slow down"* does more than comfort. It regulates.

A sentence such as *"I have to get this right immediately"* can mobilise urgency.

A sentence such as *"I am activated right now, and my thinking may be narrowing"* can restore space.

This is why language belongs alongside neurochemistry, prediction, and memory in the architecture of human experience. It is one of the mediums through which the state is organised and reinforced.

The Mirror-Linguistic Hypothesis also highlights something more subtle: language works not only through direct statement, but through implication.

A person may never be told explicitly that they are a burden, yet may receive that message through sighs, timing, delay, eye contact, clipped reassurance, performative patience, or the repeated mood in which their needs are met. Likewise, a person may never be told explicitly that they are safe, yet may feel that message through the steadiness, pace, and consistency with which they are responded to.

Language is therefore broader than literal words. It includes vocal tone, prosodic pattern, and relational timing. The nervous system listens to all of it.

This matters because human beings often overestimate the importance of the explicit while underestimating the cumulative force of the implicit. The line spoken may be mild. The atmosphere may not be. The wording may be acceptable. The pacing may not be. The message may sound neutral on paper. In the body, it may land as pressure, surveillance, uncertainty, or threat.

This is why transcripts often fail to capture relational reality.

Two people may recount the same conversation and disagree not because the words differed, but because the *field* differed. One remembers the tone. Another remembers only the content. One recalls the pressure in the pauses. Another focuses on the logic of the statements. The brain in relationship is always processing both.

The implications of this are wide.

In parenting, language trains selfhood.
In partnership, language shapes safety.
In leadership, language modulates trust and defensiveness.
In therapy, language can regulate or retraumatise.
In education, language can widen thought or collapse it into performance anxiety.
In the media, language can orient populations towards reflection or reactivity.
In spirituality, language can deepen contact or dissociate people from embodied truth.
In politics, language can build solidarity, dependency, polarisation, or fear.

The question is never only, *What was said?*
It is also, *what did it do to the receiving system?*

This is why the hypothesis matters.

It offers a way of thinking about language that is both embodied and ethical. It asks us to stop treating speech as though its only function were semantic exchange and to recognise its role in shaping nervous-system conditions, cognitive availability, and relational possibility. It makes the consequences of language harder to ignore.

This does not mean all language can or should be softened. Clarity sometimes requires firmness. Boundaries sometimes need directness. Truth can be disruptive. But even disruptive truth lands differently depending on whether it is spoken from steadiness, contempt, panic, domination, or care. Precision and kindness are not opposites. Nor are honesty and nervous-system awareness.

In fact, some of the most effective language is effective precisely because it does both:
It says what is true,
and it creates enough regulation for truth to be metabolised.

This may also help explain why some people become attached to certain speakers, teachers, ideologies, or communities beyond the explicit content being offered. Often, the language itself regulates something. The cadence may soothe. The certainty may stabilise. The repetition may calm the prediction error. The framing may reduce ambiguity. The person may not only agree with the message. They may be attached to the state that the message reliably produces.

That can be helpful or dangerous. It can be part of healing. It can also be part of capture. This is why language and power can never be separated.

Who gets to name reality?
Whose words define what counts as normal, irrational, mature, sick, spiritual, dangerous, successful, compliant, or broken?
What kinds of speech are rewarded?
What kinds are punished?
What tones become associated with truth?
What pacing becomes associated with authority?

These are not merely linguistic questions. They are questions of nervous-system conditioning and social organisation.

This chapter stands near the centre of Part III because language is one of the main bridges between private brain function and public influence. It is where biology, relationship, power, and meaning converge. It is how the social brain becomes programmable without anyone needing to write literal code. Repeated phrases, relational tones, cultural frames, and institutional vocabularies can shape what brains come to expect, fear, trust, defend, or normalise.

The Mirror-Linguistic Hypothesis helps us see that more clearly.

Language is not just what humans think with.
It is also part of what humans are shaped by. It can steady or destabilise. Reveal or distort. Regulate or dysregulate. Invite reflection or bypass it. Open the person or close them.

And once that becomes clear, the next question becomes even sharper: If language can shape the nervous system so powerfully, what happens when repetition, ideology, media systems, schooling, social reward, and technological environments all begin working together to train the brain in patterned ways?

That takes us directly into the programmed brain.

Brain Observation

Notice one phrase you hear often, from others, from the media, or in your own self-talk. Ask yourself: what state does this phrase tend to create in the body? Does it soften, narrow, pressure, clarify, soothe, or intensify?

Everyday Experiment

Choose one short sentence you often say to yourself under stress. Write it down.

Then rewrite it in a way that keeps the truth but changes the signalling tone. For example:

- "I'm failing" becomes "I'm under pressure and narrowing"

- "I have to fix this now" becomes "I feel urgency, but I can slow down"

- "I always get this wrong" becomes "I am activated, and my thinking is becoming harsh"

Read both versions slowly and notice what changes in your body, breath, and mental space.

Visual Aid

Create a simple black-and-white page titled:

Phrase / Message | How It Landed in My Body | What It Seemed to Signal

Fill in a few example rows, such as:

- "We need to talk" | tight chest, alertness | possible conflict, uncertainty
- "Take your time" | slower breathing, more space | safety, permission
- "Calm down" | irritation, pressure | dismissal, control
- "I'm here" | softening, relief | support, steadiness
- "I have to get this right" | tension, urgency | pressure, fear of failure

Leave extra lines for your own examples. At the end, underline any repeated signals such as threat, safety, dismissal, urgency, permission, or belonging.

Phrase / Message
How It Landed in My Body

Phrase / Message	How It Landed in My Body	What It Seemed to Signal
"We need to talk"	tight chest, alertness	possible conflict, uncertainty
"Take your time"	slower breathing, more space	safety, permission
"Calm down"	irritation, pressure	dismissal, control
"I'm here"	softening, relief	support, steadiness
"I have to get this right"	tension, urgency	pressure, fear of failure
•		
•		
•		
•		
•		
•		

Ethical Question

If language can regulate or destabilise people before they have consciously analysed its meaning, what responsibility comes with the power to frame, name, and repeatedly speak into other human nervous systems?

Chapter 13 - The Programmed Brain

The word *programmed* unsettles people for a reason.

It sounds mechanical. It suggests that something intimate and human has been shaped from the outside. It raises questions about freedom, autonomy, authenticity, and control. Many people instinctively resist the idea because to admit that the brain can be programmed feels uncomfortably close to admitting how influenceable human beings really are.

And yet, once we have followed the argument of this book up to this point, the idea should no longer sound so foreign.

If the brain is plastic, it can be shaped.
If it predicts, it can be trained in what to expect.
If it remembers reconstructively, it can be organised around a repeated narrative.
If it regulates in a relationship, it can be conditioned by tone, atmosphere, and attachment.
If language lands somatically, it can install patterns deeper than surface opinion.
If attention is repeatedly captured, salience itself can be engineered.

In that sense, programming need not mean science fiction, implants, or cartoonish mind control.

It can mean something far more ordinary and therefore far more powerful: the repeated shaping of expectation, interpretation, reaction, and habit through the conditions a brain lives inside.

Human brains are programmed every day.

They are programmed by family atmosphere.
By schooling.
By reward and punishment.
By ritual.
By ideology.
By the media.
By repetition.
By social belonging.
By fear.
By shame.
By desire.
By screens.
By authority.
By cultural stories repeated so often, they begin to feel like nature.

This does not mean people are empty machines passively receiving commands. The brain is active, interpretive, resistant in some places, absorbent in others. It does not install every message equally. But it is trainable.

Much of what later feels like "normal thinking" may be the result of patterns repeated long enough to disappear into the background.

This is why conditioning matters.

Conditioning is one of the clearest and simplest examples of programming. The organism learns that certain cues predict certain outcomes, and over time, the response becomes easier, faster, and more automatic.

This can happen through direct experience, through observation, through social reinforcement, through emotional association, or through repeated symbolic exposure. The brain learns not only from what is explained explicitly, but from what is linked repeatedly.

If praise follows compliance, compliance becomes attractive.
If ridicule follows difference, difference becomes costly.
If silence follows vulnerability, vulnerability becomes dangerous.
If approval follows performance, performance becomes tied to worth.
If fear is repeatedly linked to certain people, symbols, or ideas, the body may begin reacting before conscious evaluation begins.

These are not merely intellectual lessons. They are conditioned responses woven into perception, anticipation, and behaviour.

Conditioning is especially powerful because it rarely feels like conditioning from the inside. It feels like common sense. It feels obvious. It feels natural. The person says, "That is just how things are," without noticing how much repeated shaping lies beneath the conclusion.

This is one of the reasons early environments matter so much. A child raised in a household where anger dominates may learn that emotional climate is unpredictable and that constant scanning is wise. A child raised in a household where image matters more than truth may learn to perform before they learn to feel honestly. A child repeatedly exposed to contempt may internalise harshness as normal. A child rewarded only for achievement may confuse love with usefulness. Later, these patterns may be experienced as personality rather than training.

But conditioning does not end in childhood.

Adult brains continue to be shaped by the systems in which they live. Workplaces condition speed, caution, performative confidence, or silence. Social groups condition belonging through shared language, values, jokes, taboos, and enemies. Media environments condition outrage, fear, tribal identity, urgency, and habit loops. Consumer culture conditions dissatisfaction by linking self-worth to lack, acquisition, and comparison.

Institutions condition obedience not only through formal rules, but through atmosphere, consequence, and the narrow range of what can be named safely.

This is where the word *programmed* becomes especially useful. It points not only to what a person believes, but to the patterning of the whole system.

Programming operates through repetition.

This is one of its simplest laws.

A message heard once may be resisted or forgotten. A message repeated with emotional charge, social reinforcement, authority cues, and environmental consistency begins to settle differently. Over time, it becomes easier to predict, easier to retrieve, easier to inhabit. It no longer feels like an idea being inserted. It feels like the natural background of reality.

This is why slogans matter.
Why routines matter.
Why symbolic repetition matters.
Why repeated headlines matter.
Why school rituals matter.
Why repeated moral narratives matter.
Why repeated emotional climates matter.

The brain is not only learning *what* is being repeated. It is learning that this is the pattern to orient around.

That is one reason propaganda has always relied so heavily on rhythm, repetition, framing, and emotional association rather than on argument alone. A population does not have to be reasoned into a narrow field. It can be trained into one. If certain frames are repeated often enough, alternative interpretations begin to feel less available.

If certain emotional pairings become habitual, the body starts doing part of the work before conscious thought begins.

The same dynamics exist in smaller, more intimate forms.

A family can become a tiny propaganda system.

A relationship can become a conditioning environment.

A workplace can train fear and self-censorship without ever calling itself coercive.

A friendship group can enforce conformity through tone and belonging rather than explicit rules.

Programming does not require a visible puppet master. It often emerges from systems, atmospheres, and repeated contingencies that shape what becomes easy, costly, praised, ignored, or punished.

This is one reason schooling deserves attention here.

Formal education does far more than transfer knowledge. It also trains habits of attention, authority response, timing, performance, and compliance. This is not to say all schooling is inherently oppressive.

It is to say that schooling, like any repeated environment, shapes the brain through more than content. It teaches what counts as success, what kind of speech is rewarded, what pace is normal, what forms of curiosity are welcome, what kinds of bodies can sit still, what kinds of minds are treated as difficult, and how a person must organise themselves to belong within the institution.

Some people emerge from such systems more confident and structured. Others emerge fragmented, shamed, over-performant, or alienated from their own rhythms. The point is not that the institution gave them only information. It trained the conditions under which they learned to think.

The same is true of digital life, though in an even more accelerated form.

Digital systems programme the brain through reward schedules, fragmentation, emotional capture, interruption, social comparison, novelty exposure, endless optionality, and algorithmically shaped relevance. They do not merely offer information. They alter baseline expectations about pace, stimulation, response time, affirmation, and attention span.

A person repeatedly immersed in fast, emotionally loaded, endlessly updating environments may find slower forms of thought harder to access. Reading deeply may feel effortful. Silence may feel empty rather than restorative. Conversation may begin to compete with notification logic. Reflection may lose ground to reaction. This is not because the person is weak. It is because the brain adapts faithfully to repeated conditions.

This is programming through architecture rather than argument.

The feed does not need to tell you what to think directly if it can train how you attend, what you crave, how long you can stay with difficulty, and what kind of stimulus now feels normal.

This is one reason modern programming often operates through salience engineering rather than explicit indoctrination. Salience engineering means shaping what stands out, what feels urgent, what gets repeated, and what the system begins to treat as relevant. If attention is trained, thought will follow. If emotional tone is trained, interpretation will follow. If urgency is made constant, reflective awareness will struggle for room.

Programming also works through identity reinforcement.

A person does not merely repeat ideas. They begin to attach those ideas to who they are, who their people are, and what belonging requires. Once that happens, disagreement is no longer just disagreement. It becomes a threat to coherence and tribe. The brain defends what feels like identity more fiercely than what remains abstract. This is why ideologies become powerful when they move from proposition to personhood.

The person no longer says, "I believe this."
They say, implicitly or explicitly, "This is who I am."
And from there, revision becomes far harder.

This can happen in politics, religion, lifestyle, health culture, spiritual communities, family roles, academic frameworks, activist circles, and personal mythology alike. The stronger the social rewards and moral certainty around the identity, the more difficult it becomes to examine the programming that helped form it.

There is another layer still: trauma loops.

Trauma does not only wound through what happened. It can also train repeated ways of scanning, bracing, withdrawing, pleasing, over-explaining, numbing, and anticipating. A person repeatedly conditioned by threat may become programmed towards hypervigilance. A person shaped by volatile approval may become programmed towards people-pleasing. A person raised where feeling was punished may become programmed towards dissociation or performance. Again, these words are not meant to dehumanise. They are meant to clarify that repetition becomes a pattern, and pattern becomes expectation.

Many adult struggles are not simply bad choices repeated. They are nervous systems carrying programmes written under older conditions.

This is why shame often fails as a tool for change. Shame intensifies the old pattern rather than dissolving it. It deepens fusion with the programming: *This is just me. This is all I am.* What is needed instead is often awareness, environmental change, relational correction, and repeated new experiences strong enough to make another programme more available.

That does not mean human beings are prisoners of programming. If that were true, this book would collapse into fatalism. The point is not that programming is total. The point is that it is real, and that freedom begins not with denying it, but with seeing it more clearly.

To see the programme is to loosen its invisibility.

A person begins to ask:

What in me is habit rather than truth?

What in me is repetition rather than essence?

What in me was rewarded into existence?

What in me is fear rehearsed so often it now feels like identity?

What in me is genuinely chosen, and what in me is still an inherited pattern?

These questions do not destroy the self. They make a deeper self-encounter possible.

This is also where the chapter intersects with moral responsibility. If brains are programmable, then those who design systems, shape institutions, control messaging environments, or repeatedly influence others carry responsibility for what kinds of patterns they are helping to install.

What kind of attention does a platform train?

What kind of selfhood does a school reward?

What kind of nervous system does a leader evoke?

What kind of reality does a repeated narrative produce?

What kind of citizen, child, patient, worker, partner, or believer is a system helping to create?

These are not secondary questions. They are central to any serious ethics of influence.

Because programming is not always obvious coercion. Often, it is the slow installation of expectation.

Over time, people come to believe:
This is just how I am,
This is just how people are,
This is just how life works,
This is just how things have to be.

And when that happens, the programme has disappeared into identity, culture, and reality itself.

This is why Chapter 13 sits where it does in the book.

The previous chapters of Part III have established that the brain is relational and that language shapes physiology and interpretation.

This chapter expands the frame to show that once those truths are understood, programming becomes visible everywhere. It is not a fringe concept. It is a daily one.

The social world is full of shaping forces.

The deeper question is not whether the brain is being programmed, but by what, by whom, in what direction, and under what ethical conditions.

This is not a reason for paranoia. It is a reason for literacy.

Because once a person begins to recognise programming, they can begin to ask more conscious questions about what they are rehearsing, what is shaping them, what is rewarding them, and what kind of brain their daily environment is helping to produce.

And that naturally leads us into the next chapter. Because one of the most powerful programming environments in modern life is not ideology in the old sense, but the attention economy itself.

If the brain can be conditioned through repetition, salience, novelty, and emotional capture, then what happens when entire systems are built to compete for attention every waking hour? That takes us directly into attention hijacking.

Brain Observation

Notice one repeated behaviour, phrase, belief, or emotional response in your life that feels "normal." Ask yourself: where might this have been trained, family, school, work, media, culture, religion, peer group, or past survival?

Everyday Experiment

Choose one repeated influence in your day, a social feed, a news format, a certain conversation pattern, a workplace rhythm, or even a recurring self-statement.

Reduce or interrupt it for twenty-four hours if possible, or consciously observe it in real time.

Notice what becomes more visible when the repetition is broken.

Does your body soften, become restless, seek the old pattern, or reach automatically for it?

Visual Aid

Create a simple black-and-white page titled:

Pattern I Notice | Where It May Have Been Trained | What Keeps It Going Now

Fill in a few example rows, such as:

- apologising too quickly | family tension, conflict avoidance | fear of disapproval, habit
- checking headlines repeatedly | uncertainty, media rhythm | need for certainty, stimulation
- tying worth to productivity | school and work performance culture | praise, pressure, identity
- going silent when upset | childhood emotional invalidation | self-protection, learned withdrawal

Leave extra lines for your own entries.

At the end, underline any repeated sources such as fear, belonging, authority, shame, repetition, or reward.

Pattern I Notice

Where It May Have Been Trained

Pattern I Notice	Where It May Have Been Trained	What Keeps It Going Now
apologising too quickly	family tension, conflict avoidance	fear of disapproval, habit
checking headlines repeatedly	uncertainty, media rhythm	need for certainty stimulation
tying worth to productivity	school and work performance culture	praise, pressure, identity
going silent when upset	childhood emotional invalidation	self protection, learned withdrawal
•		
•		
•		
•		
•		
•		

Ethical Question

If human beings can be shaped so powerfully by repeated environments, narratives, and reward structures, where does education end and programming begin?

Chapter 14 - Attention Hijack and the Economy of Capture

Our attention has become one of the most valuable resources in modern life.

This is not just because attention helps people focus. It is because attention determines what enters awareness, what gains emotional weight, what is repeated, what becomes memorable, and what begins to shape reality from the inside. Where attention goes repeatedly, interpretation follows. Where interpretation follows, behaviour, identity, and expectation often follow too.

That is why modern systems compete so aggressively to capture it.

Attention is no longer merely something a person gives.

It is something that markets, platforms, institutions, media systems, and persuasive environments study, engineer, and monetise. Entire industries now depend on keeping minds engaged, returning, reacting, checking, scrolling, refreshing, comparing, anticipating, and remaining vulnerable to interruption.

In that sense, the battle for attention is not peripheral to modern culture. It is one of its organising realities.

To understand why this matters, we need to begin with a simple point:

The brain does not treat all information equally.

It must select. It must foreground. It must decide what is salient enough to notice and what can remain in the background. This is a normal and necessary function of cognition. Without selective attention, life would become unmanageable. But once salience can be deliberately engineered from the outside, attention stops being only a private cognitive process and becomes a social battleground.

This is where the idea of attention hijack becomes useful.

Attention hijack refers to the repeated capturing of mental focus through stimuli designed to exploit novelty, fear, outrage, reward anticipation, interruption, social relevance, or unresolved uncertainty.

The brain is drawn towards these signals because, at an evolutionary level, they often mattered. Novelty might indicate opportunity or danger. Social signals might indicate inclusion or threat. Sudden changes in tone, movement, or urgency might require a response. In ancestral environments, this responsiveness could support survival.

In modern attention economies, it becomes a point of leverage.

The result is that the same brain built for living reality can become trapped in cycles of engineered salience.

A notification is not only a sound. It is a cue.
A headline is not only information. It is a hook.

An infinite scroll is not only convenient. It is an unresolved continuation.

A trending outrage is not only a story. It is an emotional capture with a social reward attached.

What is being competed for is not just time. It is the organising principle of consciousness itself.

This matters because attention is not neutral.

What a person repeatedly attends to begins to shape:

- What feels important

- What feels threatening

- What feels normal

- What becomes familiar

- What becomes difficult to ignore

- and what the brain starts expecting from the world

A person who repeatedly attends to an alarm becomes more ready for the alarm.

A person who repeatedly attends to comparison becomes more vulnerable to inadequacy.

A person who repeatedly attends to interruption may find depth harder to sustain.

A person whose attention is continually fragmented may retain less, reflect less, and react more.

This is not a moral weakness. It is the predictable consequence of training.

The modern economy of capture works through several overlapping levers.

The first is novelty.

The brain is drawn to what changes. Novelty can signal opportunity, reward, relevance, or threat. A new message, a new alert, a new headline, a new clip, a new image, a new controversy, a new possibility — all of these tug at the attentional system. Digital platforms exploit this relentlessly. They do not need every item to be meaningful. They only need it to be new enough to trigger orientation and "just one more" anticipation.

The second lever is intermittent reward.

If every check produced the same flat result, the behaviour would weaken. But when reward is irregular, a useful message here, a like there, a dramatic post now, a dull stretch followed by something emotionally charged, the brain remains more engaged. This is one reason compulsive checking patterns are so powerful. The uncertainty itself becomes stimulating. The next scroll might matter. The next refresh might reward. The next alert might change something.

This is not only about pleasure. It is about anticipation.

The third lever is emotional activation.

Outrage, fear, moral disgust, scandal, humiliation, tribal threat, and conflict all hold attention efficiently because they narrow the field. A calm mind can choose among many things.

An activated mind becomes more easily channelled. Emotional arousal increases salience. It makes the stimulus feel consequential. It also increases the chance that the person will react, share, defend, compare, or return.

This is why emotionally loaded content spreads so efficiently. It does not merely inform. It alters the state.

The fourth lever is social surveillance.

Human beings are profoundly attentive to signs of status, approval, exclusion, visibility, and response. Has someone replied? Who liked this? Who ignored it? Who is being attacked? Who is being elevated? What are others saying? What am I missing? The social brain is always listening for cues of belonging and position. Attention systems that continuously expose the person to these cues intensify self-monitoring and comparison.

This can produce a subtle but chronic state of relational vigilance.

The fifth lever is unfinishedness.

The brain dislikes unresolved loops. A headline that implies more than it says, a video cut at a moment of suspense, a notification that withholds detail, a stream with no natural endpoint — these all exploit the mind's tendency to seek closure. The person keeps going not because each piece is valuable, but because the structure makes stopping feel incomplete.

This is why infinite feeds are so psychologically different from finite texts or deliberate study. They remove the natural rhythms that help attention regulate itself.

Once these levers combine, the result is not merely distraction. It is environmental training.

The person may begin to expect stimulation constantly. Silence may feel empty rather than restorative. Longer thought may feel effortful. Reading may become harder. Waiting may become intolerable. Reflection may lose ground to reactivity. Boredom, once a doorway into imagination or rest, becomes something to kill immediately. The brain adapts to the pace of the feed, the rhythm of interruption, and the emotional temperature of the platform.

This is how the economy of capture becomes a way of shaping consciousness.

It changes not only what people think about, but how they can think at all.

A fragmented attentional environment tends to produce:

- shallower processing

- lower tolerance for ambiguity

- increased impulsivity

- more rapid emotional shifts

- poorer working memory

- weaker consolidation

- stronger dependence on novelty

- and reduced capacity for sustained depth

Again, this does not happen in the same way for everyone. People differ in temperament, use patterns, regulation, context, and awareness. But the general force is real enough to matter culturally.

This also helps explain why many people feel both overstimulated and undernourished.

They consume more signals but integrate less meaning. They move through more content but retain less coherence. They feel busy without feeling informed, connected without feeling met, engaged without feeling grounded. The attentional system is occupied, but not necessarily fulfilled.

That distinction matters.

Capture is not the same as nourishment. Engagement is not the same as depth. Stimulation is not the same as learning. Visibility is not the same as relationship. Immediate salience is not the same as lasting importance. The brain, however, must learn those distinctions, and it can only learn them if there is enough space to notice what different attentional environments are doing.

This is where attentional literacy becomes essential.

A person begins to ask:
What kinds of stimuli pull me most quickly?
What state am I usually in when I reach for more input?

What does a certain platform or information rhythm do to my body?
When do I feel informed, and when do I merely feel activated?
What kinds of attention leave me clearer, and which leave me scattered?

These questions are not anti-technology. They are pro-awareness.

The issue is not that all digital life is corrupt or that all stimulation is bad. The issue is whether a person is consciously participating in their attentional life or being continuously shaped by systems designed to outcompete reflection.

This is also why the economy of capture is ethical, not merely technical.

When systems are deliberately designed to exploit vulnerability in reward anticipation, social monitoring, outrage, uncertainty, and interruption, the question is no longer only whether they are effective. It becomes a question of whether they are humane. A platform can succeed financially while degrading the attentional conditions required for depth, discernment, regulation, and citizenship. A media system can maximise engagement while steadily training panic, tribal certainty, and compulsive checking. A communication environment can be profitable while making reflection more difficult. In that sense, the economy of capture is not just about consumer preference. It is about what kinds of minds are being cultivated at scale.

This chapter sits where it does because the programmable brain becomes especially visible in the field of attention. Repetition, reward, and emotional salience all meet here.

The person may believe they are just choosing what to look at, when in reality, much of the environment has been built to make certain choices far easier than others.

And because attention is the gateway through which so much else enters consciousness, what captures it repeatedly begins to shape identity, belief, emotion, and behaviour.

This also sets up the next chapter.

Because once attention has been trained and salience organised, another force becomes more powerful still: the need to defend what the attended world has come to mean.

We not only capture information. We attach to it. We organise identity around it. We defend the narratives that make their world feel coherent.

That takes us to belief, identity, and the need to be right.

Brain Observation

Notice one moment today when your attention was captured quickly and almost automatically. Was it by novelty, fear, outrage, comparison, uncertainty, social relevance, or boredom relief?

Everyday Experiment

Choose one recurring attentional cue for a single day: notifications, breaking news, social feeds, or another fast-loop source. Either turn it off temporarily or delay engagement by ten minutes each time it appears. Notice what happens in the gap: restlessness, curiosity, anxiety, relief, reflex reaching, or greater space.

Visual Aid

Create a simple black-and-white page titled: What Captured My Attention | What Made It Hard to Ignore | What State It Left Me In

Fill in a few example rows, such as:

- breaking news alert | urgency, uncertainty | activated, watchful

- social media scroll | novelty, endless continuation | scattered, stimulated

- message notification | social relevance, anticipation | alert, slightly tense

- long-form reading | depth, chosen focus | calmer, more coherent

Leave extra lines for your own entries. At the end, underline any repeated hooks such as novelty, threat, comparison, boredom relief, or the need for reassurance.

What Captured My Attention		
What Made It Hard to Ignore		
Pattern I Notice	Where It May Have Been Trained	What State It Left Me In
apologising too quickly	family tension, conflict avoidance	fear of disapproval, habit
social media scroll	uncertainty, media rhythm	scattered, stimulated
message notification	school and work performance culture	praise, pressure, identity
long-form reading	childhood emotional invalidation	calmer, more coherent
•		
•		
•		
•		
•		
•		
•		

Ethical Question

When platforms, media systems, and institutions deliberately compete for human attention using psychological vulnerabilities, at what point does persuasion become extraction?

Chapter 15 - Belief, Identity, and the Need to Be Right

By the time a belief becomes emotionally important, it is rarely just a belief.

It becomes part of the way a person orients themselves in the world. It begins to organise belonging, certainty, memory, meaning, and moral position. It shapes what feels obvious, what feels intolerable, what feels threatening, and what feels like proof. Once that happens, disagreement is no longer experienced only as an intellectual difference. It can feel like an attack on coherence itself.

This is why the need to be right runs deeper than argument.

People do not only defend ideas because they have weighed them carefully and found them superior. Often, they defend them because those ideas have become tied to identity, tribe, safety, self-respect, emotional regulation, or the very structure of how reality now makes sense. To lose the belief would not feel like updating a thought. It would feel like losing footing.

That is why the brain protects belief so fiercely.

A belief can become a shelter.
A map.
A badge of belonging.
A stabiliser of uncertainty.
A defence against shame.
A way of maintaining moral innocence.

A structure that tells the person who they are and where they stand.

Once belief begins functioning in those ways, truth and identity become difficult to separate.

This is one of the reasons cognitive dissonance feels so uncomfortable.

Cognitive dissonance is often described as the discomfort that arises when a person holds inconsistent ideas or when new evidence conflicts with existing beliefs. That is true, but the lived reality is deeper than a mere intellectual mismatch. When the conflicting information threatens a belief that is tied to identity or belonging, the discomfort can feel almost bodily.

It may produce defensiveness, anger, dismissal, rationalisation, minimisation, selective attention, or sudden certainty. The goal of the system becomes not necessarily to discover truth, but to reduce the distress of contradiction.

In other words, the brain often protects coherence before it protects accuracy.

This is not because people are foolish. It is because coherence helps the organism function. A stable narrative reduces uncertainty.

A shared worldview helps social coordination. A moral identity reduces shame and self-conflict. The trouble is that these useful functions can harden into rigid defence, especially when the person has little room for ambiguity, relational safety, or self-reflective distance.

This is where identity enters.

Identity is not merely the list of things a person calls themselves. It is the organising story through which they make their life continuous and legible. It includes roles, affiliations, wounds, values, loyalties, social locations, memories, and repeated ways of interpreting the world. Some parts of identity are necessary. Without identity, there would be little continuity, little orientation, little sense of self over time. But identity can also become over-fused with belief.

When that happens, a challenge to the belief feels like a challenge to the self.

A person no longer says only:
"I think this is true."

At a deeper level, they may be saying:
"This is what makes me intelligible to myself."
"This is what keeps me connected to my people."
"This is what protects me from shame."
"This is what tells me I am on the right side."
"This is what makes the world feel survivable."

That is why people can become attached to narratives over reality. The narrative does more than explain. It regulates.

This is also why group belonging matters so much.

Human beings are not neutral processors of evidence. They are social creatures whose brains have long depended on inclusion, shared meaning, and relational safety. To belong to a group is not merely to hold certain ideas. It is to participate in a shared field of language, norm, emotion, taboo, permission, and status. The group does not only tell the individual what to think. It helps tell them what it means to be good, sane, normal, brave, intelligent, loyal, dangerous, or naïve.

This is why people can remain inside group narratives even when cracks appear.

The cost of revision may be more than intellectual. It may threaten friendships, family bonds, professional standing, moral certainty, spiritual identity, or the feeling of being part of something larger. For many people, changing their minds is not just difficult because the evidence is unclear. It is difficult because the social and emotional cost of change feels too high.

Again, this does not mean everyone is consciously calculating tribal loss. It means the brain often registers such loss before conscious reasoning fully articulates it.

This is where the need to be right becomes more than ego.

At the surface, needing to be right can look like pride, stubbornness, or arrogance. Sometimes it is. But often beneath it lies something more vulnerable: the need to remain coherent, innocent, safe, respected, or not cast out. A person may cling to certainty not because they are strong, but because they cannot yet tolerate what uncertainty would expose.

This is important because it changes how we understand both conflict and persuasion.

When people argue, they are not always contesting evidence alone. They may be defending identity structures, group membership, emotional regulation, or a worldview that keeps fragmentation at bay. That does not mean every belief is equally valid. It means that changing minds requires more than supplying information. The deeper the identity attachment, the more the challenge will be felt as a personal threat.

This is one reason facts alone so often fail.

A person can encounter contradiction and still emerge more entrenched. Why? Because contradiction is not received in a neutral chamber. It lands inside a system already organised by prediction, memory, emotion, group loyalty, and self-protective interpretation. The more threatened the system feels, the more it may use intelligence to defend its previous model rather than revise it.

This helps explain why high intelligence does not protect against dogmatism.

A clever person can build more elaborate rationalisations. A verbally skilled person can defend a fragile identity with great sophistication. A well-read person can recruit sources selectively to stabilise the conclusions they need emotionally. Intelligence can deepen honesty, but without humility and metacognition, it can also deepen self-deception.

This is why certainty is not a reliable sign of truth.

Often, certainty reflects emotional closure rather than epistemic strength. It marks the point at which ambiguity has become intolerable enough that the mind has settled on a stable interpretation and begun defending it. Some truths do deserve confidence. But the feeling of confidence itself is not proof that such truth has been reached.

The social brain intensifies this further through tribal perception.

Once people identify strongly with a group, they often begin to see the world through shared moral framing. The same event can appear heroic from one group's position and outrageous from another. The same policy can seem like protection or oppression depending on the narrative architecture surrounding it. Group identity influences which facts feel salient, which harms are visible, which motives seem plausible, and which questions can be asked without social penalty.

This is why entire populations can inhabit radically different realities while looking at the same events.

They are not simply disagreeing over neutral data. They are perceiving through different identity-laden frameworks of relevance, danger, and legitimacy. Each group begins with different assumptions, different stories of innocence and threat, different emotional investments, and different permissible conclusions. From within each frame, the others may seem irrational or corrupt. But from the standpoint of the social brain, much of this is the predictable result of belonging structures shaping cognition.

This is also why moral language becomes so charged.

People rarely attach to beliefs only because they are useful. They also attach to them because they confer righteousness, victimhood, superiority, purity, realism, awakening, or resistance. A belief that allows a person to feel morally clear will often be defended more strongly than one that is merely practical. To be wrong in such cases would not just mean factual error. It might mean guilt, shame, complicity, or betrayal.

The stronger the moral loading, the harder the revision.

This can happen across every ideological spectrum. It can happen in religion, politics, health culture, spiritual movements, activist communities, intellectual circles, family mythologies, and even self-help language. Once a person's goodness becomes fused with a narrative, questioning the narrative begins to feel like endangering the self.

This is why humility matters so much.

Humility is not passivity or indecision. It is not pretending that nothing matters or that all views are equally sound. It is the disciplined recognition that the brain is vulnerable to identity fusion, emotional certainty, social conditioning, and motivated reasoning. Humility allows a person to say:
"This matters deeply to me, but my attachment to it may also

be shaping how I see."

"I feel morally convinced, but I may still be defending more than I realise."

"I want to be right, but I also want to remain open to what my certainty might be protecting."

That kind of humility is difficult because it asks the person to remain in contact with uncertainty without collapsing.

This is where the earlier themes of the book return again: regulation, metacognition, state, prediction, and social learning.

A dysregulated brain tends to defend harder.
A threatened identity tends to close faster.
A socially reinforced narrative becomes more persuasive through repetition.
A person without reflective distance becomes more fused with their current certainty.
A person who can notice their need to be right in real time has more chance of widening.

This widening is not only intellectual. It is moral and relational.

It allows a person to remain human in disagreement.
To question without dehumanising.
To argue without making identity vulnerable.
To revise without total collapse.
To recognise that another person's rigidity may be serving a nervous-system function even when the content of their belief remains harmful or false.

This does not mean abandoning truth for empathy. It means that truth-seeking without understanding identity dynamics often becomes shallow.

A person who wants to understand how belief works must understand that beliefs are often carried by:

- attachment

- social reward

- fear of exclusion

- shame avoidance

- self-narrative

- moral status

- and the stabilising force of repetition

That is why the need to be right is rarely just about being right.

It may be about:
not being humiliated,
not being cast out,
not losing coherence,
not revisiting pain,
not surrendering innocence,
not becoming uncertain in a world already felt to be unstable.

This is one reason people can become more extreme under pressure. When identity is threatened, moderate positions may feel insufficiently protective. The system seeks stronger coherence, stronger tribe, stronger certainty, stronger language, stronger enemies. Polarisation often feeds on this. The more unstable or overwhelming the wider environment becomes, the more tempting rigid belonging structures can feel.

That is why Part III ends here.

This part of the book has shown that the brain is not merely private or biological. It is profoundly social and programmable. We began with the brain in relationship, moved into language as embodied signalling through the Mirror-Linguistic Hypothesis, explored the programmed brain through conditioning and repeated environments, and then entered the modern economy of attentional capture. This final chapter brings those threads together by showing what happens once socially trained, linguistically framed, and attention-shaped patterns become fused with identity itself.

At that point, the social brain becomes not only influenceable, but self-defending.
It protects what has shaped it.
It rationalises what regulates it.
It clings to what keeps its world coherent.
And it treats a threat to belief as a threat to self.

This is why understanding the brain requires more than neuroscience alone. It requires culture, ethics, language, relationships, power, and philosophy. It requires asking not only how people think, but what their thinking is protecting.

And now the inquiry must move further.

Because once we understand how the brain is shaped socially and how identity protects its own narratives, deeper questions begin to press forward.

If belief can become part of selfhood, what exactly is the self?
If continuity can be defended so fiercely, how stable is identity really?
What do inheritance, culture, and consciousness add to the picture?
And how far do current models of the brain actually reach before mystery reappears?

That is where Part IV begins.

Part IV, The Deeper Questions, shifts the inquiry from social shaping towards ontology, inheritance, culture, selfhood, consciousness, and the limits of reductionist explanation.

If Part III explored how the brain is programmed by the worlds it inhabits, Part IV asks what kind of being this brain belongs to in the first place.

We move now from influence to identity, from conditioning to continuity, from the social field to the deeper mysteries beneath it.

Brain Observation

Notice one belief you hold strongly. Ask yourself: what part of this belief feels factual, what part feels emotional, and what part feels connected to who I believe myself to be?

Everyday Experiment

Choose one opinion or belief you feel certain about. Without trying to abandon it, write two short paragraphs:

1.   Why this belief feels true to me

2.   What might losing this belief cost me emotionally or socially

The aim is not to weaken conviction artificially, but to observe whether the belief carries identity, belonging, certainty, or self-protection alongside evidence.

Visual Aid

Create a simple black-and-white page titled: Belief / Position | What It Gives Me | What It Might Protect Me From

Fill in a few example rows, such as:

•   "I must stay productive" | purpose, structure, self-worth | feeling inadequate, slowing down

•   "People cannot be trusted" | caution, control | vulnerability, disappointment

•   "My group sees things clearly" | belonging, certainty, moral clarity | exclusion, ambiguity, self-doubt

•   "I always need to be right" | control, protection, coherence | shame, uncertainty, loss of status

Leave extra lines for your own entries. At the end, underline any repeated protections such as shame avoidance, belonging, certainty, innocence, or fear of exclusion.

Belief / Position

What It Gives Me | What It Might Protect Me From

Belief / Position	What It Gives Me	What It Might Protect Me From
I must stay productive	purpose, structure, self-worth	feeling inadequate, slowing down
People cannot be trusted	caution, control	vulnerability, disappointment
My group sees things clearly	belonging, certainty, moral clarity	exclusion, ambiguity, self-doubt
I always need to be right	control, protection, coherence	shame, uncertainty, loss of status
•		
•		
•		
•		
•		
•		

Ethical Question

If the need to be right is often tied to belonging, identity, and emotional regulation, how should we approach disagreement in a way that seeks truth without needlessly triggering defensive collapse?

PART IV - The Deeper Questions

By this point in the book, the brain should no longer appear as a simple object.

We have explored its architecture, its signalling life, its chemistry, its reconstructive memory, its emotional intelligence, its plasticity, its relational shaping, its linguistic field, and its susceptibility to social programming. We have seen that the brain is embodied, adaptive, social, and influenceable. We have seen that what feels natural may be conditioned, and that what feels personal may be carried forward from biology, experience, relationship, and repeated environment.

And yet, even with all of that in view, certain questions remain.

In some ways, they become sharper.

Because once we have looked at the brain structurally, chemically, emotionally, relationally, and socially, we arrive at a threshold where the inquiry can no longer remain only functional. It must become philosophical, ontological, cultural, and existential.

What, exactly, is the self that the brain appears to sustain?
How stable is identity, if continuity is partly constructed and partly defended?
What role do inheritance, genetics, and epigenetics play in shaping who we become?
How do different cultures understand mind, consciousness,

and the human being?

Is the brain best understood as a computer, a receiver, an interface, or something stranger still?

And how far can current material explanations go before they meet mystery?

This is the terrain of Part IV.

If earlier parts of the book examined what the brain is, how it functions, and how it is shaped, this part turns towards what the brain may be participating in. It is not a retreat from science, but an expansion beyond simplistic reductionism. It does not abandon rigour, but it refuses to pretend that rigour requires flattening every question into a mechanism alone.

We begin in **Chapter 16, The Brain, the Self, and the Illusion of Continuity**, where the inquiry turns towards one of the most intimate problems in human life: who, or what, is the "I"? This chapter explores the narrative self, the embodied self, the observing self, and the ways continuity may be both necessary and partly constructed. It asks how identity is sustained, why fragmentation feels so threatening, and why the sense of being one stable person across time may be more dynamic than it appears.

From there, **Chapter 17, Genetics, Epigenetics, DNA, RNA, and Biological Inheritance**, widens the question of selfhood by asking what is inherited and what is shaped. This chapter explores the relationship between biology and environment, predisposition and expression, stress and adaptation, and sensitivity and development. It moves beyond crude determinism without denying inheritance, showing that human beings are neither written in full by genes nor untouched by them.

In **Chapter 18, The Brain, Culture, and Cross-Civilisational Ways of Knowing**, the frame widens further still. Western neuroscience has revealed extraordinary detail, but it is not the only tradition to have asked what mind, awareness, and consciousness are. This chapter explores contemplative traditions, symbolic systems, indigenous perspectives, ritual, meditation, and cross-cultural interpretations of cognition and selfhood. It asks what other civilisational frameworks may see that modern reductionism may overlook, and how different cultures shape what counts as knowledge in the first place.

That naturally leads into **Chapter 19, Is the Brain a Computer, a Receiver, or Something Stranger?**, where one of the most compelling and easily abused comparisons is examined directly. This chapter explores the parallels and limits between brains and artificial systems, including symbolic computation, neural networks, machine learning, pattern recognition, and the language of information processing. It also opens the careful speculative territory around quantum metaphors and the possibility that the brain may participate in deeper fields of relation than current technological analogies fully capture.

Finally, **Chapter 20, Consciousness Beyond Mechanism**, closes this part by entering the hardest question of all. Here, the inquiry turns explicitly towards the problem of consciousness: subjectivity, awareness, experience, the felt quality of being alive, and the limits of current explanatory models. Materialist, emergentist, idealist, panpsychist, and spiritual interpretations all enter the field here. This chapter does not pretend to solve the mystery. It does something more honest: it holds it open without abandoning seriousness.

Taken together, these chapters move the book into its deepest philosophical terrain.

They do not reject neuroscience. They place it within a larger horizon. They ask whether explanation alone is enough, whether the self is more fluid than identity suggests, whether inheritance is more dynamic than determinism allows, whether culture shapes cognition more deeply than science often admits, and whether consciousness may remain irreducible no matter how much structure and signalling we eventually map.

This part matters because many modern books on the brain stop too early. They explain function and assume the deepest questions have already been answered. But human life is not exhausted by mechanism. Even the most precise account of signalling, memory, regulation, and behaviour leaves something unresolved: the lived fact of subjectivity itself, the strange continuity of selfhood, the role of meaning, the tension between biology and freedom, and the possibility that reality is richer than any one explanatory frame can hold.

This is why Part IV belongs here.

It follows the previous parts naturally. Once the brain is understood as shaped by biology, body, relationship, language, conditioning, and culture, the deeper question cannot be avoided:

What kind of being is this that can be shaped in all these ways and yet still ask what it is?

That is where we now go.

Chapter 16 - The Brain, the Self, and the Illusion of Continuity

Few experiences feel more immediate than the sense of being *me*.

It appears obvious. It seems to sit beneath everything else, stable and familiar. Thoughts change, moods shift, roles come and go, beliefs evolve, relationships alter, the body ages, memory distorts, environments change — and yet through all of this, most people still feel that there is someone continuous at the centre of experience.

A self. An "I". A being who has remained, in some essential way, the same person throughout the unfolding of life.

But once we begin to examine that feeling more closely, it becomes less straightforward than it first appears.

The self is real as experience.
But it may not be as simple as structure.

This chapter is not an argument that the self is an illusion in the crude sense that nothing exists, no one is here, or identity is meaningless. Rather, it is an inquiry into how the brain helps generate, maintain, defend, and revise the feeling of continuity we call the self. It asks whether the "I" is a single stable thing, or whether it is a layered process held together through memory, embodiment, narrative, attention, relationship, and repeated acts of interpretation.

This question matters because the self is not only a philosophical abstraction. It shapes daily life.

It affects how people remember, how they defend their identity, how they interpret change, how they cling to certain narratives, how they organise morality, and how they fear fragmentation. The brain does not merely think about the self. It helps produce the continuity through which the self is felt.

At one level, this continuity is necessary.

Without some durable sense of "I", life would be almost impossible to organise. There would be no stable point from which to make plans, take responsibility, sustain relationships, or recognise one's own history across time. The self gives coherence. It allows a person to say:

I was there.

I did that.

I believe this.

I regret that.

I want to become something more than I have been.

The self, in this sense, is part of how continuity is lived.

But continuity is not the same as permanence.

A person at ten, twenty, forty, and seventy is not psychologically identical. Their bodies have changed. Their nervous system has changed. Their memories have been revised. Their roles have shifted. Their values may have deepened, collapsed, reformed, or inverted. Their capacities, sensitivities, and interpretive frameworks may be utterly different from those they once inhabited. And yet across those changes, some thread remains convincing enough for them to feel they are still themselves.

What is that thread?

Part of the answer lies in narrative.

Human beings do not merely live. They tell themselves what their life means. They organise memories into patterns, causes, turning points, wounds, achievements, identities, and moral lessons. The self is sustained partly through this ongoing narrative work. A person says, "This is who I am," and what often follows is a story: what happened to them, what mattered, what they overcame, what shaped them, what they value, what kind of person they now believe themselves to be.

This narrative self is powerful because it gives a life sequence and interpretation.

But narrative is not the whole self.

A person can tell a clear story about themselves while remaining disconnected from the body in which that story lives. They can narrate trauma without fully integrating it. They can explain their childhood while still being driven by states they do not observe.

They can describe themselves as one kind of person while their body, attention, and relational reactions reveal older and deeper patterns still active beneath the story.

This is why it helps to distinguish between different aspects of selfhood.

There is the narrative self — the version of self built through memory, story, identity claims, and autobiographical continuity.

There is the embodied self — the lived sense of being located, sensing, breathing, feeling, moving, bracing, softening, orienting, and existing through a body in the present moment.

There is the social self — the version of self organised through relationship, status, role, belonging, recognition, and the reflected responses of other people.

And there is what some traditions might call the observing self — the aspect of awareness that notices thoughts, feelings, roles, and identities without being reducible to any single one of them.

These are not separate entities living in different rooms. They are overlapping dimensions of how selfhood is experienced.

The trouble begins when one layer is mistaken for the whole.

A person may become fused with the narrative self and feel that the story they tell about themselves is identical to who they are. Another may become fused with the social self and organise identity almost entirely around external reflection. Another may live primarily through defensive embodiment, feeling selfhood as threat management rather than spacious presence. Another may over-identify with the observing self and use detachment to avoid lived human contact. In each case, continuity is preserved, but in a narrowed way.

This is one reason the self often feels more stable than it actually is.

The brain is constantly integrating experience into patterns coherent enough to preserve identity. Memory is reconstructed, narrative is updated, contradictions are softened, and roles are stitched into a story that feels sufficiently continuous. This is adaptive. Too much fragmentation would be disorienting. But it also means the self is partly a work of ongoing maintenance.

The person is not only *being* themselves. They are also repeatedly *making* themselves intelligible to themselves.

This can be seen in ordinary life.

A person remembers an older version of themselves and says, "I was always like that," when in fact they may be selectively reading continuity back into the past. Another says, "That wasn't the real me," distancing from a painful period while preserving a preferred identity. Another reinterprets former suffering as part of a growth arc, creating coherence from what once felt senseless. These are not necessarily dishonest acts. There are ways the self preserves continuity under changing conditions.

The brain does not like fragmentation.

It prefers patterns that can be lived with.
It prefers stories that can be inhabited.

It prefers identities that reduce uncertainty.
It prefers enough consistency to keep agency and orientation intact.

This is one reason rupture can feel so destabilising.

When a person's story about themselves is challenged — by betrayal, illness, loss, failure, trauma, awakening, radical change, or contradiction — the discomfort is not only emotional. It is ontological. The continuity of self is under strain. A person may say, "I don't know who I am anymore," and mean it literally enough at the level of lived experience. Their narrative self no longer fits cleanly, but a new one has not yet stabilised.

This can feel like a collapse.
But it can also become a transformation.

Because if continuity is partly constructed, then selfhood may be more revisable than it first appears.

That does not mean a person can invent themselves from nothing. Biology, history, relationship, and inherited pattern still matter. But it does mean the self is not frozen. Identities can soften. Stories can be revised. Defended roles can loosen. Embodied awareness can deepen. What once felt central may be revealed as adaptive rather than essential.

What once felt impossible may become available.

This is one reason therapeutic, philosophical, and spiritual work often revolves around selfhood.

Some approaches help people recognise the stories they are trapped inside. Others help reconnect selfhood to embodiment. Others help distinguish between transient states and enduring patterns. Others question whether the self is as singular as common sense assumes. Others cultivate contact with the observing self so that thought, emotion, and role can be witnessed without total fusion.

All of these, in different ways, respond to the fact that the self is both real and constructed.

Memory plays a central role here.

As Chapter 8 showed, memory is reconstructive rather than archival. Since the narrative self is built partly from autobiographical memory, this means selfhood itself is partly reconstructive. The person is not only remembering events. They are remembering themselves through those events. Over time, certain memories become central to identity, while others recede. Some are repeated until they become self-defining. Others are excluded because they threaten coherence. The self, then, is not simply what happened. It is what has been selected, organised, and interpreted as *mine*.

This can be liberating and dangerous.

Liberating, because it means selfhood can be re-read. A painful chapter need not remain the only truth. A person can widen what counts as them. They can recover forgotten strengths, revise over-narrow narratives, and recognise that what once felt like essence was sometimes a survival strategy.

Dangerous, because it means the self can also become distorted by selective remembering, cultural scripts, ideology, shame, or the need to preserve innocence and continuity at all costs.

This brings us back to the social dimension.

No one constructs the self alone. The self is mirrored, confirmed, challenged, and shaped in relationship. People learn who they are partly through how they are responded to. They become visible to themselves through the eyes, tone, language, and emotional atmosphere of others. If a child is repeatedly treated as burdensome, gifted, difficult, responsible, fragile, dramatic, useful, or invisible, those reflections may begin to enter the architecture of self. Later, the adult may call these identity truths when, in fact, they were also relational imprints.

This is why the self is not merely internal. It is relationally scaffolded.

The phrase "know yourself" sounds individual, but the self to be known has often been shaped through mirrors not of one's own choosing.

This also helps explain why social role can become so fused with identity.

A person may feel that they *are* the helper, the achiever, the outsider, the strong one, the broken one, the intelligent one, the misunderstood one, the rebel, the victim, the healer, the rational one, the spiritual one, the competent one, or the sacrificial one. These roles may once have been adaptive. They may still contain truth. But when they harden into total identity, continuity becomes rigidity.

The self then stops being a living process and becomes a defended position.

This is one of the reasons the idea of an observing self can be so important.

The observing self is not easily defined because it is less a role than a capacity of awareness. It is what is noticed rather than being identical to thought. It notices emotional state without being fully reducible to it. It notices the narrative without collapsing into the narrative completely. It does not erase embodiment or history; rather, it provides a slightly wider field within which embodiment and history can be held.

This capacity matters because without it, the person tends to become fused with the most immediate layer of self-experience. With it, they may begin to say:
I notice that shame is here.
I notice that my story is tightening.
I notice that I am defending a role.
I notice that my identity feels threatened.
I notice that I am speaking from an old version of myself.

That noticing creates room.

It does not destroy continuity. It makes continuity less tyrannical.

Different traditions describe this differently. Psychology may frame it through metacognition or self-observation. Mindfulness traditions may speak of witnessing. Philosophical traditions may distinguish between ego, personhood, subjectivity, and awareness. Spiritual traditions may speak of soul, presence, or consciousness beyond role. These frameworks differ, but many converge around a shared intuition: the self is not exhausted by the first story it tells about itself.

This does not mean continuity is unreal. It means continuity may be more dynamic and layered than common sense assumes.

There is also a darker side to selfhood worth naming.

Because the same continuity that makes agency possible can also make change difficult. The self defends itself. It preserves roles that once ensured coherence. It resists evidence that would require narrative revision. It clings to familiar suffering because familiar suffering still belongs to the known self. A person may say they want freedom, but part of them may fear the identity loss that freedom would require. To become different is not only to gain something. It is also to let older forms of selfhood loosen.

This is why transformation can feel like grief.

A role dies.
A story softens.
An identity loses its authority.
A familiar defensive pattern no longer fits.

And even if the change is liberating, the person may still mourn what organised their previous life.

This grief is often misunderstood. People think they are afraid of growth. More often, they are afraid of losing continuity before a new one has stabilised.

Seen this way, the self is less like a fixed object and more like an adaptive negotiation between:
memory,
body,
relationship,
story,
awareness,
and the need for enough continuity to remain coherent.

The brain is central to that negotiation.

It helps bind autobiographical memory into sequence.
It supports role continuity.
It integrates bodily feeling into identity.
It predicts who the person is likely to be based on a prior pattern.
It reacts defensively when self-structures are threatened.
It revises, slowly or suddenly, when new integration becomes possible.

This is why the self feels both intimate and unstable.

It is intimate because it is how life is lived from the inside.
It is unstable because it is maintained by processes that are changing all the time.

That instability is not a flaw. It may be part of what makes human growth possible.

If the self were perfectly fixed, there could be no true healing.
If the self were perfectly fluid, there could be no responsibility or trust.
The human challenge is to live inside continuity without worshipping it, and to allow revision without collapsing into fragmentation.

This chapter opens Part IV because it stands at the threshold between brain science and deeper philosophy.

The brain, so far, has been approached through structure, signalling, memory, emotion, relationship, language, conditioning, and identity defence. But once selfhood comes into question, the inquiry begins to widen. The self is no longer merely a psychological topic. It becomes a problem of ontology, subjectivity, and meaning. The brain can help explain how continuity is built, but the lived fact of subjectivity still presses beyond easy reduction.

That is why the next question follows naturally.

If the self is partly constructed, partly inherited, and partly revised through life, then what exactly are we born into?

How much of who we become is written into biology, and how much is shaped by environment, stress, and adaptation?

That takes us directly into genetics and epigenetics.

Brain Observation

Notice one identity phrase you use often about yourself, such as "I'm the kind of person who...", "I've always been...", or "That's just who I am." Ask yourself whether this reflects a deep truth, a repeated role, or an old adaptation that became part of continuity.

Everyday Experiment

Write two short descriptions:

1.   Who I think I am

2.   How I tend to act when I feel unsafe, pressured, or unseen

Compare them. Notice where your narrative self and your defensive self overlap, and where they differ.

The aim is not to judge either one, but to see how continuity may be built from multiple layers rather than one single stable identity.

Visual Aid

Create a simple black-and-white page titled: Part of Me / Identity I Notice | Where It Shows Up | What It May Be Holding Together

Fill in a few example rows, such as:

- "the capable one" | work, family responsibility | worth, control, reliability

- "The Outsider" | social settings, disagreement | protection from rejection, self-definition

- "the helper" | friendships, partnership | belonging, usefulness, safety

- "the one who must not fail" | performance, visibility | protection from shame, collapse of identity

Leave extra lines for your own entries.

At the end, underline any repeated functions such as control, belonging, protection, coherence, or avoidance of shame.

Part of Me / Identity I Notice

Where It Shows Up | What It May Be Holding Together

Part of Me / Identity I Notice	Where It Shows Up	What It May Be Holding Together
the capable one	work, family responsibility	feeling inadequate, slowing down
the outsider	social settings, disagreement	protection from rejection, self-definition
the helper	friendships, partnership	belonging, usefulness, safety
the one who must not fail	performance, visibility	protection from shame, collapse of identity
•		
•		
•		
•		
•		

Ethical Question

If continuity of self is partly constructed and partly defended, how gently or firmly should we challenge the identities people live inside when those identities are limiting, distorted, or harmful?

Chapter 17 - Genetics, Epigenetics, DNA, RNA, and Biological Inheritance

If the previous chapter asked what kind of continuity the self is built from, this chapter asks a different but closely related question:

What do we inherit before experience fully begins to shape us?

We as beings do not arrive as blank slates. Nor do we arrive as fully predetermined blueprints. They are born into bodies with inherited architecture, predispositions, sensitivities, developmental tendencies, and biological constraints. At the same time, those inheritances do not unfold in isolation. Genes are not destiny in the crude sense.

Biology matters profoundly, but it does not operate outside environment, stress, nutrition, relationships, culture, and lived experience.

This is why genetics fascinates and confuses in equal measure.

It is tempting to seek certainty there. People want to know whether intelligence, temperament, mental health vulnerability, giftedness, sensitivity, addiction risk, behaviour, or identity are "in the genes." They want clean answers to complicated questions. But inheritance is not usually simple enough to satisfy that desire.

The biological story is real, but it is layered.

To explore it properly, we need to begin with the basic architecture.

At the centre of genetic inheritance is DNA, deoxyribonucleic acid, the molecular material that carries inherited biological information. DNA is often spoken of as though it were a complete master script, but that too can mislead if taken too literally. DNA contains instructions for building proteins and regulating biological development, but those instructions are not expressed in the same way under all conditions. Genes are not always "on" in the same sense. They are regulated, silenced, activated, amplified, or dampened depending on developmental stage, cellular context, environmental conditions, and a range of biochemical processes.

This is where RNA becomes important.

If DNA is often treated as the stored code, RNA helps participate in how that code is read, transmitted, and used. RNA plays multiple roles in gene expression, including helping carry instructions from DNA into processes that build proteins. Again, the metaphors of code and message are useful up to a point, but living systems are not static software. The genome does not simply run like a fixed programme from first line to last. It interacts with conditions constantly.

This leads directly to the importance of gene expression.

A person may carry a gene variant associated with a certain trait, sensitivity, or vulnerability, but that does not mean the outcome is fixed in simple terms. Expression depends on interaction. Some tendencies may become more active under stress. Others may be buffered by supportive environments. Some inherited dispositions may never dominate because other factors alter how they unfold. In that sense, inheritance is not only about what is present in the organism, but about how that organism meets life.

This is one reason the phrase "genetics loads the gun, environment pulls the trigger" became popular, even if it too can be overly dramatic. The core point remains useful: inheritance creates possibility and constraint, but outcome emerges through interaction rather than simple inevitability.

This is especially important when discussing behaviour, intelligence, and emotional life.

Temperament, for example, appears to show heritable dimensions. Some children seem more reactive, more sensitive, more novelty-seeking, more cautious, more steady, more impulsive, or more socially open from very early on. These differences are not all taught into existence. Something inherited is often at work. But temperament is not identity in finished form. It meets parenting, culture, stress, schooling, health, attachment, and opportunity.

A child with high sensitivity in one environment may become deeply insightful and perceptive. In another, the same sensitivity may become chronic vigilance or overwhelm.

The inherited trait is real.
The life built around it determines much of what it becomes.

The same applies to cognitive potential.

Discussions of intelligence often become emotionally charged because they touch status, worth, fairness, and determinism all at once. It appears that cognitive variation does have biological contributions, yet intelligence itself is not a single unitary thing, nor does inherited potential unfold apart from education, nutrition, sleep, stress load, emotional regulation, and development opportunities. A highly gifted brain in a chaotic environment may never stabilise its capacities fully. A solid but unexceptional baseline may flourish under supportive conditions and disciplined cultivation. Inheritance matters. So does the field in which inheritance is being expressed.

This is why simple biological determinism is too crude.

A person may inherit vulnerability without inheriting fate.
They may inherit strength without being guaranteed flourishing.
They may inherit sensitivity that becomes a burden in one context and brilliance in another.

This brings us to epigenetics, one of the most important developments in modern biological thought.

Epigenetics refers, broadly, to processes that influence gene expression without changing the underlying DNA sequence itself.

These processes can affect whether genes are more or less active, and they can be influenced by environment, stress, nutrition, toxins, developmental conditions, and other factors. In simple terms, epigenetics shows that the genome is not only inherited; it is also responsive.

This has profound implications.

It means that life experience can alter how biology is expressed. Chronic stress, nourishment, deprivation, trauma, social support, early developmental conditions, and even patterns of care may shape the expression of inherited potentials in ways that echo through the body and brain. It also raises the controversial and fascinating possibility that some effects of lived conditions may extend across generations more than older, simplistic models allowed.

This is one reason intergenerational questions matter.

A person may inherit not only a genetic sequence, but a biological system already shaped by the stress histories, environmental burdens, or nutritional conditions of previous generations. This does not mean everything is epigenetic destiny.

The science is complex and must be handled carefully. But it does mean inheritance may be more dynamic than many older genetic metaphors suggested.

A human being, then, is not merely born from DNA. They are born into a biological lineage already in conversation with history.

This fits powerfully with the wider themes of this book.

Because throughout these chapters, one of the recurring truths has been that the brain is neither isolated nor fixed. It is relational, adaptive, embodied, and shaped across time. Genetics and epigenetics deepen that picture by showing that even the biological substrate is less static than once imagined. Inheritance matters, but it is not untouched by the environment. Environment matters, but it is not free-floating from inheritance. The organism becomes itself through the meeting of both.

This also helps explain why some human patterns seem to repeat across families in ways that are not simply moral or psychological.

One family line may carry elevated sensitivity to stress. Another may show persistent patterns of mood vulnerability. Another may display strong novelty-seeking, addiction risk, or attentional restlessness. Some of these patterns are social and relational in transmission. Others may also have a biological contribution. The point is not to collapse one into the other, but to hold both. Family inheritance is rarely only "nature" or only "nurture." It is almost always layered.

This makes the old debate between nature and nurture increasingly inadequate.

The question is not which one wins. The question is how they interact.

A person's biological inheritance shapes how the environment lands.

Their environment shapes how inheritance is expressed.
Their stress load alters development.
Their relationships buffer or intensify biological vulnerability.
Their behaviour feeds back into chemistry and regulation.
Their choices matter, but always through a body that did not choose its starting point.

This is why moral judgement needs humility here, too.

People are often praised or blamed as though they all begin from equivalent baselines. But the truth is more uneven. One person may inherit a steadier nervous system, another a more reactive one. One may begin with easier regulation, another with heightened sensitivity. One may carry robust biological resilience, another a nervous system that is more easily shaped by stress. This does not erase responsibility, but it complicates simplistic narratives of merit and failure.

At the same time, biology should not be used as a permanent excuse or prison.

A person may have inherited sensitivity, but that sensitivity can still be worked with. A person may inherit vulnerability to anxiety, depression, addiction, or dysregulation, but that does not mean life is over before it begins. The whole point of bringing epigenetics, adaptation, regulation, and plasticity into the conversation is to show that biology matters deeply without becoming final in every respect.

This matters especially for people who have spent years trapped between two bad stories:

If The Brain Was An App, Would You Use It?

"I am just broken,"
or "none of this is biological, so I should simply be able to choose differently."

Both are often too harsh.

The more accurate story is usually:
something real may be inherited,
something real may have been conditioned,
something real may still be changeable,
And all of it deserves more nuance than blame alone allows.

There is also an existential layer here.

If a person carries biological inheritances they did not choose, what does freedom mean? If some tendencies are built into temperament, metabolism, reactivity, or vulnerability, how much authorship does a person truly have over the self they become? These are not questions genetics can answer on its own, but it intensifies them. The self is not built from pure will. It is shaped through givens as well as decisions.

And yet, the brain remains adaptive.

That is the crucial balance.

Inheritance provides starting conditions.
It does not fully determine every possible end.
Genes can bias, but they do not narrate the whole life.
Biological vulnerability is real, but so is biological responsiveness.
The system is constrained, but not frozen.

This is one reason why early life matters so much.

The developing organism is highly plastic. Stress in pregnancy, early caregiving, nutrition, toxins, attachment, and environmental predictability may all shape developmental pathways. By the time a child begins consciously narrating themselves, multiple layers of inheritance and environment are already interacting. This is not a reason for panic or parental perfectionism. It is a reminder that development begins long before deliberate self-understanding.

It is also why healing sometimes requires working on multiple levels at once.

A person may need psychological insight, yes.
But also better sleep.
Better nutrition.
Reduced inflammatory load.
Safer relationships.
More stable routines.
Stress reduction.
Body-based regulation.
Changes in the environment.

Because the inherited organism is always in dialogue with the life it is living.

This has implications for how we understand illness, too.

Some conditions may have strong heritable components. Others may emerge largely through environmental conditions.

Most involve some degree of interaction. A person may inherit a vulnerability that becomes visible only under prolonged stress. Another may inherit resilience that partially protects them even in difficulty. Biology is not irrelevant, but neither does it negate context.

This is why the deeper lesson of genetics and epigenetics is not fatalism. It is complexity.

Human beings are not blank pages.
But neither are they closed books.
They are living lineages becoming themselves through interaction.

This also returns us to the wider ethos of the book.

If the brain is an app, it is not downloaded into empty hardware. It arrives through a lineage of biological instructions, predispositions, and developmental possibilities already shaped by previous lives, environments, and adaptive histories. But the app is also updated for use. It is shaped by context, repetition, relationship, culture, and stress. Its starting architecture matters. So does how it is lived.

That is why the question of inheritance belongs in Part IV.

Earlier chapters have shown how the brain is shaped by body, memory, language, relationships, and social programming. This chapter widens the temporal horizon, showing that some shaping begins before personal memory ever forms. The self is not born only from present experience. It emerges through biological continuity as well.

And once that becomes clear, another question begins to press forward.

If biology and environment meet so deeply in shaping mind and self, how have different cultures, traditions, and civilisations made sense of that process? Has modern neuroscience become the only legitimate way of knowing the human being, or are there other maps, spiritual, philosophical, contemplative, symbolic, indigenous, that still hold something essential?

That is where we go next.

Brain Observation

Notice one trait in yourself that you often explain as "just how I am": sensitivity, intensity, steadiness, restlessness, caution, emotional depth, quick overwhelm, drive, or something else. Ask whether you tend to see it only as personality, only as history, or whether it may also have inherited biological dimensions.

Everyday Experiment

Make a simple two-column note for one recurring trait you recognise in yourself:

1. How this trait may have helped me

2. How this trait may become difficult under stress or certain environments

For example, sensitivity may help with perception and empathy, but under overload, it may become exhaustion or vigilance. This helps shift the trait from a fixed label into context-dependent understanding.

Visual Aid

Create a simple black-and-white page titled:

Trait / Tendency | How It May Be Inherited or Temperamental | How Environment Shaped It Further

Fill in a few example rows, such as:

- high sensitivity | early reactivity, strong emotional registration | family stress made it hypervigilant

- strong drive | temperament, reward sensitivity | praise and performance reinforced it

- social caution | shy baseline, threat sensitivity | repeated exclusion deepened withdrawal

- restlessness | novelty-seeking temperament | digital overstimulation amplified it

Leave extra lines for your own entries. At the end, underline any repeated environmental influences such as stress, praise, unpredictability, criticism, belonging, or overstimulation.

Trait / Tendency | How It May Be Inherited or Temperamental

Trait / Tendency	How It May Be Inherited or Temperamental	How Environment Shaped It Further
high sensitivity	early reactivity, strong emotional registration	family stress made it hypervigilant
strong drive	temperament, reward sensitivity	praise and performance reinforced it
social caution	shy baseline, threat sensitivity	repeated exclusion deepened withdrawal
restlessness	novelty-seeking temperament	digital overstimulation amplified it
•		
•		
•		
•		

Ethical Question

If some traits are partly inherited and others shaped by environment, how should we speak about responsibility in a way that neither erases biology nor strips people of agency?

Chapter 18 - The Brain, Culture, and Cross-Civilisational Ways of Knowing

No brain develops outside culture.

Even when people speak as though the brain is a purely biological object, what they count as intelligence, normality, maturity, illness, selfhood, consciousness, truth, and knowledge is always shaped by a wider civilisational frame. The brain may be a physical organ, but the meanings attached to its functions are never merely physical. Different societies ask different questions of the human mind. They organise attention differently. They name inner experience differently. They reward different states, different modes of selfhood, different relationships to silence, authority, ritual, memory, and perception.

This means that no account of the brain is complete if it ignores culture.

Modern neuroscience has given extraordinary insight into structure, signalling, memory, plasticity, attention, emotion, and behaviour. It has mapped networks, studied lesions, measured activation, tracked chemical effects, and revealed patterns that no previous civilisation could have described in quite the same way.

That achievement deserves respect. But it also carries a temptation: the temptation to assume that because a framework is technically precise, it is therefore total.

If The Brain Was An App, Would You Use It?

It is not.

The brain can be measured in many ways.
But human experience cannot be exhausted by measurement alone.

This chapter, then, is not an argument against neuroscience. It is an argument against cultural narrowness. It asks what happens when modern scientific frameworks are treated as the only valid map of the mind, while older, non-Western, indigenous, contemplative, spiritual, and symbolic traditions are dismissed as primitive, vague, or merely metaphorical. It asks whether other civilisational ways of knowing may still carry insights into consciousness, selfhood, regulation, meaning, and embodied life that modern reductionism has not fully integrated.

Different cultures have not only produced different stories about the brain. They have produced different *relationships* with the mind itself.

In many contemporary Western settings, the mind is often treated as private cognition located in the individual, while the brain becomes the biological substrate of that cognition. The self is imagined as an individual unit, and knowledge tends to be valued when it is measurable, repeatable, and externally demonstrable.

These priorities have produced immense scientific power, but they are not neutral. They reflect a cultural style of inquiry.

Other traditions have oriented differently.

Some contemplative traditions begin not with external measurement, but with sustained first-person observation. They investigate attention, suffering, craving, identity, emotional regulation, and the dynamics of awareness from within lived experience. They do not necessarily use the language of neurons, but they often describe patterns of mind with extraordinary phenomenological precision.

Some indigenous traditions do not sharply divide mind from land, body, ancestry, ritual, and community. Awareness is not always treated as a private event sealed inside the skull, but as something relational, ecological, and embedded in a wider field of meaning.

Some spiritual and symbolic traditions understand language, ritual, image, music, and ceremony not merely as decorative cultural expressions, but as ways of shaping consciousness, regulating the community, and orienting the individual towards realities that exceed ordinary cognition.

Some classical philosophical traditions treat the mind not simply as a problem of mechanism, but as a question of ethics, perception, virtue, illusion, and the nature of being itself.

What all these traditions remind us of is that the human brain is always interpreted through a worldview.

This matters because a worldview shapes what can even be noticed.

If a culture values constant verbal output, it may pathologise silence.

If a culture prizes individual performance, it may reward certain cognitive styles over others.

If a culture reveres rational detachment, it may dismiss embodied knowing.

If a culture lives closer to ritual, land, and rhythm, it may preserve states of attention modern systems rarely cultivate.

If a culture treats dreaming, trance, contemplation, or ceremony as meaningful, it may map consciousness differently than a culture that values waking productivity above all else.

None of this means every non-modern framework is automatically right, nor that all cultural perspectives are equally precise in all domains. It means that the human being has been studied from more than one angle, and that some of those angles may still matter.

Meditative and contemplative traditions offer one of the clearest examples.

Long before modern neuroscience, traditions such as Buddhism, Hindu contemplative systems, Taoist practices, certain Christian mystical traditions, Sufi disciplines, and other paths of sustained inward observation were investigating attention, desire, attachment, suffering, ego-formation, perception, and altered states of consciousness.

Their language differs, sometimes dramatically, from scientific discourse. But the questions they ask are not trivial:

What is awareness when stripped of constant identification?
What happens when attention is trained?
How does craving organise suffering?
How do thought and self fuse?
What remains when narrative quiets?

These are not the same as questions about synaptic transmission, but they are questions about mind and consciousness nonetheless.

In recent decades, neuroscience and contemplative practice have begun to overlap more fruitfully in some areas. Studies of meditation, attention, compassion practices, breath regulation, and long-term contemplative training suggest that disciplined inward practice can alter brain function, emotional regulation, attentional stability, and even structural features over time. This does not prove every spiritual claim, but it does suggest that some older traditions preserved methods of working with the mind that modern scientific language is only now beginning to study more closely.

This raises an important issue: first-person knowledge.

Modern science is extraordinarily powerful at third-person observation.

It can measure, compare, quantify, and externally verify. But consciousness is also lived from the first-person position. There is something it feels like to be aware, to suffer, to desire, to observe thought, to lose oneself in ritual, to become calm, to dissociate, to awaken, to grieve, to attend deeply. Any total theory of the brain that dismisses first-person knowledge risks producing precision without fullness.

This does not mean the subjective report is always accurate. It means it is indispensable.

Different cultures also encode knowledge through ritual rather than explanation alone.

Ritual can appear irrational to a hyper-secular or purely instrumental worldview, but from another angle, it may be understood as embodied regulation, communal synchronisation, emotional processing, symbolic orientation, and intergenerational memory carried through action rather than abstract statement. Chant, breath, posture, repetition, rhythm, fasting, feast, mourning, dance, silence, sacred language, and collective ceremony all alter the human state. They shape attention. They signal belonging. They modulate emotion. They can anchor identity, reinforce moral order, or open altered modes of consciousness.

In that sense, ritual is not merely cultural theatre. It is often nervous-system technology in pre-modern form.

The same can be said for music, myth, symbol, and story.

A modern rationalist culture may reduce myth to false explanation, but myth often carries psychological, existential, and collective truths that cannot be reduced neatly to literal accuracy. Symbolic systems can shape inner life powerfully. Archetypes, narratives of descent and return, death and rebirth, sacrifice and transformation, heroism and betrayal, order and chaos — these patterns organise human consciousness across cultures because they help structure meaning. The brain is not nourished by data alone. It also lives by image, metaphor, and story.

This is one of the reasons cultural collapse often produces not only political or economic instability, but psychic instability. When shared symbols lose coherence, the collective mind can become fragmented. Attention becomes easier to capture. Identity becomes more brittle. People seek substitute myths in politics, media, celebrity, conspiracy, or ideological absolutism.

A brain deprived of meaningful cultural structure may become more vulnerable to reactive programming.

This is not an argument for romanticising tradition uncritically. Traditions can preserve wisdom, but they can also preserve hierarchy, domination, exclusion, dogma, and rigidity. Cultural inheritance is not automatically healthy. Some traditions widen human life, others constrain it. Some spiritual systems deepen consciousness; others exploit it. Some rituals regulate and integrate, others enforce fear or submission.

The point is not to idealise the non-modern. It is to avoid assuming that modernity is the sole custodian of truth.

Indigenous frameworks deserve special care here.

Many indigenous knowledge systems do not begin from the assumption that the human mind is separate from ecology, ancestry, ritual, and collective life. The self is not always organised as a radically individual unit. Knowledge may be carried in oral tradition, land-based practice, relational obligation, seasonal rhythm, dream, symbol, or ceremony. Such systems are often dismissed by cultures that privilege abstract formalisation, yet they may preserve forms of attentional discipline, ecological intelligence, intergenerational continuity, and relational orientation that industrial societies have badly weakened.

Again, this does not mean uncritical appropriation. It means epistemic humility.

What if some cultures knew things not because they had scans, but because they had long traditions of refined observation, communal ritual, ecological embeddedness, and non-fragmented ways of situating the human being?

This question matters even if the answers remain partial.

Culture also shapes what counts as pathology.

One culture may treat hearing voices as an exclusively medical symptom. Another may interpret certain experiences through spiritual, ancestral, or ritual frameworks. One culture may medicalise certain attentional patterns. Another may see them as sensitivity, divergence, or vocation. One may elevate constant productivity as normal. Another may build more cyclical rhythms of work and stillness. One may pathologise intense interiority. Another may make space for contemplation.

This does not mean all cultural interpretations are equally safe or useful. It means diagnostic frameworks are never entirely free from worldview.

Even the line between normal and abnormal cognition is culturally negotiated.

This becomes especially important when considering consciousness.

Modern neuroscientific models can describe correlations between brain states and conscious states with growing sophistication. But whether consciousness is best understood as a product, correlate, interface, field relation, emergent property, or something else remains deeply contested. Different civilisational frameworks have proposed different answers for centuries. Some see consciousness as fundamental. Others are emergent. Others are layered. Others are entangled with soul, spirit, cosmos, or collective order.

The modern impulse is often to dismiss these older models as prescientific. But the dismissal is sometimes too quick. Even when such frameworks are not empirically precise in modern terms, they may still be grappling with dimensions of lived subjectivity that a purely reductive model cannot settle.

This is where cultural pluralism becomes philosophically useful.

Different traditions may each illuminate different layers of the human being:

Science can map the mechanism,
Contemplation can refine first-person awareness,
ritual can regulate and synchronise collective life,
A symbol can encode existential truth,
Philosophy can question assumptions,
and spiritual traditions can preserve questions that modern utilitarian culture tends to forget.

No single mode needs to monopolise reality.

This is why Chapter 18 belongs where it does.

After exploring the self and biological inheritance, we now widen further into the civilisational field in which the brain is interpreted. The point is not to dilute science, but to keep the inquiry proportionate to its subject. The human being is not only a nervous system. It is also a cultural, symbolic, ritual, relational, historical, and meaning-seeking being.

A brain without culture is not a real brain. It is an abstraction.

Once that becomes clear, another question rises naturally.

If culture shapes how the brain is interpreted, and if modernity increasingly compares the brain to machines, code, networks, and computation, then how accurate are those comparisons really? Is the brain best understood as a computer? A receiver? An interface? Or does each metaphor both reveal and conceal something essential?

That is where we go next.

Brain Observation

Notice one assumption you hold about the mind or self that feels "obvious." Ask yourself whether it comes from direct experience, modern education, cultural habit, spiritual background, or repeated social language.

Everyday Experiment

Choose one mental state, focus, anxiety, calm, longing, shame, curiosity, grief, or stillness, and describe it twice:

1.   in scientific or psychological language

2.   in symbolic, spiritual, poetic, or cultural language

Compare the two. Notice what each reveals and what each leaves out.

Visual Aid

Create a simple black-and-white page titled: Experience / State | Modern Framing | Older / Cultural / Symbolic Framing

Fill in a few example rows, such as:

- anxiety | nervous-system activation, threat response | loss of inner ground, spiritual unrest

- grief | emotional processing, attachment loss | rite of passage, soul rupture, mourning

- deep calm | parasympathetic regulation, attentional stability | stillness, presence, inner alignment

- repetitive craving | reward loop, conditioned reinforcement | hunger of the self, misdirected seeking

Leave extra lines for your own entries. At the end, underline any entries where the two framings seem to complement rather than cancel one another.

Experience / State	Modern Framing	Older / Cultural / Symbolic Framing
anxiety	nervous-system activation, threat rose	loss of inner ground, spiritual unrest
grief	emotional processing, attachment loss	rite of passage, soul rupture, mourning
deep calm	parasympathetic regulation, attentional stability	stillness, presence, inner alignment
repetitive craving	reward loop, conditioned reinforcement	hunger of the self, misdirected seeking
•		
•		
•		
•		
•		

Ethical Question

When one culture's way of knowing becomes dominant, what kinds of human experience risk being dismissed, pathologised, or misunderstood?

Chapter 19 - Is the Brain a Computer, a Receiver, or Something Stranger?

Few metaphors have shaped modern thinking about the brain more strongly than the idea that it is a computer.

The comparison is understandable. Both brains and computers process information. Both operate through signalling systems. Both appear to receive input, transform it, store patterns, and generate outputs. Both can be described in terms of networks, coding, memory, error correction, learning, and problem-solving. As artificial intelligence has advanced, the comparison has only become more seductive. Neural networks, pattern recognition, machine learning, prediction, feedback loops, and optimisation all seem to echo aspects of what brains do.

But metaphors become dangerous when they become invisible.

What begins as a helpful comparison can quietly become a worldview.

A person starts by saying the brain is *like* a computer, and ends by assuming that the brain *is* one in all the ways that matter.

Once that happens, certain questions shrink, certain kinds of evidence are privileged, and certain dimensions of lived experience become harder to see.

This chapter asks whether the computer metaphor is enough.

If The Brain Was An App, Would You Use It?

It does not reject it outright. It does not deny that modern computing has illuminated important aspects of cognition. But it asks a more careful question:
What does the metaphor reveal, and what does it conceal?

Because if the brain is more than a computer, then understanding that difference matters deeply.

At one level, the comparison is useful.

A computer receives input, processes signals, stores information in various forms, runs operations, and can alter its outputs according to rules and feedback. Likewise, the brain receives sensory input, processes signals, forms memories, runs predictive models, updates according to experience, and generates behaviour. This overlap is real enough to make computational models powerful in neuroscience and AI research.

Machine learning systems, in particular, have helped illuminate certain principles relevant to the brain:

- pattern recognition

- statistical inference

- optimisation through repeated exposure

- generalisation from prior data

- adaptive updating

- sensitivity to training conditions

In those respects, the analogy has value.

But we must be careful not to confuse functional similarity with ontological identity.

A calculator can perform operations.
A brain can reason.
That does not make them the same kind of thing.

The brain is not a detached processor floating outside life. It is a living organ embedded in a body, shaped by chemistry, metabolism, hormones, development, injury, sleep, relationships, pain, pleasure, movement, and mortality. A computer does not hunger. It does not grieve. It does not feel shame. It does not orient towards safety. It does not carry attachment history in the same way. It does not interpret the world through a body trying to survive, belong, and make meaning.

This difference is not decorative. It is foundational.

The brain does not only compute. It lives.

That means any comparison to computing must be held within a wider context of embodiment.

A digital system can process vast amounts of information without fatigue in the biological sense. It does not become foggy after poor sleep, narrower under social rejection, more defensive under shame, or more expansive in the presence of trust. It does not metabolise stress through inflammation, posture, breath, endocrine shifts, or bodily memory. It does not regulate in relationship or dysregulate under emotional overload in the way we do as embodied creatures.

This is one reason the hardware-software metaphor begins to strain.

People often say:
The brain is the hardware,
The mind is the software.

Again, there is a limited use here. It helps distinguish physical substrate from functional process. But the metaphor becomes misleading when it implies that the mind can be treated like separable code running on generic machinery. Our brains are not standardised devices. They are developmental, living tissues shaped by countless interactions from conception onward. The "software" is not cleanly separable from the body running it, because the body is constantly reshaping the conditions under which the mind emerges.

The better question may not be whether the brain computes.
It clearly does something computational in some respects.
The better question is whether computation alone is enough to describe what is happening.

Take memory.

A computer stores and retrieves according to the designed architectures. But as we have already seen, the brain does not store memory like a hard drive. Memory in us is reconstructive, emotional, selective, embodied, and shaped by meaning. The fact that both systems can "remember" does not mean they remember in the same way.

Take a prediction.

A machine learning model can be trained to predict likely outcomes based on data. The brain also predicts. But our predictions are shaped by shame, hope, trauma, belonging, symbolic imagination, bodily state, and relational history. Prediction in us is not merely statistical. It is lived and felt.

Take attention.

A computer can allocate processing resources. But our attention is not only about processing. It is about salience, care, fear, desire, moral weight, and existential consequence. We do not only notice what is computationally relevant. We notice what matters to a nervous system and a self organised around meaning.

This is where the metaphor begins to leave things out.

The brain is not only solving problems.
It is participating in a world.
It is inside a body.
It is inside time.
It is inside mortality.
It is an inside relationship.
It is inside a story.

That does not make it mysterious in a lazy sense. It makes it richer than computation alone.

This is one reason some people have proposed a different metaphor: the brain as receiver rather than computer.

The receiver model appears in various forms across philosophy, spirituality, and speculative consciousness studies. In its simplest version, it suggests that the brain may not generate consciousness in the same total way a machine runs a programme, but may instead filter, shape, constrain, or receive aspects of consciousness from a broader field. Under this view, the brain is less like a factory producing awareness from nothing and more like an interface or tuning system that organises consciousness into the particular form of experience we call a person.

This idea is provocative, but it must be handled carefully.

It can become vague very quickly if used irresponsibly. It can also be invoked too easily to bypass the real evidence that brain injury, chemistry, development, and structure profoundly alter experience. Clearly, the brain matters. Damage to specific areas changes language, identity, memory, perception, mood, and awareness. That makes any simplistic "the brain doesn't matter" spiritualism untenable.

And yet, the receiver metaphor persists because it addresses something the computer metaphor often struggles with: subjectivity itself.

If consciousness is not easily explained as mechanical output, then some thinkers begin to ask whether the brain is not the sole producer of awareness, but its organiser, limiter, or mediator. This is not a settled scientific view. It remains speculative. But it survives because the hard problem of consciousness remains unresolved. The receiver idea is not proven. It is one of several ways people have tried to address what current reductionist models have not fully explained.

This is also where the comparison to quantum computing sometimes enters.

The phrase "the brain is a quantum computer" is often used far too casually. In many cases, it functions more as poetic shorthand than a precise claim. Quantum theory involves phenomena such as superposition, entanglement, probability amplitudes, and non-classical behaviour at extremely small scales. Quantum computing uses some of these principles in highly specialised engineered systems. To leap from that directly to "therefore the brain works like a quantum computer" is far too quick.

Still, the comparison remains fascinating because the brain does seem to exceed many older mechanical metaphors. It is massively parallel, adaptive, energy-efficient, probabilistic in some aspects, and capable of integrating countless variables in ways that still humble artificial systems. Some researchers and theorists have explored whether quantum effects may play some role in consciousness or neural processing, though these ideas remain highly debated and far from settled.

If The Brain Was An App, Would You Use It?

The key point is this:
The brain may be stranger than our current analogies allow, but strangeness is not a licence for sloppy explanation.

We need precision and wonder together.

The brain may involve forms of organisation not yet fully understood, while still requiring rigorous care in how we speak about them. Not every mystery is evidence for the spiritual. Not every unexplained feature will turn out to be quantum. Not every limit of current science justifies any alternative we find comforting.

But the limits of current models do matter.

Because if the computer metaphor explains everything important, then consciousness becomes a technical problem awaiting enough processing power and formal description. If it does not, then we may need frameworks that can hold embodiment, computation, subjectivity, relational life, and perhaps deeper ontological questions all at once.

This is where the idea of the brain as an interface may be more helpful than either extreme.

An interface does not have to mean mere receiver in a mystical sense, nor mere computer in a reductive one. It suggests mediation. It suggests a structure through which different domains meet:
body and world,
sensation and meaning,

memory and anticipation,

self and environment,

biology and consciousness.

The interface metaphor has an advantage because it preserves several truths at once:

- The brain clearly processes

- It clearly shapes experience

- It clearly constrains and organises consciousness

- But it may not be exhaustively understood by current mechanical analogies

This aligns with much of what this book has argued from the beginning. The brain is not a simple object. It is an embodied, adaptive, relational, predictive, symbolic, and meaning-making interface. The computer metaphor captures part of this. The receiver metaphor captures another part. Neither alone seems sufficient.

There is also an ethical dimension here.

How we imagine the brain changes how we imagine ourselves.

If we see ourselves as biological machines only, we may become tempted to reduce suffering to malfunction, morality to optimisation, and meaning to information processing. If we see ourselves only as receivers of a higher field, we may neglect biology, trauma, development, and the realities of embodiment. Both extremes can become distortions.

If The Brain Was An App, Would You Use It?

What we need is a model broad enough to honour mechanism without collapsing into reductionism, and open enough to hold mystery without drifting into fantasy.

This is especially urgent in the age of AI.

The more artificial systems imitate certain cognitive outputs, the more tempted people become to flatten the distinction between synthetic performance and lived awareness. A language model may generate coherent text. An image model may produce astonishing visual synthesis. A machine may outperform us in narrow domains of prediction, recognition, and search. But none of this settles the question of consciousness. Simulation of certain functions is not identical to lived subjectivity.

This matters because we may increasingly confuse intelligence with awareness, processing with experience, or output with personhood if we rely too heavily on surface similarity.

A machine can appear intelligent.
That does not mean it is conscious in the way we are.
A brain can be computational.
That does not mean it is only computational.

This chapter belongs near the end of Part IV because it brings several tensions together:
science and speculation,
mechanism and mystery,
technology and biology,
performance and consciousness.

It asks us not to choose prematurely between rigid reductionism and ungrounded mysticism, but to stay with the possibility that the brain is a real biological system whose deepest participation in consciousness may still exceed our current metaphors.

That leaves us at the edge of the hardest question of all.

If the brain is not fully explained by machinery, and if subjectivity remains irreducible in ways current models struggle to capture, then what is consciousness itself? Is it produced, mediated, fundamental, emergent, or something no single framework can yet contain?

That is where we go next.

Brain Observation

Notice which metaphor for the brain feels most natural to you: machine, computer, interface, receiver, network, storyteller, survival system, or something else. Ask yourself what that metaphor helps you see, and what it may be hiding.

Everyday Experiment

Write down one experience that feels difficult to reduce to computation alone, grief, awe, intuition, longing, shame, beauty, prayer, dream, or deep presence. Then write a second explanation of the same experience using technical language only. Compare the two. Notice what the technical framing clarifies and what it leaves untouched.

Visual Aid

Create a simple black-and-white page titled: Brain Metaphor | What It Helps Explain | What It Leaves Out

Fill in a few example rows, such as:

- computer | information processing, prediction, patterning | embodiment, subjectivity, felt meaning
- receiver | filtering, mediation, altered consciousness | clear mechanism, biological specificity
- interface | relation between body, world, and awareness | exact ontology still unresolved
- survival system | threat detection, adaptation, pattern defence | wonder, symbol, higher reflection

Leave extra lines for your own entries. At the end, underline any entries where the metaphor feels useful but incomplete.

Brain Metaphor	What It Helps Explain	What It Leaves Out
computer	information processing, prediction, patterning	embodiment, subjectivity, felt meaning
receiver	filtering, mediation, altered conscuuness	clear mechanism, biolojical specificity
interface	relation between body, world, and awareness	exact ontology still unresolved
survival system	threat detection, adapaation, pattern defence.	wonder, symbol, higher reflection
•		
•		
•		
•		
•		

Ethical Question

How does the metaphor we choose for the brain shape the kind of world we build around it, medically, technologically, spiritually, and morally?

Chapter 20 - Consciousness Beyond Mechanism

We can describe the brain in astonishing detail.

We can map regions, networks, chemicals, oscillations, pathways, injuries, developmental patterns, and behavioural correlations. We can study perception, memory, attention, language, selfhood, adaptation, and social shaping. We can observe what changes when certain circuits are damaged, when certain chemicals are altered, when sleep is lost, when trauma occurs, when meditation is practised, when stimulation increases, when a relationship heals, or when identity becomes threatened.

All of this matters.

And yet, even after all of it, one fact remains strangely unresolved:

There is still something it is like to be here.

There is the felt quality of experience itself.
The redness of red.
The ache of grief.
The pressure of shame.
The warmth of love.
The immediacy of pain.
The interiority of thought.
The simple fact that awareness is not only happening functionally, but is also *lived*.

This is the threshold where the problem of consciousness begins.

Consciousness is one of the most familiar facts of life and one of the hardest to explain. We know it from the inside before we ever theorise about it. We wake into it, suffer within it, remember through it, wonder inside it, and attempt to study it using the very awareness we are trying to understand. It is both immediate and elusive, undeniable and difficult to define.

That is why this final chapter of Part IV must end here.

Because once we have explored the brain through architecture, signalling, memory, emotion, relationship, language, programming, identity, inheritance, culture, and metaphor, the deepest question remains:
What is consciousness itself, and how does it relate to the brain?

Modern science has made major progress on the *correlates* of consciousness. We can observe that certain brain states tend to accompany wakefulness, dreaming, anaesthesia, focused attention, dissociation, and different perceptual or emotional conditions. We can track patterns that become more or less available when awareness changes. We can study disorders of consciousness, altered states, and the effects of injury. We can say a great deal about what is happening *with* consciousness.

But correlation is not the same as explanation.

To say that a certain pattern of neural activity accompanies conscious experience is not yet to explain why there is conscious experience at all. It tells us something important about relationships, but not necessarily about origin. This is where the problem becomes philosophically difficult.

A brain process can be described from the outside. Consciousness is lived from the inside.

The gap between those two perspectives is not easy to close.

This is sometimes called the hard problem of consciousness. The phrase points to a simple distinction. Some problems are "easy" in the sense that they concern functions that can, at least in principle, be broken down into mechanisms: how we discriminate stimuli, report experiences, shift attention, store memory, regulate action, or integrate information. Those are not easy in practice, but they are easier in kind. They concern what systems *do*.

The hard problem asks something else:
Why should any of that doing be accompanied by felt experience at all?

Why is there awareness rather than only process?
Why does information processing come with subjectivity?
Why is there something it is like to be a brain in activity, rather than merely activity?

No consensus answer yet exists.

One response is materialism.

Materialist views, in broad terms, hold that consciousness arises from physical processes. On this view, the brain does not merely correlate with awareness; it somehow generates it. Consciousness may be an emergent property of sufficiently complex biological organisation, much as liquidity emerges from certain arrangements of molecules, even though no single molecule is itself wet. Many scientists and philosophers remain committed to some version of this because it aligns with the broader success of physical explanation across many other domains.

There is strength in this position.

Brain changes do alter experience.
Drugs change consciousness.
Sleep changes consciousness.
Injury changes consciousness.
Development changes consciousness.
The evidence that brain and consciousness are deeply linked is overwhelming.

And yet the materialist position still faces a genuine challenge: even if complexity and emergence are invoked, how exactly does subjective experience arise from matter? Saying that it emerges can feel like naming the mystery rather than dissolving it.

Another response is emergentism, which overlaps with materialism but tries to hold more clearly that consciousness may be a genuinely new level of reality arising from lower-level processes without being reducible to them in simple terms. On this view, consciousness is real and causally significant, but dependent on the right kind of organised physical system. The difficulty here is similar: emergence may be plausible, but the felt leap from process to subjectivity still seems underexplained.

A different family of responses moves in another direction.

Some philosophical views suggest that consciousness is not produced out of non-conscious matter in the way we often imagine. Instead, consciousness may be in some sense more fundamental.

This is where views such as panpsychism enter the conversation. Panpsychist ideas vary widely, but in broad terms, they suggest that consciousness, or proto-experiential being, may be more basic to reality than modern materialism tends to assume. Rather than matter somehow producing consciousness from nothing but a complex arrangement, consciousness may be present in a more primitive form at deeper levels of reality, becoming richer in organised systems such as brains.

This view has appeal because it does not require subjectivity to emerge from absolute non-subjectivity in one sudden explanatory leap. But it also raises difficult questions:
If consciousness is fundamental, what kind of consciousness are we talking about?
How do simple proto-experiential units become unified into one coherent stream of awareness?
Does this solve the mystery, or relocate it?

Still other views fall under broad forms of idealism, where consciousness is treated not as derivative of matter, but as more primary than matter itself. In such frameworks, the physical world may be understood as arising within consciousness, or as inseparable from it at a deeper level. These views have long philosophical and spiritual histories. They often resonate with contemplative traditions and with certain interpretations of mystical experience. Their strength is that they take subjectivity seriously from the start rather than treating it as an awkward by-product. Their weakness, for many critics, is that they seem to overturn the common assumptions of physical science too radically or too quickly.

There are also dual-aspect and neutral monist approaches, which suggest that what we call mind and matter may be two aspects of some deeper reality not adequately captured by either term alone. These views attempt to avoid the stark split between matter-only and mind-only accounts. They propose that both the physical and the experiential may be different expressions of a deeper substrate.

None of these views has settled the debate.

That alone should teach us something important: the problem of consciousness is still open.

This openness matters because we now live in a culture that often mistakes technical confidence for explanatory completeness. If a scan lights up, if a network is mapped, if a neural correlate is identified, people can quickly assume the mystery is over. But a correlate is not the whole story. Measurement is not the same as metaphysical resolution. A model may become more precise while the deepest ontological question remains unanswered.

This is why humility is not optional here.

Consciousness is not merely a technical puzzle. It is the interior fact from which all technical inquiry is even possible. We are trying to use consciousness to explain consciousness. That does not make the effort impossible, but it should make us slower to pretend victory.

There is another dimension here that matters greatly for this book: altered states.

Across cultures and throughout history, we as a species have explored consciousness through dreams, trance, meditation, prayer, contemplation, fasting, psychedelics, ritual, breathwork, silence, music, grief, crisis, and awe. Some of these states are pathological in context. Others are transformative. Some collapse orientation. Others deepen it. What matters here is not romanticising altered states, but recognising that ordinary waking consciousness is not the only mode of mind available to us.

This complicates reductionism even further.

If consciousness can shift so radically while remaining recognisably conscious, what does that suggest about the relationship between the brain and awareness? Are altered states simply different brain modes? Certainly, at one level, they are. But are they *only* that? Or do some of them reveal that our ordinary mode of consciousness is itself a filtered, limited, adaptive state rather than the total measure of reality?

That question cannot be settled easily.

But it matters because many contemplative and spiritual traditions have long claimed that ordinary waking identity is narrower than awareness itself. The self, on such views, is not the whole of consciousness but one organised mode within it. These claims cannot simply be waved away because they are difficult to measure. Nor should they be accepted uncritically. They belong to the domain of serious inquiry.

The same is true of near-death experiences, mystical episodes, profound meditative absorption, deep trauma states, and other extreme alterations of consciousness. These experiences do not automatically prove any one metaphysical framework. But they do challenge simplistic assumptions about what consciousness is allowed to be.

There is also an ethical dimension to all this.

How we understand consciousness changes how we understand personhood.

If consciousness is treated as nothing more than output, we may become more willing to reduce ourselves and one another to function. We may begin to treat depth, meaning, and subjectivity as secondary. We may design systems that optimise behaviour while neglecting interior life. We may confuse intelligence with awareness, performance with presence, and simulation with sentience.

On the other hand, if consciousness is treated only as a mystical essence while biology is ignored, we may neglect trauma, embodiment, illness, regulation, and the realities of the nervous system. We may spiritualise suffering that needs care, or bypass physiology in the name of transcendence.

This book has tried to resist both errors.

It has been argued throughout that the brain matters profoundly.
It has also been argued that the mechanism alone may not exhaust the human story.

Consciousness sits at the point where that tension becomes unavoidable.

The brain clearly shapes the field of awareness.
But whether it fully explains awareness remains unsettled.
The self is clearly organised through neural, relational, and narrative processes.
But whether awareness itself is reducible to those processes remains open.

This openness should not frustrate us too quickly. It may be part of what keeps inquiry alive.

After all, something is fitting in the fact that the deepest mystery of the mind remains unsolved. We as a species can send instruments into space, sequence genomes, image the living brain, build artificial systems of astonishing complexity, and still find ourselves humbled by the simplest inner fact: *I am aware.*

Not only that, but I process.
Not only do I behave.
Not only that, but I respond.
But that I experience.

That experience remains the centre of the mystery.

This chapter closes Part IV because it is the deepest question into which all the previous questions finally open.

We began Part IV with the self and the illusion of continuity, moved into genetics and inheritance, widened into culture and civilisational ways of knowing, and then questioned the metaphors by which modernity understands the brain. Here, at the end, everything converges.

The self, inheritance, culture, metaphor, and philosophy all bend towards the question of consciousness.

And the most honest answer, at least for now, is not premature certainty but serious openness.

We know much more than we once did.
We also do not yet know enough to close the question.

That is not a weakness. It is a threshold.

And from that threshold, the final movement of this book becomes clear.

If The Brain Was An App, Would You Use It?

Because once we recognise that the brain is powerful, adaptive, social, influenceable, biologically shaped, culturally interpreted, and still open to mystery, the next question is no longer only *what it is.*

It becomes:

How should we live with it?
How should we work with it?
How should we protect it from misuse?
How should we cultivate it wisely?

That is where Part V begins.

Part V, Using the App Ethically, turns from structure and mystery towards practice, responsibility, and conscious participation. If the earlier parts of the book explored what the brain is, how it functions, how it is shaped, and what deeper questions it opens, the final part asks what it means to use such a system with greater awareness, restraint, dignity, and care.

We move now from explanation to stewardship.
From inquiry to responsibility. From what the brain is to how we might live with it more wisely.

Brain Observation

Notice one moment today when awareness itself becomes obvious, not just what you were thinking, but the simple fact that you were aware of thinking. Stay with that for a few seconds. What changes when attention shifts from content to consciousness itself?

Everyday Experiment

Set a timer for three minutes and sit without trying to improve anything. Do not force stillness. Simply notice:

- sounds
- body sensations
- thoughts arising
- emotions shifting
- awareness of all of this happening

Afterwards, write one sentence describing the difference between *having thoughts* and *being aware that thoughts are happening.*

Visual Aid

Create a simple black-and-white page titled: Experience of Awareness | What I Can Describe Mechanically | What Still Feels Unexplained - Fill in a few example rows, such as:

- seeing a sunset | visual processing, light perception, emotional response | why beauty feels like more than data
- grief after loss | attachment disruption, stress response, memory activation | the depth of subjective ache
- sudden intuition | pattern recognition, subconscious integration | why it arrives with felt certainty
- deep stillness in meditation | attentional stability, parasympathetic regulation | the sense of spacious presence

Experience of Awareness	What I Can Describe Mechanically	What Still Feels Unexplained
seeing a sunset	visual processing, light perception, emotional response	why beauty feels like more than data.
grief after loss	attachment disruption, stress response, memory activation	the depth of subjective ache
sudden intution	pattern recognition, subconscious integration	why it arrives with felt certainty
deep stillness in meditation	attentional stability, parasympathetic regulation	the sense of spacious presence.
•		
•		
•		
•		
•		

Leave extra lines for your own entries. At the end, underline any examples where explanation helps, but does not fully dissolve the mystery.

Ethical Question

If consciousness remains partly mysterious, how careful should we be before designing technologies, institutions, or ideologies that treat awareness as though it were fully understood and fully controllable?

PART V - Using The App Ethically

If the earlier parts of this book asked what the brain is, how it functions, how it is shaped, and what deeper questions it opens, this final part asks something more practical, moral, and immediate:

How do we live with such a system well?

Because by now, the brain should no longer appear as a neutral instrument.

We have seen that it is embodied, predictive, adaptive, relational, programmable, biologically shaped, culturally interpreted, and still open to mystery. We have seen that attention can be captured, emotion can narrow thought, memory can be reconstructed, language can regulate or destabilise, and repeated environments can shape what becomes normal, desirable, frightening, or true. We have seen that knowledge of the brain can be used to heal, educate, deepen self-awareness, and widen discernment. But we have also seen that the same knowledge can be used to manipulate, extract, condition, and control.

That is why this final part turns from explanation to responsibility.

To understand the brain without asking how to work with it ethically would leave the inquiry unfinished. Knowledge alone is not enough. We must also ask what kind of relationship we want with our own minds, what kind of environments we are helping to create for others, and what kind of intelligence deserves to guide the use of such knowledge.

This final part, therefore, gathers the earlier themes of the book and turns them towards conscious practice. It is less concerned with describing the brain from a distance and more concerned with how we, as a species, might relate to it with greater clarity, restraint, dignity, and care. It asks what it means not simply to study the app, but to use it wisely.

We begin in **Chapter 21, Working With the Brain Instead of Against It**, where the focus turns to the practical conditions under which clearer thinking becomes more possible. This chapter explores sleep, attention, novelty, movement, nutrition, emotional regulation, learning methods, repetition, silence, and relational safety. It does not approach these as lifestyle slogans, but as real conditions that affect whether the brain becomes more coherent or more fragmented in daily life.

From there, **Chapter 22, Everyday Experiments in Awareness** brings the experiential structure of the book fully into view. This chapter gathers the spirit of the chapter-end observations and experiments into a more deliberate form, using simple demonstrations of framing, memory distortion, emotional interpretation, attentional capture, sensory bias, language-state shifts, and everyday cognitive filtering. The aim is not performance, but literacy: helping the reader notice how the brain constructs reality in ordinary life.

In **Chapter 23, Intelligence, Wisdom, and the Moral Use of Knowledge**, the inquiry becomes more explicitly ethical. This chapter asks what separates being clever from being conscious, and why knowledge without discernment can become manipulation. It explores humility, responsibility, influence, power, and the difference between understanding the brain in order to deepen life and understanding it in order to exploit vulnerability.

Finally, **Chapter 24, Reclaiming the Human Mind**, closes the main body of the book by bringing brain, body, language, consciousness, culture, and technology back into one frame. This chapter asks what it means to reclaim attention, inner life, depth, and agency in a world increasingly shaped by distraction, persuasion, artificial systems, and engineered stimulation. It returns the inquiry to the central question running beneath the whole book: not only what the brain is, but who or what is using it.

Taken together, these chapters make Part V the practical and ethical culmination of the entire work.

If Part I gave us the living architecture,
Part II: The signalling and adaptive system,
Part III: The Social and Programmable Brain,
and Part IV, the deeper philosophical questions,
Then Part V asks how we live with all of that knowledge without becoming either naïve or cynical.

This matters because the final responsibility of understanding is stewardship.

Not control for its own sake.
Not optimisation without wisdom.
Not intelligence without conscience.
But a more careful relationship with perception, memory, attention, language, emotion, technology, and influence.

In that sense, the final part of this book is not an appendix to the rest. It is the point towards which the earlier chapters have been moving all along.

Because once we understand the app more clearly, the question is no longer whether we use it.

We already do.

The real question is whether we use it:
consciously or automatically,
ethically or manipulatively,
wisely or carelessly,
in service of life or in surrender to capture.

That is where the final part now begins.

Chapter 21 - Working With the Brain Instead of Against It

One of the quiet tragedies of modern life is that many of us spend years working against the very system we are trying to use.

We push when restoration is needed.
We consume when silence is needed.
We demand clarity while feeding fragmentation.
We expect emotional steadiness while living in overstimulation.
We seek depth through exhaustion.
We want memory, attention, discernment, and calm, while repeatedly building the opposite conditions around ourselves.

Then we blame ourselves for struggling.

By this point in the book, one thing should already be clear: the brain is not a machine that simply obeys conscious intention. It is a living, embodied, adaptive interface shaped by state, repetition, chemistry, memory, relationship, prediction, and environment. That means the question is no longer only what the brain is. It is also how we, as beings, create the conditions in which it functions more clearly or more poorly.

This chapter is about that question.

Not in the sense of productivity tricks or fashionable optimisation language. Not as another set of performative self-improvement demands. But in a deeper and more humane sense, what does it mean to stop living in ways that constantly place the brain in conflict with itself? What does it mean to work with attention instead of endlessly scattering it, with regulation instead of glorifying overload, with repetition instead of expecting transformation from insight alone, and with the organism's real rhythms instead of treating those rhythms as an inconvenience?

To work with the brain instead of against it is not to become rigid or perfect. It is to become more literate in certain conditions.

The quality of thought depends on conditions.
The quality of memory depends on conditions.
The quality of attention depends on conditions.
The quality of emotional life depends on conditions.
The quality of learning depends on conditions.
And many of those conditions are not mysterious. They are ordinary, cumulative, and often neglected.

The first of these is sleep.

Sleep is not an optional maintenance window for the body while the "real" person waits to continue. It is one of the primary conditions under which the brain restores, consolidates, recalibrates, and integrates. During sleep, memory is processed differently. Emotional load is reorganised. Waste clearance mechanisms become more active. Attention, learning, mood stability, and cognitive flexibility all depend on the quality of this cycle.

Yet modern life treats sleep as negotiable.

People boast about functioning on too little of it. They override fatigue with stimulation. They keep themselves cognitively "on" long after the system is signalling for down-regulation. Then they wonder why memory fragments, emotional tolerance narrows, thinking becomes harsher, and perception becomes more threat-biased.

Sleep loss not only makes us tired. It alters the conditions of interpretation.

A poorly rested brain is often less patient with complexity, less stable in attention, more reactive under pressure, and more likely to reach for urgency, certainty, or stimulation. A well-rested system is not automatically wise, but it is usually more available for wisdom.

This means sleep is not a luxury at the edges of clarity. It is part of clarity itself.

The second condition is attention.

Attention, as we have already seen, is one of the most valuable functions of the brain because it determines what enters awareness strongly enough to begin shaping meaning. But attention is also trainable. We become more able to sustain it, and more vulnerable to losing it, according to how we repeatedly live.

If we constantly interrupt ourselves, our attentional system adapts to interruption.
If we constantly seek novelty, it adapts to novelty.

If we repeatedly split focus across multiple low-grade inputs, it becomes less comfortable with depth.

If we repeatedly give ourselves periods of uninterrupted concentration, reading, stillness, or observation, another pattern begins to strengthen.

This is one reason modern attention often feels so unstable. Many of us are not only distracted by accident. We are living in environments that reward attentional fragmentation constantly, and then we internalise that fragmentation as normal. Working with the brain means treating attention as something to be stewarded rather than endlessly spent.

That does not require monastic withdrawal. It does require boundaries.

Moments without input.

Intervals without checking.

Spaces in which one thing is allowed to remain one thing.

Time during which the nervous system is not repeatedly instructed to orient, compare, and react.

The third condition is novelty.

The brain is drawn to novelty because novelty can matter. It may signal opportunity, relevance, reward, or threat. But the modern world floods us with novelty far beyond anything earlier environments prepared us for. New messages, new clips, new headlines, new updates, new opinions, new images, new alerts — all of them compete to feel urgent enough to matter.

This trains restlessness.

The system begins to expect change constantly. Familiarity feels flat. Depth feels slow. Waiting becomes irritating. Reflection starts to feel under-stimulating. In such conditions, it becomes harder to remain ordinary and discover what only slowness reveals.

Working with the brain does not mean eliminating novelty. Novelty can support learning, curiosity, and cognitive flexibility. It means restoring proportion. It means noticing when stimulation is no longer feeding vitality but eroding steadiness.

The fourth condition is movement.

Thought does not happen in abstraction from the body. Movement changes blood flow, mood regulation, attention, interoception, and stress response. We as a species are not designed only to sit under cognitive load while the body remains static. Walking, stretching, rhythmic motion, breathing changes, and basic physical engagement with the world all alter the conditions in which the brain functions.

This is why some of the clearest thinking happens while moving rather than while forcing thought in stillness. A walk can regulate what static rumination cannot. Repetitive motion can settle what argument alone cannot. The body often helps metabolise states that would otherwise harden into mental noise.

Movement is not merely about fitness. It is one of the ways cognition is supported through embodiment.

The fifth condition is nutrition and metabolic steadiness.

This does not mean reducing the whole human person to diet language. It means recognising the obvious without embarrassment: the brain depends on fuel, rhythm, and physiological steadiness. Blood sugar instability, undernourishment, poor hydration, excessive stimulants, and erratic cycles of intake all affect attention, mood, patience, memory, and interpretation.

Many states that are moralised as weakness are worsened by depletion.

A brain underfed or overstimulated is not processing from the same baseline as one that is more stable. This is not a complete explanation of anyone's life, but it is part of the conditions of life. Working with the brain includes basic respect for the organism's needs rather than acting as though cognition should float above them.

The sixth condition is emotional regulation.

This book has returned to this point repeatedly because it is central. Regulation does not mean suppression. It does not mean becoming emotionally flat or detached. It means developing enough capacity for emotional states to be noticed, felt, and worked with without them wholly taking over interpretation.

When regulation is low, the brain narrows quickly. Ambiguity becomes harder to bear. Memory becomes more selective. Thought becomes more defensive. Identity becomes more rigid. The person becomes easier to hook, easier to frighten, easier to provoke, and easier to capture with certainty.

When regulation is stronger, something else becomes possible. The person can remain with more information without immediate collapse into reaction. They can observe shame, fear, anger, and urgency without treating those states as the complete truth. They can tolerate reflection longer. They can hold complexity with less fragmentation.

Working with the brain means respecting regulation as one of the central conditions of intelligence.

This is not a soft add-on to cognition. It is part of cognition.

The seventh condition is learning through repetition.

One of the reasons people become discouraged so easily is that they expect insight to behave like installation. They hear something true once, feel it deeply, and then assume change should follow automatically. But the brain does not usually transform that way. It learns through repetition, context, and reinforcement. A single insight can be powerful, but its power often lies in the way it reorganises future repetitions.

This matters for healing, concentration, communication, and thought.

A new pattern often feels weak at first, not because it is false, but because it is under-rehearsed. An older pattern feels natural not because it is wise, but because it is well-practised. Working with the brain means expecting this. It means not demanding instant embodiment from every good idea. It means allowing repetition to do its quieter work.

The eighth condition is silence.

Silence is now so rare that many people encounter it almost as deprivation rather than as nourishment. But silence is nothing. It is one of the conditions in which previously drowned-out processes become audible. Fatigue becomes noticeable. Emotion becomes clearer. Thought slows enough to be observed rather than only inhabited. The nervous system gets a chance to stop constantly orienting outward.

Without silence, many of us lose contact with our own baseline.

We live in layers of sound, text, commentary, stimulation, and subtle demand, then wonder why our interior life becomes harder to hear. Working with the brain means allowing intervals in which input is not continuous, and consciousness is not immediately colonised by the next thing.

Silence is not an absence of life. It is often the space in which life becomes legible again.

The ninth condition is relational safety.

We do not think, remember, and interpret in the same way under all relational conditions. A safe relationship can widen the field. A contemptuous or unstable one can narrow it dramatically. Learning, speech, risk-taking, creativity, emotional honesty, and intellectual openness all change depending on whether the person feels met or threatened.

This means the brain not only works privately. It works with society.

Who are we around when trying to learn?
What kinds of conversations do we repeatedly inhabit?
What emotional climates do we normalise?
What tones become familiar?
Do the relationships around us invite coherence or performative survival?

Working with the brain instead of against it includes becoming more discerning about relational atmosphere. Not every environment deserves equal access to the inner field. Not every tone deserves to become normal. Not every conversation deserves indefinite residence in the body.

There is also a deeper issue beneath all of this.

Many of us have been trained to approach the mind adversarially.

We speak inwardly with contempt.
We bully ourselves into action.
We demand clarity while producing fear.

We shame ourselves for dysregulation.

We call ourselves lazy when we are depleted.

We call ourselves weak when we are overwhelmed.

We call ourselves broken when older adaptations are still active.

This is another way of working against the brain.

Harshness can produce short-term compliance, but it often degrades the very conditions that bigger change requires. A person who lives in chronic inner attack rarely becomes clearer in a stable way. They become more defended, more exhausted, or more split. Working with the brain means learning a firmer but less punitive relationship to one's own system.

Not indulgence.

Not an excuse.

But intelligent cooperation.

This chapter is not suggesting that every difficulty can be solved by sleeping more, walking more, eating better, and avoiding notifications. Life is more complex than that. Trauma is real. Injustice is real. Illness is real. Deep suffering is real. Some conditions require far more than an improved routine. But it is equally true that many of us are making an already difficult life harder by repeatedly undermining the conditions under which the brain can function with any coherence at all.

That deserves honesty.

It also deserves compassion.

Because once we understand how much the brain depends on conditions, we begin to see that working with it is less about domination and more about stewardship. It asks:

What does this system need to think more clearly?

What repeatedly narrows it?

What helps widen it?

What am I feeding daily — clarity or fragmentation, regulation or stimulation, steadiness or capture?

These are practical questions, but they are also ethical ones.

To work with the brain instead of against it is to treat the mind not as a machine for extraction, but as a living field worthy of care. It is to stop asking the system to produce depth while depriving it of the very conditions depth requires. It is to recognise that the quality of perception, memory, emotion, and thought is not only a matter of talent or will, but of relationship to one's own inner ecology.

This chapter opens Part V because it provides the practical threshold. Before we move into deliberate experiments in awareness, intelligence and wisdom, and the reclaiming of the human mind, we must first face something more basic:

Many of us are fighting the tool we are trying to use.

The first ethical act is to stop doing that where we can.

Not because the brain is fragile in some sentimental sense, but because it is powerful enough to build a world and vulnerable enough to be damaged by the conditions in which it is repeatedly asked to operate.

And once that becomes clear, the next step follows naturally.

If working with the brain requires attention, observation, and literacy of state, then one of the best ways to deepen that literacy is not only through theory, but through experiment.

That is where we go next.

Brain Observation

Notice one area of daily life where you are repeatedly asking your mind for something while feeding it the opposite condition. It might be wanting focus while remaining in constant interruption, wanting emotional steadiness while living in overstimulation, or wanting memory while running on exhaustion.

Everyday Experiment

Choose one condition to support for three days only:

- better sleep timing
- ten minutes of uninterrupted reading
- one short walk without audio
- Reduced notifications for an hour
- a slower meal without screen input
- one pause before reactive reply

Do not treat it as a life overhaul. Treat it as an experiment in conditions. At the end of the three days, note whether your attention, mood, clarity, or reactivity changed even slightly.

Visual Aid

Create a simple black-and-white page titled:

What I Want From My Brain | What I'm Feeding It Daily | What Might Support It Better

Fill in a few example rows, such as:

- clearer focus | constant checking and interruption | protected attention window

- better memory | poor sleep and overstimulation | steadier rest, slower input

- calmer mood | endless headlines and tension | reduced exposure, more regulation

- deeper thinking | fragmented screen time | silence, reading, single-tasking

Leave extra lines for your own entries. At the end, underline any repeated conflicts where your desired state and your daily conditions are pulling in opposite directions.

What I Want From My Brain	What I'm Feeding It Daily	What Might Support It Better
clearer focus	constant checking and interroption	protected attention window
better memory	poor sleep and overstimulation	steadier rest, slower input
calmer mood	endless headlines and tension	reduced exposure, more regulation
deeper thinking	fragmented screen time	silence, reading, single-tasking
•		
•		
•		
•		
•		

Ethical Question

If we know enough about the brain to recognise what supports clarity and what degrades it, what responsibility do we carry for the conditions we repeatedly create for ourselves and for others?

Chapter 22 - Everyday Experiments in Awareness

There is a limit to what can be learned about the brain through description alone.

We can read about attention, memory, perception, emotional bias, prediction, framing, and nervous-system state. We can understand the theory. We can agree with the principles. We can even recognise ourselves in them. But until these processes are *noticed directly*, much of the knowledge remains conceptual rather than lived.

This is why experiments matter.

Not laboratory experiments in the strict scientific sense, but simple, safe, observable demonstrations through which we can catch the mind in the act of constructing reality. These experiments matter because the brain is persuasive. It presents its interpretations as though they were immediate facts. It hides its own edits. It gives us conclusions without always showing us the process that produced them.

Every day, experiments interrupt that illusion.

They allow us to see how quickly context changes perception.
How easily memory shifts.
How rapidly tone alters meaning.
How strongly emotional state shape thought?
How often attention moves before intention arrives.
How readily the mind fills in gaps and then defends the result.

This chapter gathers that spirit deliberately.

Across the book, each chapter has ended with a Brain Observation, an Everyday Experiment, and an Ethical Question. That structure was never ornamental. It reflects a core conviction of this work: if we want to understand the brain in a truly useful way, then we must not only study it from the outside. We must also observe it in motion, within ordinary life, where it is shaping what feels obvious, urgent, meaningful, and real.

That is what this chapter is about.

It is not here to overwhelm the reader with endless exercises. It is here to show that awareness becomes deeper when theory is tested against direct observation. The goal is not performance. It is literacy. We are learning to notice the app running while it is running.

One of the clearest places to begin is perception.

Look at an optical illusion long enough, and the brain reveals something important: perception is not passive reception.

A still image seems to move. Two equal lines seem unequal.

A figure flips between interpretations. Nothing "out there" changed.

What changed was the organisation of what was being seen. This is not a trivial curiosity. It is a doorway into one of the book's central claims: what feels immediate is often constructed.

An everyday experiment in perception might be as simple as this:

Look at an ambiguous image, then place two different captions beside it. Notice how quickly the apparent meaning changes. The image remains the same. The interpretive field does not.

This teaches humility.

The same principle applies to framing.

Read two headlines about the same event written in different emotional tones. One uses dangerous language. One uses stabilising language. One foregrounds conflict. One foregrounds complexity. The facts may overlap, but the felt reality changes.

The brain is not only processing information. It is responding to tone, implication, urgency, and pre-loaded narrative.

This matters because collectively we live in framing environments all the time.

The experiment is simple, but the insight is not: often, we do not merely react to events, but to how events are linguistically and emotionally packaged before we encounter them.

Memory offers another important field of experimentation.

Most of us trust memory far more than we should. We remember something vividly and assume vividness proves accuracy. But as this book has already argued, memory is reconstructive, not archival. A useful experiment is to write down a personal memory in detail, then revisit it after time has passed and write it again without checking the first version. What changes?

What stays?

What becomes more emotionally charged?

What disappears? Often, the shift is not dramatic, but it is enough to reveal that remembering is an act of rebuilding.

This does not make memory meaningless. It makes it human.

The experiment matters because it shows how easily narrative continuity is stabilised through revision we barely notice.

Then there is emotional interpretation.

A powerful experiment is to attempt the same reasoning task under two different states. Solve something when calm, then compare it with solving under emotional activation: after annoyance, hurry, tension, or mild stress.

The difference is often revealing. Thought may become narrower. Patience may collapse. Certainty may rise even as clarity falls.

This matters because it shows that emotion is not simply added onto cognition afterwards. It alters the conditions under which cognition is happening.

The lesson is not "never think while emotional".

That would be impossible and false.

The lesson is more subtle: if we do not account for state, we often mistake the state-shaped thought for pure logic.

Language offers another rich field.

Say the same sentence internally in two tones:
first harshly,
then calmly.

For example:
"I need to finish this."
Spoken inwardly with pressure, it may tighten the body.
Spoken inwardly with steadiness, it may organise without collapsing the system.

Nothing in the literal meaning changed. The signalling environment did.

This is one of the clearest ways to observe the principles behind the Mirror-Linguistic Hypothesis in ordinary life. Language is not only semantic. It is regulatory. The body hears how something is said, even when the words stay the same.

Music can also be used as an experiment.

Play one piece of music that reliably activates the system — urgency, nostalgia, grief, intensity, longing, and another that settles or widens it.

Then notice what happens to thought speed, body posture, memory associations, and emotional framing. Music is often treated as entertainment, but it is also a state technology.

It changes timing, chemistry, atmosphere, and interpretation. A person entering the same room under two different sonic conditions may, in some sense, inhabit two different worlds.

This matters because so much of daily life is already being scored by sound without us noticing its effects.

Another experiment concerns attention fragmentation.

Track how often you reach for your phone in one hour without deciding to. Not when you consciously need it. When the hand moves almost before awareness catches up. The number can be humbling. The point is not guilt. The point is visibility. Attention capture often happens beneath declared intention. Once seen, it becomes harder to pretend the loop is purely chosen.

You can deepen this by delaying each reach for ten seconds. In those ten seconds, notice the urge itself. Is it boredom relief? uncertainty? social anticipation? discomfort with stillness? Fear of missing something? The experiment turns a habit into an observable event.

That is the pattern across all these exercises:
They reveal a process where there was previously only a conclusion.

There are also experiments in social contagion.

Spend time in one dysregulated environment and one calmer one. This does not need to be extreme. It could be a fast, fragmented, irritated group conversation followed later by a slower, grounded interaction with someone settled.

Notice posture, breathing, thought speed, interpretation, and emotional tone in each setting. We often underestimate how much we borrow from the field around us. This kind of observation makes the social brain visible.

Another valuable area is prediction.

Watch a silent interaction between two people in public or on a muted video. Guess what is happening. Then, if possible, learn the context or compare multiple plausible interpretations. The speed with which the mind creates a story is often startling. One glance becomes "tension", "attraction", "awkwardness", "danger", "boredom", "sadness", or "authority" before the evidence warrants it. The experiment is not designed to stop interpretation. It is designed to reveal how interpretation arrives long before certainty should.

There is also the experiment of inattentional blindness.

Focus hard on one assigned feature of a scene — a colour, a movement, a repeated action — and notice how much else disappears. This can be done with a busy room, a short video, or even a page full of visual information. The brain's selective attention becomes immediately obvious. What is not being tracked may as well not exist for the duration of the task.

This is worth experiencing directly because it helps dissolve the fantasy that we are taking in everything simply because it is present.

Even ordinary conversation can become an experiment.

Read a brief text message in one emotional state, then again later in another. "Interesting." "Fine." "We need to talk." "Okay." The words remain fixed. The meaning does not. A tired, uneasy, or shame-activated system may hear a threat where a calmer system hears neutrality. This is not an abstract claim once it is seen directly. It becomes lived proof that the state shapes interpretation.

What all these experiments share is a common ethical value: They weaken naïve certainty.

Once we begin to see how constructed our experience often is, we may become less arrogant about what feels obvious. Less reactive in the face of immediate impression. Less convinced that our first interpretation is the final truth. This is not self-doubt for its own sake. It is discernment.

Discernment does not emerge from distrusting everything. It emerges from seeing more of the process by which trust is formed.

This chapter matters because knowledge becomes much harder to misuse when it is embodied honestly.

A person who has directly observed attentional capture, memory drift, emotional narrowing, and framing effects is less likely to treat those forces as distant theories relevant only to other people. The work becomes personal without becoming self-obsessed.

That is one reason this chapter sits in Part V.

By the time we reach this part of the book, the question is no longer merely what the brain is. It is how we work with it responsibly. Experiments are part of that responsibility because they make self-awareness concrete. They move us from passive reading into active observation. They turn the mind from a hidden operator into something we can, at least at times, witness more clearly.

This does not produce mastery.
But it does produce literacy.
And literacy changes the relationship.

Once we can see the mind constructing, framing, predicting, remembering, and reacting in real time, another question naturally follows:

What kind of intelligence is needed to use that knowledge well?

Because cleverness alone is not enough. It never was.

That takes us into the next chapter.

Brain Observation

Notice which kind of experiment reveals the most to you: perception, memory, framing, emotional state, attention capture, language tone, or social atmosphere. What does that preference suggest about where your own self-observation most easily begins?

Everyday Experiment

Choose one experiment from this chapter and repeat it three times across one week. Do not chase a dramatic result. Watch for small consistencies. The aim is to observe not whether the mind ever distorts, but how regularly it does so in ordinary life.

Visual Aid

Create a simple black-and-white page titled: Experiment I Tried | What Changed | What It Revealed About My Mind

Fill in a few example rows, such as:

- optical illusion with caption change | image meaning shifted quickly | perception follows framing

- same message read under stress and calm | threat feeling reduced when calmer | state shapes interpretation

- delayed phone check | urge felt stronger than expected | attention is partly habitual

- rewriting a memory later | detail and tone changed | memory is reconstructive

Leave extra lines for your own entries. At the end, underline any repeated findings such as prediction, emotional bias, attentional capture, memory drift, or language effect.

What I Want From My Brain	What I'm Feeding It Daily	What Might Support It Better
clearer focus	constant checking and interroption	protected attention window
better memory	poor sleep and overstimulation	steadier rest, slower input
calmer mood	endless headlines and tension	reduced exposure, more regulation
deeper thinking	fragmented screen time	silence, reading, single-tasking
•		
•		
•		
•		
•		

Ethical Question

If simple everyday experiments can reveal how easily perception, memory, and attention are shaped, how much more careful should we be with systems designed intentionally to influence them?

Chapter 23 - Intelligence, Wisdom, & the Moral Use of Knowledge

There is a difference between understanding something and being changed responsibly by that understanding.

This difference matters more than many of us admit.

A person can know a great deal about attention, persuasion, memory, emotion, language, reward, trauma, and behaviour, and still use that knowledge carelessly.

They can become more effective without becoming more ethical.

They can become more precise in influence without becoming more humane in intention. They can sharpen their ability to guide, frame, and move other minds while remaining inwardly immature, defensive, manipulative, or spiritually shallow.

That is why intelligence alone is not enough.

This chapter turns towards one of the deepest ethical tensions in the entire book: the difference between being clever and being wise.

By now, we have explored the brain as a structure, system, signal, interface, adaptive organ, social instrument, programmable field, and philosophical mystery.

We have seen that knowledge of the brain opens extraordinary possibilities. It can help us regulate better, learn more deeply, understand one another more clearly, and reclaim some freedom from automatic reaction. But the same knowledge can also be used to exploit vulnerability, optimise compliance, bypass reflection, intensify dependence, and reshape perception without consent.

The issue, then, is no longer whether knowledge is powerful.

It is what kind of person is using it.

This is the chapter where the moral question becomes unavoidable.

What is intelligence for?
What is understanding for?
What is knowledge for, if not only to gain advantage?
What kind of maturity must accompany insight into the human mind if that insight is not to become another instrument of control?

These questions matter because modern culture often confuses intelligence with speed, accumulation, verbal fluency, memory range, or strategic advantage. A person who can explain well is assumed to understand deeply. A person who can persuade effectively is assumed to be wise. A person who can analyse a system is assumed to be trustworthy in how they will use that analysis.

But these assumptions do not hold.

A clever person may simply be better at justifying themselves.
A strategic person may be better at bypassing resistance.
A knowledgeable person may still be morally underdeveloped.

A persuasive person may be highly dangerous precisely because they understand so much without a corresponding conscience.

This is why the difference between intelligence and wisdom matters so deeply.

Intelligence can recognise patterns, solve problems, hold abstractions, detect inconsistencies, learn quickly, and manipulate variables. It can be brilliant, efficient, and creative. It can produce systems, arguments, tools, and strategies. It can forecast, compare, infer, and optimise.

But wisdom asks something further.

Wisdom asks:
To what end?
At what cost?
Under what moral constraints?
What does this understanding do to others?
What kind of life does this knowledge help create?
What remains unseen by brilliance when humility is absent?

Wisdom is not opposed to intelligence. It is what intelligence becomes when joined to depth, humility, conscience, and proportion.

This distinction becomes especially important in a book like this one because so much of what we have explored can be turned in different directions.

Understanding prediction can support better communication or better propaganda. Understanding emotional regulation can support healing, or emotional bypass and behavioural control.

Understanding attention can help us protect it or design systems to capture it more efficiently. Understanding language as embodied signalling can help create safer, clearer relationships or more manipulative and suggestive environments.

The knowledge itself does not decide.

The person using it matters.
The system using it matters.
The values guiding it matter.

This is why the moral use of knowledge cannot be treated as an optional afterthought. It belongs at the centre.

One of the risks of studying the brain is that people may begin to see others too instrumentally. Once patterns become visible, the temptation emerges to treat people as systems to optimise, nudge, frame, regulate, predict, or move.

This can happen in marketing, politics, therapy, education, parenting, leadership, spiritual communities, relationships, and even self-help culture.

The language may differ, but the underlying temptation is similar: once I know how the mind works, I can get better results.

But results are not always wisdom.

A person may produce obedience, but not flourishing.

They may produce attention, but not understanding.

They may produce loyalty, but not freedom.

They may produce persuasion, but not truth.

They may produce efficiency, but not dignity.

That is why the moral question cannot be reduced to whether something works.

Many damaging things work.

Fear works.

Shame works.

Repetition works.

Addiction loops work.

Manipulative framing works.

Emotional extraction works.

Tribal signalling works.

Identity capture works.

The fact that something works on the brain does not make it good for the person, the relationship, the culture, or the future.

This is where discernment becomes essential.

Discernment is not simply intelligence with a calmer tone. It is the capacity to recognise not only what is possible, but what is fitting. It asks not only whether a tool can be used, but whether it should be, and in what way. It includes ethical proportion. It includes moral imagination. It includes the ability to sense when knowledge is becoming power without responsibility.

Discernment also requires inward honesty.

Because one of the hardest truths to accept is that we can use knowledge of the mind not only to influence others, but to defend ourselves from truth. A person may study psychology to avoid vulnerability. They may study language to control impressions. They may study neuroscience to reduce moral discomfort into a mechanism. They may study consciousness in order to feel superior rather than sincere. They may study trauma to justify every reaction without truly working through any of it.

Knowledge can become armour.

That is one reason humility matters so much here.

Humility is not weakness, indecision, or false modesty. It is the recognition that understanding does not automatically purify the one who understands.

It is the awareness that insight into the brain can enlarge the ego just as easily as it can soften it. It is the refusal to assume that because we can describe a mechanism, we have transcended its distortions in ourselves.

A person may understand projection and still project.

They may understand cognitive bias and still live inside it. They may understand emotional contagion and still spread dysregulation. They may understand attentional capture and still design systems that rely on it.

They may understand the nervous system and still use that knowledge to dominate rather than support.

Humility does not erase these dangers, but it makes them more visible.

This is also why power belongs in the conversation.

Knowledge of the brain is never socially neutral. It enters systems already shaped by hierarchy, incentive, ideology, profit, fear, and status. A corporation may learn how to hold attention longer.

A political campaign may learn how to trigger faster loyalty. A school may learn how to improve learning or how to improve compliance.

A therapist may use insight to liberate or to subtly dominate.

A parent may use knowledge to regulate with greater care, or to control with greater sophistication.

The more powerful the knowledge, the more serious the responsibility.

That is why we must ask:
Who benefits from this use of knowledge?

Whose dignity is being protected or reduced?
Is this helping a person become more conscious, or more manageable?
More free, or more dependent?
More whole, or more strategically useful to someone else?

These are not abstract ethical questions. They are daily ones.

They appear in the tone we use.
In the systems we design.
In the technologies we normalise.
In the institutions we build.
In the educational practices, we justify.
In the ways we speak to children, partners, audiences, patients, voters, customers, and ourselves.

This is where the distinction between being clever and being conscious becomes most important.

Cleverness often seeks leverage.
Consciousness asks what leverage does to the soul of the interaction.

Cleverness asks how to increase the effect.
Consciousness asks whether the effect honours the person.

Cleverness asks how to gain compliance, engagement, loyalty, or response.
Consciousness asks what kind of internal world is being created in the other while this happens.

This is why wisdom is not merely knowledge plus age. It is knowledge disciplined by ethical awareness.

A wise use of brain knowledge tends to do certain things:

- It widens rather than narrows

- It clarifies rather than confuses

- It respects consent

- It supports agency

- It avoids unnecessary domination

- It seeks truth without humiliating

- It recognises vulnerability without exploiting it

- It values human depth over behavioural efficiency alone

This does not mean wisdom is always soft. It can be direct, firm, and boundary-rich. But it does not casually instrumentalise inner life.

This matters especially in an era where so much knowledge is now operationalised through systems rather than only individuals.

Algorithms do not need moral intention to become morally consequential.

Behavioural design does not need explicit cruelty to degrade agency. Institutions do not need to call themselves manipulative to become shaping forces that reward fragmentation, dependence, or emotional capture.

When knowledge of human cognition is embedded into systems, ethical responsibility becomes more diffuse, and therefore even more necessary to name.

We as a species are now capable of building environments that know how to move the mind.

That should sober us.

Because if we can direct attention, amplify compulsion, engineer persuasion, and shape emotional climate at scale, then wisdom is no longer a private virtue alone. It becomes a civilisational necessity. A culture with increasing psychological power and decreasing moral depth becomes highly dangerous.

This is one of the reasons intelligence alone has never been enough to save societies.

A civilisation can become technically brilliant while spiritually and ethically stunted. It can know how to build, calculate, optimise, measure, predict, and scale, while losing proportion, reverence, restraint, and care. It can become extremely good at affecting minds without becoming any better at honouring them.

That is one of the dangers this book has been circling from the beginning.

It is not only that the brain can be misunderstood.
It is that it can be understood in ways that are then used without wisdom.

This is why the moral use of knowledge begins inwardly.

Before asking whether others are manipulating, exploiting, or shaping minds irresponsibly, we must also ask:
How do I use what I know?
Do I use insight to become more honest or more defensive?
Do I use language to clarify, or to gain the upper hand?
Do I use psychological understanding to support freedom, or to

increase my ability to manage people?

Do I study the mind to deepen contact with life, or to gain control over it?

These are difficult questions, but they are necessary ones.

And they lead into another important distinction:
The difference between knowledge and formation.

Knowledge can be acquired quickly. Formation takes longer. Knowledge can be downloaded. Formation must be lived. Knowledge can inform the mind. Formation alters the person. In that sense, wisdom depends less on how much one can explain and more on what kind of inner life one has become through what one knows.

This is why regulation, humility, discernment, and moral restraint are not side topics. They are part of the ethical formation required to hold brain knowledge well.

Without them, understanding becomes dangerous.

With them, understanding can become a form of service.

This chapter belongs where it does because Part V is not only about practical techniques. It is about orientation. Chapter 21 asked how we can stop working against the brain in our daily conditions. This chapter asks what kind of intelligence should guide any practical use of what we have learned. It makes explicit that the final measure of understanding is not merely whether it improves performance, but whether it deepens responsibility. Once that becomes clear, the final chapter of the book naturally comes into view. Because if cleverness is not enough, and if wisdom requires that we reclaim a more dignified relationship with mind, body, language, attention, culture, and technology, then the closing question becomes larger still:

What would it mean, in this age, to truly reclaim the human mind?

That is where we go next.

Brain Observation

Notice one situation in which you used understanding to gain an advantage, socially, emotionally, rhetorically, or strategically. Ask yourself whether the same understanding could have been used more honestly or humanely.

Everyday Experiment

Over the next two days, notice one moment when you are tempted to use insight about another person to manage, impress, soften, steer, or out-position them. Pause and ask:

- Is this truthful?

- Is this necessary?

- Does this respect their dignity?

- Am I trying to connect, or to control?

You do not need to become perfect. The experiment is simply to notice the moral edge where knowledge becomes leverage.

Visual Aid

Create a simple black-and-white page titled: What I Understand | How It Could Be Used Well | How It Could Be Used Poorly

Fill in a few example rows, such as:

- emotional triggers | greater sensitivity and care | manipulation, pressure, compliance

- language tone | clearer communication and regulation | suggestion, intimidation, control

- attention patterns | protecting focus and designing better habits | capture, extraction, addiction loops

- trauma knowledge | compassion, pacing, safety | excuse-making, identity fixation, exploitation

Leave extra lines for your own entries. At the end, underline any areas where the same knowledge could serve healing or manipulation, depending on intention and ethics.

What I Understand	How It Could Be Used Well	How It Could Be Used Poorly
emotional triggers	greater sensitivity and care	manipulation, pressure, compliance
language tone	clearer communication and regulation	suggestion, intimidation, control?
attention patterns	protecting focus and designing better habits	capture, extraction, addiction loops
trauma knowledge	compassion, pacing, safety	excuse-making, identity fixcition, exploitation
•		
•		
•		
•		
•		

Ethical Question

If knowledge of the mind always increases power in some form, what inner qualities must grow alongside it to keep that power from becoming corruptive?

Chapter 24 -Reclaiming the Mind

The deeper question beneath this entire book has never been only what the brain is.

It has been:
What kind of life are we building through it?
What kind of world is acting upon it?
and what kind of inner freedom remains possible once we begin to understand how much it is shaped by body, memory, language, technology, relationship, biology, culture, and repetition?

That is why this final chapter must turn towards reclamation.

Not because the human mind has been lost in some absolute sense, but because many of us now live at a distance from it. We live inside acceleration, interruption, persuasion, overstimulation, performative identity, emotional capture, and environments designed to outcompete stillness.

We are flooded with signals and starved of integration. We are trained towards reaction more often than reflection. We are taught to manage appearances while losing touch with atmosphere, body, depth, and the slower forms of knowing that help a life become coherent.

In that sense, reclaiming the human mind is not a grand slogan. It is a practical and moral necessity.

Reclamation begins with a simple recognition:

The mind does not disappear all at once.
It is eroded gradually.

It is eroded by endless partial attention.
By chronic overexposure.
By identity scaffolds, we no longer question.
By algorithmic pacing.
By environments that reward performance over presence.
By language that narrows rather than opens.
By emotional climates that train vigilance as normal.
By technologies that stimulate response while weakening inward steadiness.
By knowledge severed from wisdom.
By speed without digestion.
By information without silence.
By contact without depth.

None of these alone needs to destroy our inner life. But together, repeated long enough, they can produce a kind of subtle dispossession. A person still functions. They still speak, work, scroll, reply, choose, and consume. But the sense of inward authorship begins to thin.

Thought becomes increasingly borrowed. Attention becomes increasingly guided from the outside. Mood becomes easier to move through invisible levers. Identity becomes more performative.

Depth becomes harder to access. The person is still living, but less often from the centre of themselves.

This is what reclamation pushes against.

It is not anti-technology.
Not anti-science.
Not anti-culture.
Not anti-relationship.
Not anti-intelligence.

It is anti-unconscious surrender.

To reclaim the human mind is to refuse to let every force that can shape attention, emotion, memory, language, and selfhood do so without being noticed. It is to become more deliberate about what enters the inner field, what repeats there, what gains authority there, and what kind of person is being formed through that repetition.

This does not require purity. It requires participation.

One of the first elements of reclamation is attention.

Attention is where so much begins. It is the gate through which experience becomes salient enough to shape perception, mood, memory, and meaning. A mind that cannot hold attention for long is easier to guide from outside. A mind trained to chase novelty loses some capacity for depth. A mind repeatedly fragmented may still be intelligent, but it often finds it harder to gather itself into coherence.

So reclaiming the human mind means reclaiming attention not as a private productivity technique, but as a moral and existential faculty.

What do I repeatedly give my mind to?
What am I rehearsing without realising?
What am I allowing to define relevance?
What part of my inner life is now being organised by systems whose interests are not the same as mine?

These are not small questions. They are among the most important questions of modern life.

The second element is language.

Language does not merely describe the world we inhabit. It helps build it. It frames experience, regulates states, creates moral atmospheres, normalises assumptions, narrows possibilities, and shapes the felt meaning of events. Reclaiming the human mind, therefore, requires more careful speech — outwardly and inwardly.

What kind of language do we live in?
What kind of language do we turn against ourselves?
What phrases have become mental furniture?
What tones have become internalised as normal?
What labels have quietly hardened into identity?

To reclaim the mind means taking language seriously again.

Not just politically or rhetorically, but physiologically and ethically. It means recognising that repeated contemptuous speech changes the atmosphere of a person. That weaponised certainty degrades thought. That language without care can become programming. That language with steadiness, precision, and dignity can become part of repair.

The third element is embodiment.

A mind severed from the body becomes easy to manipulate because it loses one of its deepest reference points. If we are cut off from sensation, breath, fatigue, tension, hunger, contraction, and the subtler rhythms of internal life, we become more dependent on outer signals to tell us what is true, what matters, and how we feel. We become easier to capture through intensity because we no longer sense ourselves clearly enough to notice when something is pulling us out of our own centre.

Reclaiming the human mind means restoring some contact with the body, not in a self-help fashion, but as orientation.

The body is not infallible.
It is not always correct about the world.
But it is part of how we remain real to ourselves.

A person who can feel their own contraction, fatigue, overwhelm, urgency, and softening has more chance of noticing how perception is being altered in real time. A person cut off from that inner feedback is more likely to confuse every triggered state with external truth.

The fourth element is relationship.

None of us reclaims the mind alone in some purified individual sense. We are shaped in relationships, and much of what narrows or widens us happens there. Some relationships intensify performance, self-monitoring, and emotional confusion. Others return us to steadiness, thoughtfulness, and breath. Some make us more fragmented. Others make us more whole.

This means reclaiming the human mind includes asking:
Who helps me hear myself more clearly?
Who intensifies noise?
What conversations strengthen presence?
What atmospheres train self-betrayal?
What kinds of contact make me more performative, more defended, more scattered?
What kinds make me more sincere, more embodied, more thoughtful?

This is not about superiority or social sorting for its own sake. It is about recognising that relational environments are cognitive and moral environments too.

The fifth element is memory and identity.

As we have seen, memory is reconstructive, and selfhood is partly maintained through continuity work. This means reclaiming the mind includes becoming less naïvely fused with the stories that organise us. Not because the story is bad, but because the story can become a prison when it is never examined.

Many of us live inside inherited narratives:
about who we are,
what is possible,

what we deserve,
What kind of person must we be?
what must be defended,
What kind of world are we in?

Some of these narratives support life. Some merely preserve familiarity. To reclaim the human mind means being willing, at times, to interrupt continuity long enough to ask whether the story still serves truth.

This is delicate work.
Because identity protects us.
And the loosening of identity can feel like a threat.

But without some loosening, reclamation remains superficial. A person may protect their attention more carefully and remain trapped in a story that does not belong to their deepest life. The outer app is being managed, but the inner authorship remains compromised.

The sixth element is discernment around technology.

This book has not argued that all technology is dehumanising. Technology can extend learning, connection, creativity, access, and even forms of reflection. But the issue is not whether technology exists. It is how it shapes the conditions of the mind. Some tools augment human depth. Others trade on human weakness. Some support agency. Others quietly erode it while appearing convenient.

Reclaiming the human mind, therefore, requires a more mature relationship with tools.

Not idolising them.
Not demonising them.
But asking:
What is this tool training me?
At what pace does it normalise?
What kind of attention does it reward?
What kind of self does it assume?
What kind of dependence does it cultivate?
Does it support my authorship, or slowly replace it?

These questions are now part of psychological hygiene.

The seventh element is silence, depth, and slowness.

A mind cannot be reclaimed entirely at the same pace that fragmented it. Something slower must return. Some form of stillness, even brief. Some space in which cognition is not always colonised by incoming demand. Some intervals in which thought can deepen rather than only react. Some return to reading, listening, walking, journalling, making, praying, contemplating, or simply sitting long enough for subtler layers of the mind to become legible again.

This is not nostalgia. It is a nervous system and attentional necessity.

Without slowness, we lose proportion.
Without silence, we lose self-audibility.

Without depth, we lose inner hierarchy and begin to live as though every stimulus deserves equal significance.

The eighth element is moral seriousness.

The human mind is not only something to be protected from noise. It is something through which moral life is lived. What we repeatedly expose ourselves to affects what feels normal. What we normalise affects what we can see clearly. What we see clearly affects what we tolerate, resist, excuse, or refuse to name in ourselves.

This means reclaiming the mind is not merely therapeutic. It is ethical.

A degraded mind is easier to mislead.
An overstimulated mind is easier to govern through reaction.
A fragmented mind is easier to polarise.
A captured mind is easier to make useful to systems that do not honour human depth.

So reclamation is not withdrawal from the world. It is part of responsible participation in it. It is how we preserve some ability to think, feel, judge, and relate without being wholly consumed by the machinery acting upon us.

There is also a deeper spiritual dimension here, whether one names it spiritually or not.

To reclaim the human mind is, in part, to remember that we are more than reflex, more than programming, more than borrowed narrative, more than stimulus-response loops. Not separate from biology, but not exhausted by it. Not free from conditioning, but not identical to it. Not beyond the nervous system, but not reducible to its most frightened patterns either.

Something in us can still observe.
Something can still choose more consciously.
Something can still slow down enough to refuse total capture.
Something can still widen.

This "something" may be described differently by different traditions:
awareness,
presence,
witnessing,
soul,
conscience,
the observing self,
reflective consciousness.

The term matters less than the fact that it remains available, however buried, however clouded. Reclaiming the human mind means strengthening contact with that deeper authorship.

This is not mastery.
It is stewardship.

It does not mean we become invulnerable to influence, distortion, grief, fatigue, or fear. We remain beings in bodies, in culture, in time. But it does mean we can become less passively governed by forces we never examine. We can become more responsible for the inner conditions through which we meet the world.

That is why this chapter closes the main body of the book.

We began with the brain as architecture, moved through chemistry and memory, through social shaping and programming, through selfhood and inheritance, through culture, metaphor, and consciousness, and now arrive at the practical and existential question that has been there from the beginning:

What would it mean not merely to understand the mind, but to inhabit it more consciously?

The answer is not a formula. It is a way of living.

It is:
more care with attention,
more honesty about the state,
more respect for embodiment,
more discernment in language,
more humility in knowledge,
more seriousness about technology,
more courage around identity,
more protection of silence,
more depth in relationships
more responsibility in what we normalise,
and more willingness to remain human in a world increasingly organised around automation, stimulation, and control.

This does not close the mystery.
It closes the argument in the right place.

Because the deepest question of the book was never simply "What is the brain?"

It was always also:
Who is living through it?
Who is training it?
Who is capturing it?
Who is caring for it?
Who is shaping the conditions in which it becomes itself?
And what kind of species do we become depending on how we answer those questions?

That is why the main text ends here.

Not with technological triumph.
Not with reductionist certainty.
Not with spiritual fog.
But with an invitation.

An invitation to reclaim some authorship.
Some inward dignity. Some steadiness of attention.
Some care in language. Some ethical seriousness in knowledge.
Some courage in the face of speed. Some depth in an age designed to flatten. From here, only one final movement remains. The conclusion returns us to the title with new eyes.

If the brain was an app, would you use it?

Brain Observation

Notice one place in your life where your mind feels most like your own, and one place where it feels most captured by pace, expectation, noise, or repetition. What is different about the conditions?

Everyday Experiment

For one hour, create a small reclaiming space. No unnecessary notifications, no multitasking, no reactive checking, no background noise unless chosen deliberately. Use the hour for one thing only: reading, writing, walking, reflecting, sitting, or making. At the end, note whether your mind resisted, softened, or deepened.

Visual Aid

Create a simple black-and-white page titled: What Helps Me Feel More Human | What Pulls Me Away From Myself | What I Want To Reclaim

Fill in a few example rows, such as:

- deep reading | endless scrolling | sustained attention
- honest conversation | performative interaction | sincerity
- quiet walking | constant input | inner space
- slower mornings | rushed digital checking | grounded beginning

Leave extra lines for your own entries. At the end, underline any repeated themes such as silence, depth, pressure, speed, validation, or disconnection.

What Helps Me Feel More Human	What Pulls Me Away From Myself	What I Want To Reclaim
deep reading	endless scrolling	sustained attention
honest conversation	performative interaction	sincerity
quiet walking	constant input	inner space
slower mornings	rushed digital checking	grounded beginning
•		
•		
•		
•		
•		

Ethical Question

If the human mind can be reclaimed only through deliberate care, what does that suggest about the kind of civilisation we are building when depth, silence, and inward authorship are increasingly treated as optional?

Conclusion - If the Brain Was an App

If the brain was an app, would most of us know how to use it?

That question may sound playful at first, but by now it should feel far less innocent.

Because the deeper I have gone into this work, the more obvious it has become that we are not simply living with a remarkable system. We are living *through* one, and usually with only partial awareness of how much it is shaping what we call reality, identity, memory, emotion, behaviour, and meaning. We do not merely think through the brain. We interpret, defend, react, imagine, attach, predict, learn, distort, and become through it.

That is what this book has tried to make visible.

It has not tried to flatten the brain into a machine, nor float it into vagueness. It has tried to hold a more difficult balance. The brain is biological, but not merely mechanical. It is adaptive, but not neutral. It is social, but not passive. It is programmable, but not beyond reclamation. It is tied to chemistry, body, history, and inherited pattern, yet it also opens onto questions of selfhood, consciousness, mystery, and moral responsibility that mechanism alone does not settle.

That tension matters.

Because one of the great errors of our time is that we often move towards extremes. On one side, there is reductionism: the belief that once we can map the circuitry, describe the chemistry, and name the networks, the human being has been explained. On the other side, there is a form of spiritual abstraction that can become careless with biology, trauma, regulation, and the body's real conditions. I have tried not to collapse into either. The truth, as I have found it so far, is harder and richer than both.

We are embodied beings whose inner life cannot be understood apart from the state.
We are social beings whose minds are shaped in relationships.
We are linguistic beings whose worlds are framed by tone, timing, and implication.
We are programmable beings whose attention can be captured and whose patterns can be trained.
And we are conscious beings who still cannot be fully explained by current models alone.

This is not a contradiction to solve. It is the condition of being alive.

As I have moved through this wider body of work, I have noticed something in my own life that has shaped this book profoundly. The more I learned to regulate emotion rather than be unconsciously driven by it, the more my memory deepened. The more I learned to slow down my reactions, the more discernment sharpened. The more I stopped confusing urgency with truth, the more space opened for curiosity. The more I paid attention to how language, physiology, atmosphere, diet, attention, and nervous-system state affected my thinking, the more I realised that intelligence is not merely a matter of information. It is also a matter of conditions.

That changed my relationship with knowledge itself.

Learning stopped being only about accumulation. It became participation. It became a way of observing the interface through which life is lived. It became less about forcing answers and more about recognising the kinds of states in which answers are distorted, defended, or made unavailable. In that sense, what I have called consciousness expansion has not been some theatrical awakening, nor an identity position to perform. It has been more practical and more intimate than that. It has involved becoming more aware of the layers through which experience is filtered, and more careful about what I repeatedly feed those layers.

That is part of what this book has been offering.

Not a final doctrine.
Not a closed system.
Not a promise that everything can be fixed if we simply optimise well enough.
But a more serious literacy of the mind.

A literacy that asks:
What is this system doing when I think I am simply seeing?
What has it learned from stress, family, culture, technology, and repetition?
What is it protecting?
What is it predicting?

What language is it living inside?
What identity is it trying to preserve?
What kind of world is it helping me inhabit?

These questions matter because collectively we now live in an age where knowledge of the brain is no longer confined to laboratories, clinics, or philosophy. It is embedded into media systems, educational models, persuasive technologies, therapeutic language, platform design, political messaging, advertising, and increasingly into artificial systems capable of shaping behaviour at scale. That means understanding the brain is no longer only an interesting topic. It is becoming a basic form of cultural and moral literacy.

If we do not understand how attention is captured, it will be captured.
If we do not understand how emotion narrows thought, that narrowing will be used.
If we do not understand how language regulates the body, language will regulate us without our noticing.
If we do not understand how repeated environments train the mind, those environments will continue to write themselves into us beneath awareness.

This is why the question in the title matters so much.

If the brain was an app, would you use it?

Would you learn what it protects and distorts?
Would you notice how others are programming it?
Would you recognise when your own attention is no longer

your own?

Would you become more careful with what you repeat, what you expose yourself to, and what you call truth?

Would you notice the difference between intensity and clarity, between stimulation and wisdom, between information and integration?

Or would you continue letting other systems run it for you?

That is not a judgement. It is the question.

Because if there is one thing I have come to see more clearly, it is that many of us are not failing because we are weak or unintelligent. We are often trying to think clearly in conditions that degrade clarity, trying to remain steady in environments built around activation, trying to protect depth in cultures that reward speed, and trying to hear ourselves in a world that never stops speaking.

To understand that is not defeatist. It is liberating.

It means that some of what we experience as personal inadequacy is actually a systems problem, an environmental problem, a relational problem, a pacing problem, an attentional problem, or a problem of language and state. It means that reclaiming the mind is not merely a private self-help project. It is also an act of resistance against forces that benefit from fragmentation, confusion, performative identity, and chronic inner noise.

But resistance alone is not enough.

The human mind cannot be reclaimed only through critique. It must also be nourished. It must be given conditions in which depth becomes possible again. Conditions of slower attention, more honest speech, more embodied contact, more careful use of technology, more meaningful relationships, more silence, more inward responsibility, and more humility around what we think we know.

That, to me, is where the real work begins.

Not in the performance of being awakened.
Not in claiming some superior distance from manipulation.
Not in turning insight into another identity badge.
But in daily participation.

In how we sleep.
How we speak.
How we breathe.
How we read.
How we respond.
How we relate.
How we remember.
How we frame.
How do we allow attention to be spent or protected?
How we use knowledge not only to become sharper, but to become more careful.

That is the ethical dimension of this entire inquiry.

Knowledge of the brain can widen life.
It can also be used to extract from life.

If The Brain Was An App, Would You Use It?

It can deepen responsibility.
It can also deepen control.
It can support healing.
It can also be weaponised into more elegant forms of manipulation.

So perhaps the final question is not only whether we would use the app.

It is whether we would use it wisely.

Whether we would use it in the service of greater awareness rather than greater automation.
In the service of discernment rather than domination.
In the service of truth rather than emotional capture.
In the service of depth rather than speed alone.
In the service of becoming more fully human rather than more efficiently programmed.

That, ultimately, is what I hope this book has moved towards.

Not certainty, but clearer sight.
Not simplification, but deeper literacy.
Not detachment from life, but a more conscious participation in it.

The brain remains extraordinary.
The mystery remains open.
The responsibility remains ours.

And perhaps that is the most honest place to end.

If the brain was an app, would you use it?

Or better still:

Now that you know a little more about how it shapes your reality, how will you choose to live through it from here?

James Miller

Glossary

1. Adaptation

The brain and body's capacity to adjust to repeated conditions, demands, and environments. Adaptation can support survival and growth, but it can also stabilise patterns that are no longer helpful.

2. Agency

The felt and lived capacity to choose, respond, and participate consciously in one's own life. Agency is shaped by state, history, environment, and awareness rather than existing as a fixed absolute.

3. Algorithmic Reinforcement

The way digital systems learn is what captures attention and then feeds back more of the same, gradually shaping preference, mood, behaviour, and perception through repetition.

4. Ambiguity

A condition in which the meaning is not yet fully clear. The brain often finds ambiguity difficult because it prefers prediction and closure, especially under stress.

5. Amygdala

A brain structure closely involved in threat detection, emotional salience, and rapid orienting to potential danger. It is important, but often oversimplified as a pure "fear centre."

6. Attention

The selective focusing of awareness on certain signals, thoughts, sensations, or events over others. Attention determines what becomes foregrounded enough to shape experience.

7. Attention Hijack

The capture of mental focus by stimuli designed to exploit novelty, urgency, fear, outrage, social relevance, or reward anticipation.

8. Attunement

The process by which one person senses, responds to, and aligns with another's state, rhythm, or emotional reality. Attunement plays a central role in regulation, development, and relationships.

9. Awareness

The capacity to notice experience as it unfolds. Awareness may be broad or narrow, steady or fragmented, reflective or reactive.

10. Behavioural Conditioning

The process through which repeated rewards, punishments, associations, and environments shape automatic responses and habits over time.

11. Belief

A pattern of interpretation held to be true, often reinforced by memory, identity, emotion, repetition, and social belonging rather than evidence alone.

12. Bias

A tendency in perception, interpretation, or judgement that inclines the mind in a particular direction. Bias is not always malicious; it often emerges from efficient patterning and a limited perspective.

13. Biological Inheritance

The genetic and physiological tendencies are passed across generations, shaping predisposition, sensitivity, development, and possible ranges of response.

14. Body State

The organism's current physiological condition, including tension, fatigue, regulation, arousal, inflammation, rest, hunger, and internal readiness. Body state strongly shapes cognition.

15. Brain-Body Loop

The ongoing feedback relationship between the brain and the rest of the body, through which internal state and perception continuously influence one another.

16. Capture Economy

A social and technological environment organised around competing for attention, emotional engagement, and repeat behavioural response.

17. Cerebral Cortex

The outer layer of the brain is associated with many higher-order processes such as language, planning, sensory integration, abstraction, and conscious reflection.

18. Chemistry of Signalling

The biochemical dimension of neural communication involves neurotransmitters, hormones, modulators, and intracellular changes that shape how signals are sent and received.

19. Cognitive Dissonance

The discomfort experienced when beliefs, actions, identity, or new information conflict. The brain often seeks to reduce this discomfort by defending coherence rather than revising honestly.

20. Cognitive Framing

The mental and linguistic structuring of an event, idea, or experience before interpretation fully settles. Frames influence what feels important, threatening, or obvious.

21. Coherence

A state in which thought, body, feeling, attention, and action are relatively aligned rather than fragmented or internally split.

22. Consciousness

The fact of lived experience itself: that something is being felt, known, perceived, or noticed. Consciousness remains one of the deepest unresolved questions in science and philosophy.

23. Conscious Interpretation

The explicit meaning the mind assigns to an experience after sensation, state, memory, and prediction have already begun shaping it.

24. Construction of Reality

The idea that experience is not a direct copy of the external world, but a working model built by the brain through sensation, prediction, memory, state, and context.

25. Context

The wider frame in which a signal, event, word, or behaviour is received. Context can change meaning dramatically, even when the surface content stays the same.

26. Control Loop

A repeating cycle of sensing, comparing, adjusting, and responding. The brain uses control-like processes constantly to regulate action, prediction, and internal stability.

27. Co-Regulation

The way one nervous system helps another settle, organise, or intensify. Regulation is not only individual; it is deeply relational.

28. Cortisol

A hormone involved in stress response, energy mobilisation, and adaptation. It is necessary for life, but chronic elevation can narrow cognition and burden the body.

29. Culture

The shared field of values, language, rituals, assumptions, meanings, and norms through which people interpret life. Culture shapes what the brain comes to expect and normalise.

30. Default Patterning

The familiar ways of thinking, feeling, reacting, and perceiving that become automatic through repetition, identity, and lived history.

31. Delayed Interpretation

A moment in which the body or nervous system reacts before the conscious mind fully understands why, revealing that meaning often forms after state shifts.

32. Discernment

The ability to distinguish between signal and noise, truth and intensity, reaction and reflection, wisdom and manipulation. Discernment depends on regulation as well as thought.

33. Dissociation

A partial disconnection from sensation, emotion, presence, memory, or embodied contact, often arising under overwhelm, trauma, or chronic stress.

34. Distributed Cognition

The idea that cognition does not occur in one tiny isolated region but across interacting networks, bodily processes, environmental cues, and social systems.

35. Dopamine

A neurotransmitter strongly involved in motivation, learning, reward prediction, novelty, and behavioural reinforcement. It is not simply the "pleasure chemical."

36. Dysregulation

A state in which the nervous system struggles to maintain workable balance, often leading to overwhelm, collapse, agitation, reactivity, or cognitive narrowing.

37. Embodiment

The lived reality is that the mind is not separate from the body, but emerges through it, with sensation, physiology, posture, movement, and internal state all shaping experience.

38. Emotional Contagion

The spread of emotional states between people through tone, expression, rhythm, posture, atmosphere, and shared nervous-system signalling.

39. Emotional Regulation

The capacity to stay in contact with feeling without being wholly ruled by it. Regulation involves flexibility, not suppression.

40. Emotional Salience

The degree to which something feels affectively charged and therefore more likely to capture attention, memory, and behavioural response.

41. Emergence

The appearance of a more complex quality or property from interacting parts, often used in discussions of how consciousness or cognition may arise from neural processes.

42. Environment

The total field in which the brain lives and learns, including physical surroundings, relationships, cultural atmosphere, routines, media, sensory input, and social conditions.

43. Epigenetics

Processes that influence gene expression without changing the DNA sequence itself. Epigenetics helps explain how biology and environment interact over time.

44. Error Correction

The process by which the brain updates its model when reality does not fully match its predictions. Healthy learning depends on tolerating and integrating such a mismatch.

45. Executive Function

Higher-order capacities such as planning, inhibition, working memory, decision-making, and flexible problem-solving are often associated with frontal brain networks.

46. False Memory

A memory that feels real but has been altered, reconstructed, suggested, or reshaped over time. False memory shows that remembering is not a simple playback.

47. Filtering

The selective reduction, prioritisation, or exclusion of information. The brain filters constantly because the total incoming world is too vast to process equally.

48. Flow State

A mode of absorbed, coherent, and often high-functioning attention in which self-consciousness may recede, and action feels more integrated with awareness.

49. Framing Effect

The way presentation alters meaning. The same information can produce different reactions depending on wording, tone, sequence, or emotional packaging.

50. Gene Expression

The process by which genetic information is activated, suppressed, or translated into biological function. What is inherited is not always expressed in the same way.

51. Glia

Support cells in the nervous system, once underestimated, are now known to play important roles in regulation, maintenance, signalling support, and brain health.

52. Habit Loop

A repeating behavioural cycle often involving a cue, response, and reinforcement. Habit loops can support life or quietly imprison it.

53. Hemispheric Specialisation

The idea that the two brain hemispheres show some differences in processing style and function, though popular "left brain/right brain" myths greatly oversimplify this.

54. Homeostasis

The organism's tendency to maintain internal stability across changing conditions. The brain and body work continuously to preserve workable balance.

55. Hormonal Signalling

The slower but powerful chemical messaging system through which the body regulates stress, growth, metabolism, reproduction, energy, and many features of mental life.

56. Identity

The organised sense of who one is, shaped by memory, narrative, role, attachment, culture, and repeated self-interpretation.

57. Illusion of Continuity

The sense of being one continuous self across time, even though memory, state, identity, and interpretation are more dynamic and reconstructed than they first appear.

58. Implicit Memory

Memory is expressed through pattern, body, behaviour, or expectation without needing conscious recall. Many relational and emotional responses are shaped by implicit memory.

59. Inattentional Blindness

The failure to notice something visible because attention is engaged elsewhere. This shows that seeing depends as much on focus as on presence.

60. Inner Narrative

The ongoing story through which the mind interprets experience, identity, and events. Inner narrative can clarify life or trap a person inside defended meanings.

61. Interoception

The sensing of internal bodily signals such as heartbeat, breath, hunger, temperature, tension, and visceral state. Interoception is central to emotion and self-awareness.

62. Interpretation

The assignment of meaning to an event, sensation, memory, or signal. Interpretation is shaped by state, expectation, context, and prior learning.

63. Language as Signal

The idea that language does more than represent meaning. It also carries tone, timing, implication, and nervous-system consequence.

64. Learning

The lasting alteration of behaviour, expectation, skill, or understanding through experience, repetition, relationship, and feedback.

65. Limbic System

A loose grouping of brain structures often associated with emotion, motivation, memory, and salience. The term is useful but often used too vaguely in popular writing.

66. Meaning-Making

The process through which sensation, memory, language, emotion, and narrative are organised into significance. The brain is always involved in this process.

67. Memory Reconstruction

The rebuilding of memory at recall rather than the simple retrieval of a fixed original record. Reconstruction is shaped by state, context, identity, and later experience.

68. Metacognition

Awareness of one's own thinking. Metacognition allows a person to notice thought as a process rather than mistaking every thought for reality.

69. Mirror-Linguistic Hypothesis (MLH)

A framework proposing that language functions not only as symbolic representation but as embodied signalling capable of shaping nervous-system state, perception, and relational dynamics in real time.

70. Mirror Systems

Broadly, the brain's sensitivity to the actions, expressions, and states of others supports imitation, resonance, learning, and social understanding.

71. Neurobiology

The biological study of the nervous system, including cells, circuits, chemistry, development, structure, and function.

72. Neurochemistry

The chemical dimension of brain function, especially involving neurotransmitters, modulators, hormones, receptors, and the biochemical conditions of cognition and emotion.

73. Neuroplasticity

The brain's capacity to change through learning, repetition, injury, development, and experience. Plasticity is real, but not limitless.

74. Nervous System

The wider signalling network, including the brain, spinal cord, nerves, and regulatory pathways through which the organism senses, coordinates, orients, and responds.

75. Novelty Seeking

The tendency to orient toward what is new, stimulating, or changing. In balance, it can support learning; in excess, it can fuel fragmentation and compulsive scanning.

76. Observing Self

The aspect of awareness capable of noticing thoughts, feelings, roles, and identities without being fully fused with them.

77. Overstimulation

A condition in which sensory, emotional, informational, or social input exceeds the system's capacity to process and integrate cleanly.

78. Pattern Recognition

The ability to detect regularities, similarities, and recurring structures. It is central to survival, learning, prediction, and also to distortion when over-applied.

79. Perception

The brain constructs an experience of the world through sensation, filtering, interpretation, and prediction rather than raw direct access alone.

80. Predictive Processing

A model of brain function suggests that the brain continuously anticipates incoming information and updates itself by comparing predictions with actual signals.

81. Presence

A condition of more direct contact with what is happening in the current moment, including body, feeling, attention, and environment.

82. Priming

The way prior exposure influences later interpretation, attention, response, or perception without always being consciously noticed.

83. Procedural Memory

Memory for skills, routines, and patterns of doing, such as riding a bike, typing, or other repeated actions that become automatic.

84. Programming

The repeated shaping of perception, reaction, habit,

expectation, and belief through environments, relationships, language, media, reward, and emotional reinforcement.

85. Proprioception

The sense of the body's position, movement, and orientation in space allows coordination without constant visual monitoring.

86. Quantum Speculation

Careful philosophical or scientific speculation about whether some aspects of the brain or consciousness might involve principles not fully captured by classical models. It remains highly debated.

87. Reaction

A rapid response shaped by prior pattern, state, or prediction, often occurring before reflection fully enters.

88. Receiver Model

The idea that the brain may not only generate awareness but also mediate, filter, or organise consciousness in ways not yet fully understood. This remains speculative.

89. Regulation

The process by which the brain and body maintain or restore workable balance across emotional, physiological, attentional, and relational states.

90. Relational Field

The shared atmosphere between people is created by tone, state, history, expectation, and mutual signalling. Much of communication happens within this field.

91. Repetition

The repeated exposure or enactment through which patterns become stabilised. Repetition is one of the strongest forces in learning, conditioning, and programming.

92. Reward System

The set of brain processes involved in motivation, reinforcement, anticipation, and behavioural repetition is often strongly shaped by dopamine-related pathways.

93. Salience

The quality of standing out as important, relevant, or urgent enough to capture attention and influence processing.

94. Selfhood

The lived sense of being a person across time, shaped by embodiment, memory, narrative, awareness, role, and relationship.

95. Signal

Any piece of information, sensation, cue, word, tone, or event that the system treats as meaningful enough to shape attention or response.

96. Social Brain

The aspect of brain functioning is shaped by relationship, belonging, language, mimicry, emotional contagion, attachment, and group life.

97. State-Dependent Thinking

The principle that thought quality, interpretation, memory

access, and reasoning are influenced by the current physiological and emotional state of the organism.

98. Subjectivity

The first-person quality of lived experience: what it feels like to be aware, to perceive, to suffer, to think, or to exist.

99. Wisdom

The ethical and existential maturity that guides how knowledge is used. Wisdom joins understanding to humility, proportion, responsibility, and care.

100. Working Memory

The limited mental space used to hold and work with information in the immediate present. Working memory is crucial for reasoning, learning, and conscious problem-solving.

References & Bibliography

Note: The following list combines referenced fields, foundational thinkers, relevant scientific and philosophical domains, and selected works aligned with the themes explored in this book.

It is designed as a practical back-matter bibliography for audiobook and paperback development, and can be expanded or formalised further during final print preparation.

Books by James Miller

Miller, James. *The Inversiverse: Waking Up in a World Built to Keep You Asleep.* This Place Called Earth Ltd.

Miller, James. *My Inner Child Was Broken.* This Place Called Earth Ltd.

Miller, James. *The Resonance Matrix: The Anatomy of Influence & The Linguistic Somatic Decode.* This Place Called Earth Ltd.

Miller, James. *The Consciousness Code.* This Place Called Earth Ltd.

Miller, James. *If the Brain Was an App, Would You Use It?* - This Place Called Earth Ltd.

Neuroscience, Cognition, and Perception

Barrett, Lisa Feldman. *How Emotions Are Made: The Secret Life of the Brain.* Houghton Mifflin Harcourt.

Damasio, Antonio. *Descartes' Error: Emotion, Reason, and the Human Brain.* Putnam.

Damasio, Antonio. *The Feeling of What Happens: Body and Emotion in the Making of Consciousness.* Harcourt.

Dehaene, Stanislas. *Consciousness and the Brain: Deciphering How the Brain Codes Our Thoughts.* Viking.

Eagleman, David. *The Brain: The Story of You.* Pantheon.

Friston, Karl. Works on predictive processing, active inference, and brain function.

Gazzaniga, Michael S. *Who's in Charge? Free Will and the Science of the Brain.* Ecco.

Kahneman, Daniel. *Thinking, Fast and Slow.* Farrar, Straus and Giroux.

LeDoux, Joseph. *The Emotional Brain.* Simon & Schuster.

Mlodinow, Leonard. *Subliminal: How Your Unconscious Mind Rules Your Behaviour.* Pantheon.

Ramachandran, V. S. *Phantoms in the Brain.* William Morrow.

Sacks, Oliver. *The Man Who Mistook His Wife for a Hat.* Summit Books.

If The Brain Was An App, Would You Use It?

Sapolsky, Robert M. *Behave: The Biology of Humans at Our Best and Worst.* Penguin.

Seth, Anil. *Being You: A New Science of Consciousness.* Faber & Faber.

Nervous System, Trauma, and Regulation

Levine, Peter A. *Waking the Tiger: Healing Trauma.* North Atlantic Books.

Levine, Peter A. *In an Unspoken Voice.* North Atlantic Books.

Porges, Stephen W. *The Polyvagal Theory.* Norton.

Siegel, Daniel J. *The Developing Mind.* Guilford Press.

van der Kolk, Bessel. *The Body Keeps the Score.* Viking.

Walker, Pete. *Complex PTSD: From Surviving to Thriving.* Azure Coyote.

Schore, Allan N. Works on affect regulation, attachment, and right-brain development.

Memory, Learning, and Adaptation

Baddeley, Alan. Works on working memory and cognitive psychology.

Doidge, Norman. *The Brain That Changes Itself.* Viking.

Eichenbaum, Howard. Works on memory systems and hippocampal function.

Kandel, Eric R. *In Search of Memory.* W. W. Norton.

If The Brain Was An App, Would You Use It?

Roediger, Henry L., and McDermott, Kathleen B. Research on false memory.

Language, Meaning, and Framing

Bateson, Gregory. *Steps to an Ecology of Mind.* University of Chicago Press.

Lakoff, George. *Don't Think of an Elephant!* Chelsea Green.

Lakoff, George, and Johnson, Mark. *Metaphors We Live By.* University of Chicago Press.

McGilchrist, Iain. *The Master and His Emissary.* Yale University Press.

Sapir, Edward. Works on language and culture.

Whorf, Benjamin Lee. Works on linguistic framing and worldview.

Miller, James. Mirror-Linguistic Hypothesis working framework and associated essays.

Social Influence, Conditioning, and Persuasion

Arendt, Hannah. *The Origins of Totalitarianism.* Harcourt.

Bernays, Edward. *Propaganda.* Horace Liveright.

Cialdini, Robert B. *Influence: The Psychology of Persuasion.* Harper Business.

Ellul, Jacques. *Propaganda: The Formation of Men's Attitudes.* Vintage.

If The Brain Was An App, Would You Use It?

Festinger, Leon. *A Theory of Cognitive Dissonance.* Stanford University Press.

Fromm, Erich. *Escape from Freedom.* Farrar & Rinehart.

Goffman, Erving. *The Presentation of Self in Everyday Life.* Anchor.

Milgram, Stanley. *Obedience to Authority.* Harper & Row.

Zimbardo, Philip. *The Lucifer Effect.* Random House.

Consciousness, Philosophy of Mind, and Selfhood

Chalmers, David J. *The Conscious Mind.* Oxford University Press.

Dennett, Daniel C. *Consciousness Explained.* Little, Brown and Company.

Merleau-Ponty, Maurice. *Phenomenology of Perception.* Routledge.

Nagel, Thomas. "What Is It Like to Be a Bat?"

Varela, Francisco J., Thompson, Evan, and Rosch, Eleanor. *The Embodied Mind.* MIT Press.

William James. *The Principles of Psychology.*

Culture, Symbol, and Ways of Knowing

Campbell, Joseph. *The Hero with a Thousand Faces.* Pantheon.

Eliade, Mircea. *The Sacred and the Profane.* Harcourt.

Jung, C. G. *Man and His Symbols.* Aldus Books.

If The Brain Was An App, Would You Use It?

Watts, Alan. *The Book: On the Taboo Against Knowing Who You Are*. Pantheon.

Genetics, Biology, and Development

Dawkins, Richard. *The Selfish Gene*. Oxford University Press.

Gabor Maté and Daniel Maté. *The Myth of Normal*. Vermilion.

Meaney, Michael J. Research on stress, development, and epigenetic influence.

Sapolsky, Robert M. *Why Zebras Don't Get Ulcers*. Holt.

AI, Computation, and Mind

Bostrom, Nick. *Superintelligence*. Oxford University Press.

Hofstadter, Douglas R. *Gödel, Escher, Bach*. Basic Books.

Kurzweil, Ray. *How to Create a Mind*. Viking.

Mitchell, Melanie. *Artificial Intelligence: A Guide for Thinking Humans*. Farrar, Straus and Giroux.

Tegmark, Max. *Life 3.0*. Knopf.

Additional Interdisciplinary Themes

Research literature relating to:

- predictive processing

- embodied cognition

- affective neuroscience

- attentional capture

- memory reconstruction

- neuroplasticity

- social contagion

- co-regulation

- psycholinguistics

- trauma physiology

- consciousness studies

- cultural cognition

- symbolic and contemplative tradition

Acknowledgements

This book emerged through years of observation, reflection, writing, study, and lived inquiry. It was shaped not by one discipline alone, but by the meeting place between neuroscience, psychology, language, embodiment, systems thinking, philosophy, consciousness studies, and everyday human experience.

My thanks go first to all those, known and unknown, whose work has helped deepen public understanding of the brain, memory, emotion, perception, nervous-system regulation, consciousness, learning, development, and behaviour. Whether through formal research, philosophical inquiry, clinical insight, scientific exploration, or lived testimony, their work has contributed to the wider conversation this book enters.

I am also grateful for the more difficult parts of life that demanded a deeper honesty, the moments of contradiction, overload, uncertainty, curiosity, disorientation, and insight that forced me to look more carefully at how the mind and body actually work together. Much of what appears in these pages was not formed through study alone, but through the ongoing discipline of noticing: noticing how emotion shapes thought, how physiology shapes meaning, how attention is pulled, how memory shifts, how language changes state, and how awareness can widen when the inner conditions are steadier.

My appreciation also extends to all those who have followed and supported my wider work through

This Place Called Earth, including the readers, listeners, and viewers who have engaged with *The Inversiverse*, *The Resonance Matrix*, *The Consciousness Code*, *My Inner Child Was Broken*, and the wider body of podcast, essay, and research-based material that surrounds them. Your willingness to engage deeply with questions of language, influence, regulation, consciousness, identity, and lived experience has helped make books like this worth writing.

I also acknowledge the careful use of emerging creative and editorial tools, including AI-assisted systems, in helping refine language, structure, and developmental flow across parts of the broader writing process. Used thoughtfully, such tools can support inquiry without replacing it, and can assist in bringing complex frameworks into clearer and more readable form.

This book is offered with gratitude to all those who continue the work of paying attention, not only to the world, but to the conditions through which the world is perceived.

James Miller

About the Author

James Miller is an independent writer, researcher, systems thinker, and podcast creator whose work explores the meeting point between language, perception, nervous-system regulation, embodiment, behaviour, influence, and consciousness.

With a professional background in electronics and systems engineering, his work bridges technical systems thinking with grounded psychological inquiry and lived observation. Across books, podcast series, essays, and long-form explorations, he examines how human reality is shaped not only through thoughts and beliefs, but through state: breath, tension, timing, memory, attention, physiology, emotional charge, and the relational fields in which meaning settles.

James is the founder of **This Place Called Earth**, an independent inquiry-led platform exploring the hidden architecture beneath modern life. His writing frequently investigates how perception is shaped by repetition, framing, language, emotional regulation, cultural conditioning, and the subtle interplay between body and mind.

He is also the originator of the **Mirror-Linguistic Hypothesis (MLH)**, a developing framework proposing that language functions not merely as symbolic representation, but as embodied signalling capable of modulating nervous-system state in real time. His wider body of work explores how words, tone, rhythm, implication, narrative, and physiological readiness interact beneath conscious awareness.

His books include:

- The Inversiverse: Waking Up in a World Built to Keep You Asleep

- My Inner Child Was Broken

- The Resonance Matrix: The Anatomy of Influence & The Linguistic Somatic Decode

- The Consciousness Code

- If the Brain Was an App, Would You Use It?

Across these projects, James returns repeatedly to one central concern: how we, as a species, are shaped by systems we rarely pause to examine, and how greater awareness of language, physiology, attention, memory, emotion, and conditioning may help restore a deeper form of discernment.

About This Place Called Earth

This Place Called Earth is an independent writing, research, and media platform exploring the hidden architecture of human experience.

It was built around a simple recognition: much of what shapes modern life remains difficult to see clearly while we are living inside it. Perception, language, nervous-system state, memory, behaviour, regulation, identity, influence, technology, culture, and consciousness all interact continuously, yet they are often treated as separate subjects. This Place Called Earth exists to hold those threads together in a more integrated way.

The project brings together books, podcast series, essays, visual media, original frameworks, and long-form investigations that ask deeper questions about what it means to be human in an age of distraction, manipulation, emotional capture, technological mediation, cultural fragmentation, and accelerating pressure on attention.

Its work is grounded in several recurring principles:

- to question appearances without becoming careless

- to honour science without collapsing into reductionism

- to explore philosophy and spirituality without drifting into vagueness

- to make subtle mechanisms more readable in everyday life

- to support greater awareness of how perception, language, state, and conditioning shape lived reality

Across projects such as *The Inversiverse*, *The Resonance Matrix*, *The Consciousness Code*, *My Inner Child Was Broken*, and *If the Brain Was an App, Would You Use It?*, This Place Called Earth examines the relationship between body and mind, language and physiology, attention and influence, memory and identity, culture and consciousness.

At its core, the project is not built around offering final answers. It is built around disciplined inquiry. It invites readers and listeners to observe more honestly, think more carefully, and become more conscious of the systems through which life is filtered, interpreted, and lived.

More at: www.this-place-called-earth.com

Disclaimer

This book is intended for **educational and informational purposes only**. It reflects the author's personal experiences, perspectives, and independent inquiry, and is not a substitute for professional medical, psychological, psychiatric, legal, or financial advice.

The concepts discussed, including nervous-system regulation, trauma-related patterns, communication dynamics, and the Mirror-Linguistic Hypothesis, are presented as a framework for reflection and exploration. They are not presented as clinical diagnoses, treatment protocols, or guarantees of outcome. Readers should not use this book to self-diagnose, to discontinue or modify prescribed treatment, or to delay seeking professional help.

If you are experiencing mental health distress, persistent anxiety or depression, intrusive thoughts, trauma symptoms, suicidal ideation, or any condition that affects your safety or daily functioning, please seek support from a qualified healthcare professional. If you believe you may be at immediate risk of harm to yourself or others, contact emergency services or your local crisis support provider right away.

Any references to research, theory, or physiology are included to support discussion and should be interpreted within the limits of this book's scope. The author is not providing medical or clinical services, and no professional relationship is created by reading this book.

To the fullest extent permitted by law, the author and publisher disclaim liability for any loss, injury, or damage arising from the use of or reliance upon the information in this book. You are solely responsible for how you interpret and apply the material.

Copyright Page

© 2026 This Place Called Earth Ltd. All rights reserved.

James Miller is the author.

No part of this publication may be reproduced, stored in a retrieval system, or transmitted in any form or by any means, electronic, mechanical, photocopying, recording, or otherwise, without the prior written permission of the publisher, except for brief quotations used in critical articles or reviews.

First Edition, 2026 - Audiobook Format

This is a work of non-fiction based on the author's life experiences, perspectives, and independent research. The views expressed are the author's personal views and do not reflect those of any organisation or institution. Any resemblance to actual persons, living or dead, is purely coincidental unless otherwise stated.

AI-Generated Content Acknowledgement

This book contains content and imagery created with the assistance of OpenAI's ChatGPT, including editorial collaboration, structural formatting, and image generation. All final content was curated, edited, and approved by the author. Any AI-generated images are licensed for commercial use by the author and created explicitly for this publication.

Cover and Interior Design: James Miller - OpenAI's ChatGPT

ISBN: 979-8-90417-725-6

For permissions, questions, or speaking engagements:

Contact: j.c.miller@live.co.uk

www.ingramcontent.com/pod-product-compliance
Lightning Source LLC
Chambersburg PA
CBHW071444140726
47997CB00005B/1587